THE LITTLE SCHOOLS OF

PORT-ROYAL

T0382584

JEAN DU VERGIER DE HAURANNE,
ABBÉ DE SAINT-CYRAN,
Founder of the Little Schools of Port-Royal.

THE LITTLE SCHOOLS OF
PORT-ROYAL

BY

H. C. BARNARD, M.A., B.Litt.

SOMETIME SENIOR HULME SCHOLAR OF BRASENOSE COLLEGE, OXFORD

Cambridge:

at the University Press

1913

CAMBRIDGE
UNIVERSITY PRESS

University Printing House, Cambridge CB2 8BS, United Kingdom

Cambridge University Press is part of the University of Cambridge.

It furthers the University's mission by disseminating knowledge in the pursuit of education, learning and research at the highest international levels of excellence.

www.cambridge.org
Information on this title: www.cambridge.org/9781107512023

First published 1913
First paperback edition 2015

A catalogue record for this publication is available from the British Library

ISBN 978-1-107-51202-3 Paperback

PREFACE

WITH the exception of two French collections of reprinted extracts from Port-Royalist writers on education, there exists—so far as I am aware—no modern book which deals solely with the Little Schools. In view therefore of the importance and influence of the educational work of the Port-Royalists, it seemed to me that a detailed study of their theories and practice might be of value even at the present day.

I desire to tender my very hearty thanks to the Librarian of Sion College, London, through whose kindness I was allowed access to the unique collection of some 250 original Port-Royal works, bequeathed to the College by Mrs Schimmelpenninck. I have also to acknowledge many kind and helpful suggestions and criticisms from Viscount St Cyres and Mr Arthur Hassall, of Christ Church, and also from Mr M. W. Keatinge, Reader in Education in the University of Oxford.

H. C. B.

May 1913

TABLE OF CONTENTS

CHAPTER I

PAGE

INTRODUCTION I

CHAPTER II

HISTORY AND PERSONNEL OF THE SCHOOLS

History of Port-Royal previous to the Little Schools . . . 6
Saint-Cyran and Port-Royal 9
Saint-Cyran's love of children 12
Foundation of the schools 13
Arrest of Saint-Cyran ; dispersion of schools 15
Death of Saint-Cyran 17
Du Fossé and De Tillemont 18
Establishment of the schools in the rue S. Dominique in 1646 . 20
Port-Royal masters; Lancelot; Guyot; Coustel; Nicole; Le Fèvre 21
De Saci; Fontaine; Hamon 25
Reason for the name "Petites Écoles" 28
Dispersion of schools in 1650; the groups 30
Racine at Port-Royal 32
"Floruit" period of the Little Schools 33
The educational treatises of the solitaries 34
The Pascals at Port-Royal 37
Dispersion of schools in 1656 39
Miracle of the Holy Thorn 40
Final dispersion of schools—March 10th, 1660 41
Subsequent educational career of solitaries 42
Digression on the education of princes 43
Why the Jesuits persecuted the Little Schools 44
Subsequent history of Jansenist schools ; the Tabourin schools . 49

CHAPTER III

THE EDUCATIONAL THEORIES OF THE PORT-ROYALISTS

Theological basis of their educational theory 52
Saint-Cyran's views on the teacher's office 57
Selection of pupils 59
Intellectual education sacrificed to moral education . . 61

	PAGE
Contrast with spirit of Renaissance and of Jesuits	65
Attitude towards genius	67
Attitude towards the Drama	68
Attitude towards Music and Painting	69
Educational results of Port-Royal's theological position:	71
(a) Complete surveillance	72
(b) The Port-Royal tuition system	73
(c) Control of general environment	76
(d) Condemnation of travel	77
(e) Character and training of the masters	78

CHAPTER IV

GENERAL TEACHING METHODS

Affection for pupils	82
Moral education—indirect, as far as possible	83
Expurgation of texts	86
Patience and Perseverance	89
Teaching based on Genetic Psychology	90
Learning to be made easy and pleasant	91
Education through "Realien"	94
Manual Training	95
Discipline and Punishments	96
Prayer as an educational organon	99
Instruction in good manners	101
Emulation in the Little Schools	103

CHAPTER V

PARTICULAR TEACHING METHODS

Historical excursus on teaching in the Vernacular	107
Reading	113
Writing	118
Study of the Vernacular; literary style	119
Latin	124
Previous Latin grammars; Van Pauteren; Comenius	126
Lancelot's *Nouvelle Méthode latine*	130
"Versions"	132
Translation	133
List of Authors read	136
Prose composition	139
Latin verses	140
Emphasis on literature rather than on language	141

PAGE

Greek 142
Lancelot's *Jardin des Racines grecques* 144
History and Geography 147
Mathematics and Science 149
Modern Languages 150

CHAPTER VI
SOME DETAILS OF SCHOOL ADMINISTRATION

Time-tables 151
Recreation and physical exercises 155
Indoor games 158
Sleep and clothing 159
School fees 160
Some noted Port-Royal pupils 161
How many pupils were there? 163

CHAPTER VII
THE PORT-ROYAL GIRLS' SCHOOLS

Boys' schools to be distinguished from girls' schools . . . 167
History of girls' schools 168
Religious aim of these schools 170
The curriculum 173
Time-table 176
The prayers and the silences 181
Teaching as a means to the teacher's salvation 184
"Douceur et Sévérité" 186
Instruction in good manners 187
Punishments 188
Age and number of the pupils 190
Explanation of contemporary praise of Port-Royal girls' schools . 191

CHAPTER VIII
THE EDUCATIONAL PREDECESSORS AND SUCCESSORS OF PORT-ROYAL

Influence of the Renaissance on French education 194
The University of Paris 195
Rabelais and Montaigne 196
Ramus 200
The Jesuits; the Brethren of the Common Life 202
Comenius 204

PAGE

The Oratorians 205
Education of girls in France in early 17th century . . . 208
Descartes 209
The *Grammaire générale* 212
The Port-Royal *Logic* 213
Minor sources of Port-Royal educational theory 215
Yet Port-Royal was original 216
Followers of Port-Royal: Rollin 217
S. Jean-Baptiste De La Salle 219
Fleury 219
Locke 220
Rousseau 221
Dumarsais 222
Expulsion of Jesuits in 1762 223
La Chalotais 224
Rolland 225
Educational proposals of the Revolution 226
Influence of Port-Royal during the 19th century 228

CHAPTER IX

CONCLUSION 230

APPENDICES

A. *On the Date of the Destruction of the Port-Royal Boys' Schools* 239
B. *Bibliography:*
    I.   Original Port-Royal Authorities 247
    II. Non-Port-Royal Authorities 250
    III. Some of the more modern works consulted . . . 250
C. *Chronological Table* 252

LIST OF ILLUSTRATIONS

Portrait of Jean Du Vergier De Hauranne, Abbé De Saint-Cyran *frontispiece*
Map of the Environs of Port-Royal de Paris . . . *to face p.* 20
Map of the Remoter Environs of Port-Royal des Champs   „   49
Bird's-eye View of Port-Royal des Champs . .   „ 151

CHAPTER I

INTRODUCTION

THE contribution which France has made towards the cause of education during the last four centuries is one of her brightest glories. It is true that her services have been to a large extent devoted to secondary education and that the important work of the elementary school was for long comparatively neglected. But in the cause of higher education and of the education of girls, France maintained a widespread and unrelaxing activity at a time when other nations were content to put forth sporadic and half-hearted efforts. Again, there exists in the French language an educational literature distributed over 400 years or more; and this testifies to a sustained and deeply-felt interest on the part of the French people in the work of the school. To the German race we owe the greatest services rendered to the cause of elementary education, for no other nation can furnish a rival to Pestalozzi or Froebel. But their activity, together with that of Kant and Herbart, is confined to a period of some 50 years; for a German educationalist of real note previous to them we must go back to Ratke, or perhaps even to Sturm. Similarly in England there was a period of some 150 years during which were published Elyot's *Governour*, Ascham's *Scholemaster*, Mulcaster's *Positions*, Brinsley's *Ludus Literarius*, Milton's *Tractate*, and Locke's *Thoughts on Education*. This was succeeded by another century and a half or more which saw no educational treatise of importance published in this country. The works already mentioned produced very little effect on English secondary education; the grammar schools for the most part went on in a state of complacent satisfaction with existing methods, until they were rudely awakened in 1861 by the Public

Schools' Commission and the vigorous onslaughts of Herbert
Spencer's *Essay on Education.*

The history of French education presents a very different
picture. There is a series of school reformers and educational
writers, stretching almost continuously from the time of the Renaissance down to our own days. More than this, the reformers,
unlike so many of their English brethren, often made their
influence felt; while many of the writers on education (though
there are obvious exceptions) set forth in an attractive manner
views of great practical value to those engaged in the work of
teaching. It is at times hard to set great store by some of our
classical English educational treatises; they too frequently savour
of being mere second-rate by-products of men of genius whose
chief interests lay elsewhere. When reading Milton's *Tractate*
we seem to have the Rabelaisian curriculum for Gargantua set
forth in all seriousness as meet, not for a giant in a fairy-tale,
but for an English schoolboy—though of special aptitude, it is
true. Locke's *Thoughts on Education* are more practical and
teem with common sense; but the plan of the book is incoherent,
the same thing is often repeated several times, and the reader
wearies long before he reaches the end. Spencer's *Essay on
Education* is full of interest and is attractively written; but it
lacks in philosophic analysis and tends at times to degenerate
into a mere party pamphlet. Those of our educational writers
who were most in touch with school-realities are too little
known; Ascham certainly borrows some fame from his connection with Queen Elizabeth, but who, save the specialist, reads
Brinsley or Mulcaster?

In England, then, we lack a continuous tradition of educational thinkers and writers and we are too apt to disregard the
inheritance that we do possess. We are proud—and rightly so
—of our ancient public and grammar schools, which have educated generations of the ablest Englishmen and which to-day
help to maintain that sense of solidarity with the past which is
one of the most precious possessions of an old-established nation.
But to their uncompromisingly conservative attitude has been
largely due the stagnation of educational interest and the lack
of progress in teaching methods which characterised a large part

of English secondary education from the Tudor period until the middle of the nineteenth century.

In France at the present day there is a far keener and more general public interest in education and perhaps a greater average efficiency in teaching than with us. This is to a considerable extent the outcome of the more potent educational tradition which the French inherit. In the history of France, matters educational have more often been mixed up with politics and have thus claimed more of public attention than in our own case until within recent times. The Jesuits did an important educational work, but they also had great influence at court and among the people; the causes of their expulsion in 1762, again, were pedagogic as well as political. Some of the most learned Frenchmen of the seventeenth century concerned themselves with the education of members of the royal house or of the sons of those in authority; the University of Paris, which had a European reputation, was reformed by Henri IV; the Revolution was marked by innumerable educational projects— Mirabeau, Talleyrand, Condorcet, and the Convention in 1792 and 1793 were all concerned with proposals for educational reform; while under the Napoleonic *régime* the matter was discussed and legislated upon with vigour. In this manner, education and politics in France have tended to react the one upon the other, and this has in several ways stimulated the French people to be interested in education and to give ear to proposals of reform which were often exaggerated or impracticable. But it has also resulted in continuous educational activity and a gradual improvement of methods; often false moves have been made, retrogressive steps have been taken, and disturbance and disorganisation have troubled the peaceful work of the schools. But on the whole the movement has been one of progress and since the Renaissance there has been in France no period of educational somnolence such as that which we in this country have to deplore. Education was regarded as a matter of vital national significance by the French at a time when in England there prevailed an exaggerated *laissez-faire* policy which discouraged public and professional interest alike. It is only within the last half-century that the importance of the problem has been realised among us and even yet we have not caught up the lead set us by France and Germany.

In many ways the seventeenth century was one of the most striking periods in the whole history of French education. Its beginning was marked by the reform of the University of Paris; it saw the establishment of the elementary schools of S. Jean-Baptiste De La Salle, and the notable achievements of Madame De Maintenon in the education of girls; in the course of it secondary education was set forth in one of its most remarkable forms in the 'collèges' of the Jesuits. It was thus in France a century of exceptional activity in every department of education. In the present volume our concern is chiefly with one aspect of this many-sided movement—with the Jansenist Port-Royal schools. The Port-Royalists are in some respects the most interesting of all the French school-reformers of the seventeenth century, partly because their educational doctrines were in many respects far in advance of those of any of their contemporaries, and partly on account of their intense earnestness, their complete disinterestedness, their courage in the face of persecution, their pathetic but not inglorious fate. Moreover, though the failure of their schools—due rather to the malignant *odium theologicum* of the Jesuits than to any inherent educational weakness—seemed complete and even ignominious at the time when it occurred, yet this failure was more apparent than real. The spirit of their doctrines has had a very real influence on subsequent French education and has not yet ceased to operate. Through Rollin, the Port-Royalists inspired the University; their use of the vernacular was adopted by S. Jean-Baptiste De La Salle and has since become universal; their treatises were 'devoured' by Rousseau; their cultivation of their mother-tongue laid the foundations of modern French prose; their school-books have been in use down to our own days, not only in France, but in several other European countries; according to Compayré, their theories inspired the Circular issued in 1872 by the Minister of Public Instruction; and we may justly regard them as being in no small degree responsible for that discriminate appreciation of good literature and power of clear, forceful, and beautiful expression which is so eminently characteristic of the educated Frenchman of the present day.

The educational work of the Port-Royalists then is worthy of study, both for its own sake and for the importance of its subsequent influence in France and elsewhere. At the same time it is true to say that the doctrines and practice of the Little Schools are but little known not only in this country but even in France itself. The reason is not far to seek. Port-Royal's chief importance has been theological and literary, rather than educational. Its best known representatives are Pascal and Arnauld, not Coustel or De Beaupuis. Thus, owing to the interest which the Jansenist controversy has for the theologian, or the style of the *Provincial Letters* for the *littérateur*, the value of the Port-Royalists' contribution to education has been very generally overlooked. This is due also to the fact that the treatises, in which their educational theories are expounded and the practice of their schools is recorded, are for the most part rare and not easily accessible; again these details are to some extent scattered throughout 'Mémoires' and histories and letters where it is not easy to find them and where they are often intermingled with extraneous matter of every kind. But, for all this, a sympathetic study of the methods used in the Little Schools and of the educational theories which underlie those methods cannot fail to be a source of inspiration even to teachers of the present day, if they can be persuaded to evince some interest in the history of their profession.

CHAPTER II

HISTORY AND PERSONNEL OF THE SCHOOLS

To trace the origin of Port-Royal it is necessary to go back to the year 1204. At that date an abbey was founded at the head of the valley of the Rhodon near Chevreuse (about 18 miles to the south-west of Paris) by Eudes De Sully, Bishop of Paris, and a lady named Mathilde De Garlande. The object of this community, which consisted of twelve or fourteen women, was to ensure prayers for the safe return of Matthieu De Marly De Montmorenci, Mathilde's husband, who had gone to take part in the fourth crusade; but the nuns from the first concerned themselves also with the education of girls. The site of this abbey was known as Port-Royal, a name of which the etymology is uncertain; probably it is a corruption of 'porrois' from the Low Latin 'porra,' meaning a 'stagnant pond.' This would indeed well fit the facts of the case, for the abbey was built in a marshy and unhealthy valley by the side of one of those large ponds[1] or 'mares' which abound in the neighbourhood. The abbey was put in charge of the monks of S. Bernard who had a monastery at Cîteaux[2] near Dijon; and they acted as confessors for the nuns of Port-Royal. During the fourteenth and fifteenth centuries the community flourished and seems to have attained a certain amount of fame. But the English wars and the religious wars of the sixteenth century tended to relax the discipline of religious houses in France, and the Gallican Church had never accepted those decrees of the

---

[1] This pond can be seen in the Bird's-eye View of Port-Royal des Champs facing page 49. It was subsequently drained by the solitaries. Copies of the original print are preserved at Sion College and in the small museum at Port-Royal des Champs.

[2] This was the original house of the famous Cistercian order (*Cistercium* is the Latin name for Cîteaux). The society was founded in 1098 and placed under the rule of S. Benedict. In 1113 S. Bernard joined the order and thenceforward it spread widely and flourished greatly.

Council of Trent which dealt with ecclesiastical discipline and organisation. Hence abuses were rife, and Port-Royal did not escape the infection. At the beginning of the seventeenth century the abbey had for its 'confessor' a Bernardine monk who was so ignorant, it was said, that he could not understand the Paternoster. He knew not a word of the Catechism and never opened a book except his Breviary; for he spent his time in the hunting field. For over thirty years no sermon had been preached at Port-Royal, save at seven or eight professions. "The rule of S. Benedict was practically forgotten; even seclusion was no longer practised and the spirit of the world had entirely banished the strict conventual rules. Ignorance of religion at this monastery was deplorable; sermons were scarcely ever preached and even the confessors were no better educated than the nuns. The sacrament was taken only from month to month and at high festivals. This did not apply to the feast of the Purification because it took place during the carnival, when the house was entirely given over to revels and the confessor took part in them along with the servants[1]."

We are surely justified in conjecturing that in an abbey thus given over to worldliness, the arduous work of educating girls had for some time been given up. But at a time when things seemed at their worst an event occurred of great importance to the religious life of Port-Royal, and also indirectly to its educational work. In 1602 Jacqueline-Marie Arnauld was appointed abbess; she was at the time a child of eleven, but in the Papal Bull appointing her to this charge her age was deliberately falsified and she was described as 'religieuse professe, âgée de dix-sept ans.' Such a beginning might not seem to augur well for the moral regeneration of Port-Royal, and indeed at first Jacqueline, who assumed the name of Angélique, seems much to have disliked conventual life. But in 1608, after hearing an eloquent sermon preached by a disreputable Capuchin monk named Basil, she underwent a conversion and immediately set about reforming Port-Royal on the most rigorous lines. We are told that the community at this time consisted of ten professed nuns, of whom three were 'imbéciles,' and two novices[2]. The rule of seclusion

---

[1] Poullain, pp. 4—5.   [2] Tronchay, p. 7.

was no longer observed and there was no kind of strictness or regularity. After her conversion Angélique succeeded in introducing vows of poverty and seclusion, and it seems probable that the teaching work of the abbey was resumed[1]. Angélique came of a notable family, many members of which had become illustrious at the bar or on the field of battle. The introduction by her of the vow of seclusion at Port-Royal at first caused a rupture with her family, but this was soon healed and eventually she became the instrument whereby twenty-one other members of the Arnauld family entered Port-Royal, either as nuns or as solitaries. She was indeed a true daughter of a long line of famous soldiers and scholars; she had a gift for administration and was willing to suffer persecution rather than be false to her principles. Cousin calls her the equal of the great Dr Arnauld by her intrepidity of soul and elevation of thought; Sainte-Beuve describes her character as 'truly royal.' Her energy and steadfastness of purpose overcame all obstacles; she not only won her family to Port-Royal, of which they became the backbone, but the influence of her reforms made itself felt in other religious houses, and there was a widespread revival of those primitive austerities for which the Cistercian order had been particularly renowned. The whole movement was fostered by Richelieu himself; he attempted to make the decrees of the Council of Trent binding upon the Church of France and also secured his own nomination as general of several of the great religious orders, including that of Cîteaux.

As time went on the number of nuns at Port-Royal increased and by the year 1626 there were not less than 80. But the unhealthy site of the abbey bred fevers, and the well which supplied the convent with water was situated in the middle of the

---

[1] Cadet (*L'Éducation à Port-Royal*, note on p. 54) says that Sister Louise Sainte-Praxède De Lamoignon was appointed mistress of the 'pensionnaires' (i.e. girl boarders) in 1609. If this is true it proves that the educational work of the community was being carried on at this time. But according to the big *Nécrologe*, p. 36, and the *Supplément*, p. 327, Sister Louise Sainte-Praxède De Lamoignon was born in 1564 and entered the Abbey of S. Antoine at the age of nine. There she remained till her 60th year and did not enter Port-Royal till 1624. She died there on Jan. 20, 1638. If this is so she could not have taken charge of the Port-Royal girls' school in 1609, and I am at a loss to explain whence Cadet has got his apparently erroneous information.

nuns' burying ground; hence the infirmary was always full, and in two years 15 of the nuns had died. At the beginning of 1626 therefore the community was removed from the neighbourhood of Chevreuse to Paris; this was rendered possible by the liberality of Angélique's mother, Catherine Arnauld, who had become a widow in 1619, and who subsequently in 1629 entered Port-Royal and took the name Catherine De Sainte Félicité. The new abbey fronted on to the rue de la Bourbe (now Boulevard de Port-Royal) and was bounded west and east by the rue d'Enfer (now Avenue de l'Observatoire and rue Denfert Rochereau) and the rue du Faubourg S. Jacques[1]. A large part of the original building still survives; during the Revolution it was used as a prison and is to-day a lying-in hospital. Henceforth then we have to distinguish two Port-Royals—that near Chevreuse known as Port-Royal des Champs, and that in the rue de la Bourbe, called Port-Royal de Paris.

In 1620 one of Angélique's brothers, D'Andilly, who was at that time attached to the Court, was passing through Poitiers and there met for the first time the Abbot of Saint-Cyran, who was destined to play a most important part in the subsequent history of Port-Royal, and above all of its schools. Saint-Cyran seems to have made a great impression upon D'Andilly and a close friendship sprang up between them; through her brother Angélique soon came into contact with this remarkable man. In a letter of hers to D'Andilly, dated January 7, 1621, we read: "I received M. De Saint-Cyran's letter with an unspeakable delight. I thank you with all my heart for having procured for me the happiness of so holy a friendship[2]"; and it is interesting to notice in her letters how as time goes on and she gets to know Saint-Cyran better, her praises of him become more and more enthusiastic. Angélique evidently saw how valuable would be the influence of Saint-Cyran upon Port-Royal, but she did not dare at first to ask him to 'abase himself' by becoming confessor to the abbey. However, in 1633 there appeared a little book of devotions to the Holy Sacrament (*Le Chapelet Secret*) which had been written by Agnès, Angélique's sister and coadjutor at Port-

---

[1] See plan facing page 20.
[2] *Lettres de la Mère Angélique*, p. 13.

Royal. It created a most unexpected stir in the theological world, for it was condemned by the Sorbonne and suppressed by the Pope. At this juncture Saint-Cyran took up the cudgels on behalf of Port-Royal, and his action seems to have brought him into closer touch with the community. In 1635 the proposal was at last made to him through the Bishop of Langres, who was one of the 'superiors' of Port-Royal, that he should undertake the spiritual direction of the abbey; at first he refused, but finally, believing that he would be acting in accordance with the will of God, he accepted the position. Saint-Cyran thus became 'director' of the community, and in the following year he introduced as his second-in-command, and under the title of 'confessor,' Singlin, who also exerted an important influence upon the subsequent history of Port-Royal.

At this stage it will not be out of place to consider in brief the history and character of Saint-Cyran, for it is only in the light of a thorough and sympathetic knowledge of his life and his doctrines that the essential spirit of Port-Royal education can be understood. Saint-Cyran has been called 'the soul of Port-Royal,' and it is certain that the Port-Royal schools were not only due in the first instance to his initiative, but were carried on largely in the spirit of his ideas even after his death, by his faithful disciples.

Jean Du Vergier De Hauranne, afterwards Abbot of Saint-Cyran, was born at Bayonne in 1581. He studied at the University of Louvain and there met the famous Jansen, afterwards Bishop of Ypres and founder of a famous heresy. Jansen and De Hauranne studied together both at Paris and at Bayonne, occupying themselves chiefly with S. Augustine and developing the Jansenist doctrines of original sin and grace. Five years were spent thus and in 1616 Jansen returned to Louvain, while four years later De Hauranne was appointed Abbot of Saint-Cyran, an abbey in Brenne, to the east of Poitiers. The two friends, though separated, kept up their intimacy by means of letters or visits, and together worked out their 'new theology.' For twelve years or more they were thus occupied, and during this time Saint-Cyran wrote several theological treatises; among these most probably was the *Petrus Aurelius* which combated the attacks which were being made by English Jesuits against episcopal authority.   The book met with a very mixed reception, but, according to Sainte-Beuve, marked out its author for a position as 'director of consciences.'   This then may have been an additional reason why Saint-Cyran in 1635 was invited to become director of the abbey of Port-Royal at Paris.

Saint-Cyran rapidly became an influence of the first importance at Port-Royal; he penetrated with his spirit everything which had any kind of connection with this community.   The first fruits of his ascendancy were seen in the accession of Angélique's nephew Le Maître to Port-Royal as a 'solitary'; for from this time onwards, in addition to the regular nuns, priests and laymen who wished to retire from the world began to select Port-Royal as their retreat where they could live under the spiritual direction of Saint-Cyran.   Like the Brethren of the Common Life in the two previous centuries, as well as at a later date the Oratorians, these solitaries were not bound by any vows; they lived a life of meditation, study, and labour in the vicinity of the convent of Port-Royal, where separate lodgings for them were built.   Le Maître was at this time a young man of thirty-one who had already made a brilliant reputation at the bar; but influenced by Saint-Cyran and also perhaps by the example of his aunt Angélique, he relinquished all prospects of worldly advancement and embraced the 'religious life.'   As he rendered important services to the Port-Royal schools we shall have occasion to refer to him again.   At the same time his mother Catherine Arnauld, and his soldier brother De Séricourt, also entered Port-Royal; and with them was installed Lancelot, who afterwards played a most important part in the history of Port-Royal education.   Lancelot was of humble origin, but had met Saint-Cyran and like so many others who became acquainted with him, came immediately under his spell.   Lancelot had long desired to enter the religious life and at last succeeded in enlisting the sympathies of Saint-Cyran in this direction.   In Le Maître, De Séricourt, and Lancelot then we see the first of those 'solitaries'—the 'messieurs de Port-Royal'—in whose care, and under the inspiration of Saint-Cyran, the work of the Port-Royal boys' schools and the dissemination of their educational doctrines were carried on.

It is, however, to Saint-Cyran that the initiative for founding the schools is due. The education of children had always bulked very largely in his theories and was mainly the outcome of his theological position. Moreover, although a celibate, a bookworm, and a theologian he had a very strong natural love for children. The *Mémoires* of Fontaine are full of instances of this; in one of his letters Saint-Cyran exclaims: "I would that you could read in my heart the affection I have for children[1]," and that this was no idle sentiment is proved by Saint-Cyran's own life. He constituted himself tutor alike to the nephew of one of his friends whose mother was a widow, and to a poor joiner's son at Saint-Cyran; and even when at a later date he was cast into prison at Vincennes he still contrived to carry on in some measure his educational work. In a conversation with Le Maître soon after he was set free he says: "I give you this detail to show you how I love children. Since charity tells us that we must cherish them and take them from the breast, I devoted myself at Vincennes to looking after children at that early age, to paying nurses for them, and to having shirts and other garments bought for them. I even longed to send to the boundaries to bring in some little orphans who had neither father nor mother, to bring them up in my abbey; 'ad ubera portabimini, et super genua blandientur vobis.'...When they are grown up, I shall make them learn a trade or have them educated according to the gift of grace which I see in them. For my aim is always to take care of them, when once I have begun, so that my charity may be like the charity and grace which God bestows on us; and unless charity endures to the very end it is suitable only to reprobates[2]." Thus even when in prison, since he was allowed a certain amount of freedom, Saint-Cyran managed to give expression to his ardent love for children; we have evidence that while there he occupied himself with the education of the two sons of the lieutenant of the prison, a man who had treated him with extreme harshness. Lancelot also conjures up a charming picture for us when he tells how this austere and middle-aged

---

[1] *Suppl. au Nécr.* (1761), p. 46.   [2] Fontaine, *Mémoires*, I, p. 177.

ecclesiastic used often to become a child again and beguile the weary hours of his imprisonment by playing ball with little children of seven or eight years of age. Even more charming is a letter of his written from prison to his grand-niece and god-daughter; it is surely excusable to quote from it at length since it shows more than anything else that in Saint-Cyran we have no arid mediaeval ecclesiastic, but rather an ardent lover of children, and that his educational theories, though they be deduced from somewhat gloomy theological dogmas, are none the less ablaze with sympathy and affection for child-life. " Since I have been in this fine castle," runs the letter, "where the King has had me put, I have not ceased to pray to God for him and for you, that He may give you grace to devote yourself entirely to Him and to serve Him from your youngest days....I am very glad that you are so happy; it is a sign that the Holy Spirit is with you....I should have been glad to keep your cat which was so pretty, but my room is so small that we could not both live in it together. Keep him for me till another time, when I will ask for him; and be careful not to give him meat to eat, or he will get into bad habits. Cats and children are very much alike; they hardly ever get rid of bad habits acquired in early years.... In this world there is nothing to be loved save God; and if you love any creature, even your little pussy, let it be for the love of God who created and made him[1]."

Enough has been said to show that Saint-Cyran fully realised the importance of the factor of affection in education. It was an element rarely to be found in contemporary seventeenth century educational practice, for on every side we see a dark background of floggings and Spartan discipline against which the spirit and methods of Port-Royal, inspired by Saint-Cyran, shine out with an added lustre.

Bearing in mind this essential characteristic of Saint-Cyran's educational ideas let us return to the foundation of the Port-Royal schools. At the beginning of 1638, Le Maître, De Séricourt, and Lancelot were installed as solitaries at Port-Royal; to their care Singlin, the confessor of Port-Royal, committed five or six boys

---

[1] Saint-Cyran's *Letters* (1744), Vol. II, pp. 14 and 16.

who in turn had been entrusted to him by Saint-Cyran himself.
We are told that the education of these children had been in-
formally begun during the previous summer at Port-Royal des
Champs; but early in 1638 they were transferred to Paris and
their numbers soon increased to 10 or 12. Thus the Port-Royal
solitaries and the Port-Royal boys' schools came into existence
together and both alike were due to the initiative of Saint-Cyran.
The year 1637 or 1638 then marks the birth of Port-Royal
educational work. To quote one of the authorities : " From the
year 1637[1] date the first beginnings at Port-Royal of that cele-
brated community of solitaries who there educated in the knowledge of letters and Christian piety several children of quality
whose parents wished to avoid the irregularities too common in
young boys who go to college; everything went on under the
care of M. De Saint-Cyran who visited both regularly every
other day, giving children and solitaries alike instruction suited
to their age and condition[2]." It should be noticed however that
the education of girls by the nuns of Port-Royal had already
been for a long time in vogue. It is important to distinguish
clearly between the boys' schools and the girls' schools; in the
greater part of this book we shall be concerned with the former,
and it is not until Chapter VII that we shall treat of the educational work carried on by the nuns of Port-Royal in their
boarding-school for girls. The boys' schools were at first chiefly
in the charge of Lancelot in whom the Abbot had discovered a
special gift for teaching; but Saint-Cyran kept up a continual
supervision. As has just been said he visited the schools,
inspected the children's work, and held conferences with the
solitaries and nuns; in short he continued to fulfil his duties
as 'director' of the community.

Unfortunately this state of affairs lasted only a few months,

[1] The writer of the *Mémoires de la Vie de M. Walon De Beaupuis* (1751),
pp. 57—62, contends that the school-work of Port-Royal did not begin till about 1640
or 1641 and that the mention of Saint-Cyran's visits on alternate days refers only to
the few months between his release in February 1643 and his death in October 1643.
This theory seems very unlikely, for there is plenty of evidence that the work began
about 1637, before Saint-Cyran was imprisoned; see especially the big *Nécrologe*, p. 31,
Preface, which, although not printed till 1723, was a contemporary MS document.

[2] *Vies des Amis de Port-Royal*, p. 57.

for on May 14, 1638, Saint-Cyran was arrested by order of the King and, as was mentioned above, he was thrown into prison. We need not here examine in detail the reasons which had led to this and of which Saint-Cyran himself enumerates seventeen. M. Carré attributes his arrest to the fact that he had defended Jansen's work on Grace, entitled *Augustinus*; but this is obviously incorrect, since the *Augustinus* was not published at Louvain until 1640, two years after the death of its author.   Racine in his *Histoire abrégée de Port-Royal* specifies three reasons; jealousy on the part of certain ecclesiastics of Saint-Cyran's success as a 'director of souls'; his breach with Richelieu on the theological doctrine of attrition and the question as to the nullity of a marriage between Gaston, Duke of Orléans, and Margaret of Lorraine; and thirdly his book entitled *Petrus Aurelius*, to which reference has already been made and which had incensed the Society of Jesus against its author.   It seems obvious that, whatever may have been the charges alleged against Saint-Cyran, he was recognised by civil and ecclesiastical authorities alike as too strong a personality to be allowed to come into opposition with them.   Richelieu in his early days as Bishop of Luçon had met Saint-Cyran and had come to know him well and to esteem him highly.   When therefore in later years Richelieu rose to power, he made strenuous efforts to win the allegiance of one whom he declared to be the most learned theologian in Europe. No less than five—some say eight—bishoprics were offered to Saint-Cyran; but the Abbot refused to exchange independence for preferment.   And since his attitude was in every point un-compromising, it was inevitable that he should be regarded as a danger and should accordingly be confined where his writings and personality would cease to influence the world.

The arrest of Saint-Cyran recoiled on Port-Royal; in June 1638 the whole community was driven out of Paris by order of the Archbishop and took up its abode at Port-Royal des Champs; this had been unoccupied save by a priest to say the daily Mass since 1626 and thus it presented a suitable refuge.   In July the solitaries, twelve in number, were again dispersed and Lancelot with some of the pupils retired to La Ferté-Milon—a village about 40 miles to the north-east of Paris—where they lived in the family of M. Vitart, one of whose sons was being educated at Port-Royal and who was an uncle of the poet Racine. Later some of the solitaries were allowed to return to Port-Royal des Champs and we even find Lancelot at Port-Royal de Paris educating the two sons of M. Jérome Bignon, who is said to have originally suggested the idea of the Port-Royal schools to Saint-Cyran. But during all this time, in spite of the separations and wanderings of the solitaries, Saint-Cyran from his cell in the prison of Vincennes never ceased by his letters to supervise their educational work and to act as director to the community, so far as his own ill-health and the galling restrictions set upon him by the prison authorities would allow. His most notable achievement during this period of captivity is that he influenced the great Dr Antoine Arnauld, one of Angélique's brothers, to ally himself with Port-Royal and ultimately to enter the priesthood. From the theological standpoint Dr Arnauld ranks with Pascal in importance to Port-Royal; but he has less concern for those whose chief interest is in the Port-Royal schools. Nevertheless we have evidence that he was actually given charge of the education of a young marquis; and he certainly found time in a busy life of theological controversy to write a *Mémoire sur le Règlement des Études dans les Lettres humaines*, which enshrines for us much of the practice of the Port-Royal schools. He also collaborated in the *Logic* and the *Grammaire générale*. He had had a brilliant career at the Sorbonne and had been greatly attracted by the Augustinian doctrine of Grace. When therefore in 1640 Jansen's *Augustinus* appeared, Dr Arnauld read it with great eagerness, and was much influenced by it when writing his treatise *De la Fréquente Communion* which was published in 1643.

Richelieu died in December 1642, but it was not till February 1643 that Saint-Cyran was set at liberty. He at once defended the *Augustinus* which had appeared during his imprisonment, and in this he was aided by Dr Arnauld. His interest in the schools did not wane, for we find him publishing in March 1643 a little catechism for the use of the two sons of M. Bignon and the other Port-Royal pupils. Unfortunately this seemingly innocent school-book gave rise to religious disputes which were greatly aggravated by the appearance of Dr Arnauld's work *De la Fréquente Communion* in August 1643. This treatise was aimed at the Jesuits who had sought to compromise between the Christian and the worldly life; it emphasised the importance of spiritual worthiness before partaking of the Holy Communion. Two Jesuit fathers immediately attacked the treatise, for it was said that it offered an excuse for abstaining from communicating at Mass and that owing to it the number of communicants was dwindling; the book only just escaped condemnation at Rome.

These theological disputes overshadowed the last days of Saint-Cyran. His imprisonment had weakened his health and he enjoyed only eight more months of freedom. On October 11, 1643, he died—in harness; for as he himself was wont to say: 'Stantem mori oportet.' He was lamented with the sincerest grief by the 'religious' and the solitaries of Port-Royal, and no less, we may surely conjecture, by those children of high and low degree alike who had always claimed so large a share of his love and of his thoughts. His memory was venerated with the honours due to a canonised saint, and throughout subsequent Port-Royal literature his name is always referred to with the deepest reverence.

Saint-Cyran then is the most striking character that we meet with in the history of the Port-Royal schools, and his personality and ideas completely dominate the education given in them. The Port-Royal educational theory is deduced from Saint-Cyran's theological position, as will be seen presently; but, more than this, the personality of the man is stamped upon it in a manner that cannot be due merely to the following out of a theological dogma. He apparently exercised a kind of personal magnetism over all whom he met—witness his influence upon D'Andilly, upon Angélique, upon Lancelot, upon Dr Arnauld. The secret of this charm seems to have been firstly his ardent love for mankind, as the creation of the God whom he loved so sincerely and unreservedly; and secondly, his sympathetic understanding of human weaknesses and difficulties which made him *par excellence* a 'director of consciences.'

Angélique says of him, "This saintly man never forced people into penitence nor enjoined excessive mortifications or austerities. But by the power of the solid truths which he set forth, he touched one's heart with the respect and love owed to God; from which were born grief at having sinned and so lively a desire to expiate this that one always wished to do more than he desired."

In June 1643 there had been entered at Port-Royal a pupil named Pierre-Thomas Du Fossé. He is of special interest to us because he gives in his *Mémoires*, which are still extant, a vivid picture of life at the Port-Royal schools in these early days of their existence. Du Fossé's father, Gentien Thomas, Seigneur Du Fossé, Maître des Comptes, had been greatly attracted by Saint-Cyran, and, realising the evil influences of the contemporary Jesuit 'collèges,' sent his three sons to be educated at Port-Royal des Champs. The young Pierre Du Fossé was at this date just ten years of age. He and his brothers found at Port-Royal two other pupils already installed (the rest were at Port-Royal de Paris under the care of Lancelot); they were a young Saint-Ange and a son of D'Andilly named De Villeneuve, who was usually known as 'petit Jules.' For the five pupils there were two masters, Étienne De Bascle who had charge of their religious instruction and a M. Selle who taught secular subjects. The former of these had entered the community in 1637, having come under the influence of Saint-Cyran; owing to an unhappy marriage he had had a troubled life and by the time he reached the haven of Port-Royal was broken in health. None the less he gave himself up to the work of the schools and when he died in 1662, after their final dispersion, De Bernières, an active and generous friend of Port-Royal, said of him: "He was the joy of my heart, the love of my children, and the peace of my poor and desolate house at Le Chesnai." Of M. Selle's history we know very little as his name does not appear in the *Nécrologe*; he probably died soon after Du Fossé entered Port-Royal. M. Selle, so Du Fossé tells us, was "very clever and very capable of instructing us in the humanities," but apparently the pupils learnt less than they might from him owing to their delight in the company of Le Maître and De Séricourt, who had been in retirement at Port-Royal since 1638. We can understand the attraction which the two brother solitaries may well have possessed for the boys when we remember that Le Maître had since his conversion shown a great love for children and composed his *Règles de la traduction française* for the special benefit of Pierre Du Fossé; while De Séricourt had been a soldier in Germany where he had been taken prisoner and had escaped with the help of a rope. Such a man must have possessed a large fund of exciting anecdotes and perhaps even the austere atmosphere of Port-Royal could not prevent their being retailed occasionally for the benefit of the little boys. At any rate Du Fossé tells us that 'le petit Jules' and he had 'tout à fait la guerre dans la tête,' and they both decided to be soldiers when they grew up. In their play-time they erected a fort in the garden, flanked by four bastions and surrounded by a ditch. To cover the slopes of the fort, the children brought turf, one or two sods at a time, from a neigh-bouring valley. 'C'était une peine et une fatigue incroyables,' we are told; but at last the fort was finished. Then ensued innumerable games of attack and defence, until the fights ceased to be entirely playful and undesirable passions were aroused. At this the authorities intervened and after the first disappoint-ment had passed Du Fossé and his companions pulled down the fort 'with almost the same pleasure as that with which it had been constructed.'

During Du Fossé's first year of school at Port-Royal, work and organisation alike seem to have been somewhat lax. But these peaceful times soon came to an end. In August 1643 Arnauld's book *De la Fréquente Communion* appeared, which greatly incensed the Jesuits. Arnauld was known as a friend of Saint-Cyran and as an adherent of Jansenism; many of his family were already in retreat at Port-Royal; and therefore it was not unnatural that the Jesuits should seek to wreak their vengeance on a community, which they had already begun to regard with a jealous eye. To avoid any possible calamity Du Fossé and the other pupils were sent in 1644 to Le Chesnai near Versailles; but in the following year, when the storm had somewhat abated, they were able to return to Port-Royal des Champs.

Passing reference must here be made to Sébastien Le Nain De Tillemont who entered Port-Royal as a pupil in 1646, and who, with Du Fossé, is a type of the best result of Port-Royal education. He became a pupil of the solitaries at the age of ten, and early gave promise of the great historical genius which later inspired his writings on Church History and on the Roman Empire, and which led Gibbon to consult him as a reliable authority. He seems to have learnt at Port-Royal the value of consulting original sources, and to have studied logic and philosophy.

Meanwhile the number of nuns had been increasing in the abbey under the charge of Angélique at Port-Royal de Paris. To relieve the consequent overcrowding the abbey was divided into two parts, and some of the sisters returned to their old home at Port-Royal des Champs which was restored and enlarged. This however inconvenienced the solitaries and the pupils, since the numbers of both were growing. At this juncture a friend of Port-Royal, a M. Lambert, solved the difficulty by offering them a house in the rue S. Dominique d'Enfer[1], a street lying close to the convent of Port-Royal de Paris and to the north of it. About the end of 1646, then, the pupils and their masters left Port-Royal des Champs and took up their new quarters in Paris. It was now for the first time that boys' schools were definitely established; hitherto educational or rather tutorial work had been undertaken by the solitaries who were in retreat at Port-Royal, but in a somewhat unsystematic way, if we are to believe Du Fossé. Henceforward the numbers of staff and pupils alike increase, classes are formed and fees fixed, and the work of education is carried on along definite lines fixed by the tradition of Saint-Cyran.

The school in the rue S. Dominique d'Enfer was put in the charge of Walon De Beaupuis, who was only 25 years of age at this time. He had been born at Beauvais and had been brilliantly successful at the University. He had studied under

---

[1] It is at present called the rue Royer-Collard.

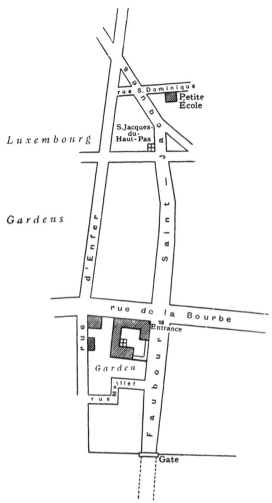

MAP OF THE ENVIRONS OF PORT-ROYAL DE PARIS.

(1) It is uncertain upon which side of the rue S. Dominique d'Enfer the Little School was situated. Its position, therefore, as given above, is conjectural.

(2) The following are the modern names of the streets given in the plan:
    rue de la Bourbe—boulevard de Port-Royal.
    rue du Faubourg S. Jacques—name unchanged.
    rue Maillet—rue Cassini.
    rue d'Enfer—avenue de l'Observatoire and rue Denfert Rochereau.
    rue S. Dominique—rue Royer Collard.

(3) The Observatory which now adjoins the back of Port-Royal was not built till 1667—72.

(4) The gardens of the Luxembourg in the 17th century were more extensive than they are at the present time.

(5) The Parish of S. Jacques du Haut Pas, in which Port-Royal stands, was and still is to some extent a stronghold of Jansenism (see especially Hallays, *Le Pèlerinage de Port-Royal*, p. 30). Saint-Cyran is buried in the choir of the parish church.

Dr Arnauld, whose book *De la Fréquente Communion* won him to the side of Port-Royal; and in 1644 he became a solitary at Port-Royal des Champs.   Although he was not ordained to the priesthood till 1666, his connection with the Port-Royal schools seems to have been as spiritual overseer and general director, rather than as one of the teaching staff.   We possess in the *Supplément au Nécrologe* a regulation for the schools which he drew up, but it is concerned less with teaching than with general rules for the daily routine.   In short, his work at the Port-Royal schools seems to have been more administrative and religious than pedagogic.

Under Walon De Beaupuis were four masters engaged in the actual work of teaching and each of these taught five or six pupils in a separate class-room.   These masters were Lancelot, Nicole, Guyot, and Coustel; and since it is through them that the educational doctrines already enunciated by Saint-Cyran were put into practice, we must stop a while to consider these men more closely.

The chief of them was Claude Lancelot.   As has been seen, he came early under the influence of Saint-Cyran, and on entering Port-Royal in 1638 had been given some educational work to do.   He was a whole-hearted disciple of Saint-Cyran; it is to his *Mémoires* that we owe most of our knowledge of the Abbot.   Throughout his life he devoted himself to educational work; in addition to teaching Greek and Mathematics in the Port-Royal schools, he is the author of the well-known 'Methods' for learning Latin, Greek, Italian, and Spanish, and he took a large part in the preparation of the *Jardin des Racines Grecques* and the *Grammaire générale*. Even after the Port-Royal schools were finally dispersed, he acted as tutor first of the young Duc De Chevreuse and afterwards of the Princes De Conti.   He lived a life of great humility, being content ever to take a subordinate position. Of his character and capabilities, his pupil Du Fossé speaks in the highest terms; he was "a man of great piety and had an unusual gift for educating the young."   He soon put an end to the lack of systematic work which had characterised instruction at Port-Royal des Champs—'ce qui, je l'avoue,' says Du Fossé, 'nous causa bien du chagrin'; but his pupil lived to remember with gratitude the services of the master to whom he owed so much.

Of Guyot we know comparatively little, the reason being that he deserted to the Jesuits after the downfall of Port-Royal, and accordingly Jansenist writers have little to say of him. There are however still extant editions of Cicero's letters and other Latin texts, prepared by him; and to the prefaces of these we are indebted for much information with regard to the educational doctrines of the Port-Royalists.

Pierre Coustel is, next to Lancelot, the most important schoolmaster produced by Port-Royal; perhaps for our purpose he is even the more important of the two, for it is to his detailed *Règles de l'éducation des Enfans* that we owe the greater part of our knowledge of Port-Royal educational theory and practice. Coustel was born at Beauvais in 1621 and was attracted to Port-Royal by his fellow-townsman Walon De Beaupuis. He had already taught in the college at Beauvais[1] and at Port-Royal was given special charge of the teaching of Latin. Although there is no evidence that he ever came into contact with Saint-Cyran, he had inherited a large portion of his spirit. He lived in obscurity, busying himself with his daily tasks. 'Tel qui le vit un jour pouvait dire qu'il l'avait vu tous les jours de sa vie,' we are told in the *Supplément au Nécrologe*[2]; and Sainte-Beuve adds: "This silent regularity and uniformity constitutes the distinguishing mark of the pure race of Saint-Cyran." All the more valuable therefore are his *Règles de l'éducation des Enfans*, which give us the deepest insight into Port-Royal educational methods as inspired by the doctrines adumbrated by Saint-Cyran.

In Pierre Nicole we have a personality which is far better known than Coustel, but which is less truly Port-Royalist. Nicole was born in 1625 and after studying philosophy and theology at the Sorbonne, entered Port-Royal where his aunt, Marie Des Anges Suireau, was already in retirement. He was

---

[1] N.B. *not* the Collège de Beauvais which was part of the University of Paris. See Desmaze, *L'Université de Paris*, p. 139.

[2] *Suppl. au Nécr.* p. 12.

entrusted with the teaching of *belles-lettres* when the schools were established in the rue S. Dominique d'Enfer; but he cannot have given his whole time to teaching, for he continued to study for the bachelor's degree in theology and to learn Greek and Hebrew.   In a Dutch manuscript quoted by Sainte-Beuve in an appendix we read: "M. Nicole only directed the studies of the young people in the Port-Royal schools.   The young gentlemen were of themselves very devoted to study; they only needed to have pointed out to them beautiful passages from their authors whether Greek or Latin.   M. Nicole was there to inspire them with a taste for this.   M. Nicole served them more as an adviser than as a master, in the sense that the word is understood to-day[1]."   However, he seems to have had gifts for teaching and ideas on a literary education which were in advance of his times.   The following quotation from his biography will give some idea of his methods: "He made M. De Tillemont read Quintilian, Cicero's *De Oratore*, and Horace's *Ars Poetica*.   He pointed out all the passages most likely to develop the mind and which most deserved attention; he explained all the figures of speech employed by these authors to make their style more ornamental or more persuasive; he developed everything conformable with the rules of the art and which most closely imitated the beauties of nature.   After this he taught him philosophy and on the subject of logic explained to him all that has since been given to the public under the title: 'The Art of Thinking[2].'   He never dictated any notes, but he used to talk very sensibly, and in order to make clear what he said, had recourse to concrete examples and suitable comparisons.   He allowed his pupil the liberty of making objections and answered them simply and concisely.   He would never break off a conversation with him without seeing clearly that the latter had entirely understood what had been said to him[3]."   In addition to his teaching work Nicole has left us a *Traité de l'éducation d'un Prince*, which will be found in the second volume of his *Essais de Morale*; it is also known that he collaborated in the writing of the *Logic*.

---

[1] Sainte-Beuve, IV, p. 599.   [2] i.e. The Port-Royal *Logic*.
[3] *Vie de Nicole*, pp. 28—29.

However, Nicole does not represent the true spirit of the Port-Royal of Saint-Cyran to anything like the same extent as Lancelot and Coustel. He had not their warm-hearted reverence for the master, and could even describe him as 'capable of producing much, but prolific in briars and thorns.' He once referred to the great Pascal himself as a 'gatherer of shells,' and seems to have possessed a not very sound judgment, for his writings sometimes lack taste and moderation. After the final dispersion of the schools Nicole gave himself up to controversial writings and allied himself with Dr Arnauld, who is also not altogether representative of the Port-Royal of Saint-Cyran. While therefore we recognise that Nicole did render valuable aid to the Port-Royal schools, his chief services to the community were undoubtedly in the realm of literature and theological controversy, and therefore he has not for us the interest possessed by Saint-Cyran, Lancelot, Coustel, and Guyot.

There is another master named Le Fèvre who, according to Du Fossé, taught in the school in the rue S. Dominique d'Enfer at this time. A careful search in the various Port-Royal histories and the *Nécrologes* and their supplements (see Appendix B) has not revealed any other reference to him. He was a master at Port-Royal for only about three or four years—from soon after the foundation of the schools in 1646 to his sudden death about 1650. But he is in some respects so truly a type of the Port-Royal schoolmaster as conceived by Saint-Cyran, that he deserves to be brought out of the oblivion which seems hitherto to have shrouded him. He is described as a complete scholar, adept at the humanities, philosophy and theology; he had also studied history, astronomy, and medicine. But above all he sought to gain the affection of his pupils and to rule them by love. "Since he knew," says Du Fossé, "how to be on terms of familiarity with us without in the least forfeiting that importance which a master should possess, he used always to introduce something pleasant into his conversations, according to the different subjects presented. And his manner towards us was so charming that, having for his object to influence us by the sentiment of honour and to make us sensible thereof, he knew so well how to win us that we loved him tenderly as our friend while we respected him none the less as our master.   The result was that there was not a pupil in the house who did not envy our position, as if it were a kind of benefice, and who did not consider himself miserable in comparison with us....We would have done anything for him so much did we love him and dread displeasing him[1]."   The schoolmaster who can win an epitaph like that from one of his pupils has not lived in vain.   Le Fèvre was not merely content to instruct his boys in class, but he was wont to share their recreation with them, when they were "in a manner even more attached to him owing to the innumerable interesting things which he told them."   Unfortunately this paragon of schoolmasters was suddenly struck down by a violent disease and died in a few days.   Surely since the death of Saint-Cyran the Port-Royal schools had not sustained a heavier blow.

During the years 1646 to 1650 the schools of Port-Royal were carried on in the rue S. Dominique d'Enfer and they apparently soon became famous; the teaching work was in the hands of the solitaries mentioned above, under the general direction of Walon De Beaupuis.   In addition to them however there were other members of the community who took some part in the teaching and who exerted an important influence upon the educational theories set forth by the Port-Royalists.

Among these was De Saci, otherwise Louis Isaac Le Maître, the younger brother of Antoine Le Maître and De Séricourt. Born in 1613, he had studied at the Sorbonne with his 'little uncle,' the afterwards famous Dr Arnauld, who was his senior by only one year.   He early showed poetic talent, and while yet young set his heart on entering the church.   Through the agency of his mother, Catherine Arnauld, he entered Port-Royal about 1638 where he soon came under the influence of Saint-Cyran.   He was at once put in charge of the tuition of his two brothers, Saint-Elme and De Vallemont.   Throughout his connection with Port-Royal he interested himself in the educational work of the community, and M. Carré says of him that next to

[1] *Mémoires*, p. 92.

Saint-Cyran he was the most important source of inspiration for all who laboured at the instruction and education of the pupils at Port-Royal. It would perhaps be more just to ascribe this position to Lancelot, but we cannot overlook De Saci's importance. In January 1650 he was made 'director' of the community—a position originally held by Saint-Cyran—and in this capacity he would have a general oversight of the educational work of the solitaires. De Saci has left us no writings of his own on the subject of education; but Fontaine in his *Mémoires* devotes a long passage to De Saci's views, and in reading it one is at once struck by its remarkable resemblance to Lancelot's remarks 'de la charité de M. De Saint-Cyran pour les Enfans.' In fact it is upon De Saci that a larger portion of Saint-Cyran's spirit descended than upon any other of the solitaires save perhaps upon Lancelot. These two—De Saci and Lancelot— were faithful to their master's ideas and so forfeited some of their claims to originality and greatness. But while with them we are still in the Port-Royal of Saint-Cyran, and it is with this Port-Royal that the Little Schools are inseparably connected. When we come to Nicole and Dr Arnauld, and even Pascal, we have already entered a somewhat different atmosphere, and amid the turmoil of theological controversy the more peaceful work of education is brought to a premature close.

Reference has already been made to Fontaine[1], to whose *Mémoires* we are indebted for much light on the educational views of both Saint-Cyran and De Saci. He entered Port-Royal in 1644 at the age of 19, and De Saci, following the example of his master who had just died, entrusted to the young Fontaine the instruction of several children. Fontaine always filled a subordinate position at Port-Royal; but though he took no great part either in teaching or in enunciating the Port-Royal educational doctrine, yet he is valuable to us because

---

[1] Monroe (*History of Education*, p. 431) cites La Fontaine (1621—1695) and Pascal (1623—1662) as "two of the most renowned pupils" of the Port-Royal Schools. The only conceivable explanation of the statement that La Fontaine was ever a pupil of the Little Schools, seems to be that Monroe has confused the author of the *Fables* with Fontaine, the solitary of Port-Royal. Pascal was educated privately by his father; he did not come into close connection with Port-Royal until 1646, when he was 23 years of age (see p. 37).

of his close connection with the more important solitaries and because he has given us in his *Mémoires* the most vivid and charming picture of Port-Royal that we possess.

Before passing on there remains one other figure to be considered, the physician Hamon, who entered Port-Royal about this period and who found time amid his professional and religious duties to help in the routine work of the schools. He had been born in 1617, and after studying medicine at Paris was converted and entered Port-Royal as a solitary in 1650. His chief occupation was to act as physician to the community, but he also lived a life of extreme asceticism, studying theology and writing religious treatises. None the less, he had a discerning taste for the beauties of style and a sound literary judgment—accomplishments which were rare among the solitaries, in spite of their learning. He does not seem to have given regular lessons at Port-Royal, but to have taken Le Maître's place in his absence; and it was thus (if we may be allowed to anticipate matters somewhat) that he came to have charge of the education of the young Racine—the most notable, if in some respects one of the least representative, of the pupils of Port-Royal. We have some charming pictures of this 'beloved physician' whose care and kindness towards the community and the sick poor of the neighbourhood were equalled only by his own learning and the austerities and mortifications which he continually practised. We see him visiting his patients mounted on a donkey and reading or knitting *en route*, that he may waste no time. Again we are shown him summoned by the grave and reverend faculty of medicine at Paris to pronounce upon the thesis of a candidate; and he appears in his peasant's clothes with long unkempt hair and a general appearance of 'humilité souriante.' It would be beside the point to enlarge upon the services which Hamon rendered to the nuns of Port-Royal at a later date and at a time of great distress and anxiety. But a few biographical details in his, as in other cases, are perhaps justified; for in order to comprehend the spirit of a school, it is of the first importance to know the character of the men who teach there and with whom the pupils come in contact. Let us therefore take note of this unkempt ascetic who was none the less 'un esprit fin et délicat, très versé dans la connaissance des langues et des littératures'; Sainte-Beuve, in an untranslatable phrase, calls him 'un roi-mage en haillons.'

We have now seen the Port-Royal schools definitely organised in the rue S. Dominique d'Enfer, and have to some small extent at any rate become acquainted with the men who were responsible for the education given in them.   It will be appropriate to consider at this stage the meaning of the name 'Petites Écoles,' by which the Port-Royal schools have been known from the time of their first establishment down to the present day.   The term was not a new one, nor was it peculiar to Port-Royal. There had grown up in Paris two distinct educational authorities; the Cathedral Chapter, as represented by the Precentor (cantor, chantre) of Notre Dame, and the University, as represented by the faculty of Arts.   The Precentor had originally been in charge of a cathedral school.   When in later days other schools were opened he himself ceased to teach, and the cathedral school probably degenerated into a 'manécanterie' designed chiefly for the professional instruction of 'enfants de chœur.' However the Precentor continued to claim authority for granting the licence to teach for all schools in Paris.   But when the University was founded at the end of the twelfth century a divided authority was at once instituted, and thus the Cathedral Chapter and the University of Paris came into collision.

The schools under the authority of the Precentor had been of two kinds—the 'écoles petites' or 'françaises' for both sexes, and the 'écoles grandes' or 'latines' for boys only.   The curriculum in the former consisted only of reading, writing, and church-singing, but in the 'écoles grandes' Latin was learnt from *Donatus de octo partibus orationis*, and Cato's *Disticha de moribus*, elementary Mathematics from the *Carmen de Algorismo*[1], and Logic from

---

[1] 'Algorism' included seven operations of elementary Mathematics as specified in the following lines:

> en argorisme devon prendre
> vii especes :
> adison, subtracion,

the *Summulae* or abridgement of the *Organon* of Petrus Hispanus. But the University, which in its faculty of Arts gave a secondary education, tended more and more to displace the 'écoles grandes' and it became quite customary for a boy to go straight from an 'école petite' to the University at a very early age. In this manner the 'écoles grandes' gradually dropped out, and by the time that the Port-Royal schools were organised matters had been compromised thus: the University was to give a secondary education, and the 'écoles petites' were supposed to confine themselves to elementary education. Thus the term 'petites écoles' distinguished these latter schools not, as formerly, from the Latin schools, but from the 'collèges' of the University.

The re-admission to France in 1603 and to Paris in 1609 of the Jesuit schools, which gave a secondary education, had again aroused the opposition of the University; and though the Jesuits had triumphed, Port-Royal was anxious not to arouse opposition either with the University or with them. Hence their schools were called 'Petites Écoles,' which implied that an elementary education only was given in them and that no competition with the University of Paris or other body giving secondary education was contemplated. In point of fact the name was a misnomer. Boys were often entered at an early age—Du Fossé and De Tillemont were both only just 10 years old when they became pupils—but they frequently came later, for Racine was 16 and had already attended the 'collège' of the town of Beauvais. Also a complete education was given, and we have several instances of pupils who stayed on at the school and became solitaires; Du Fossé and De Tillemont both illustrate this. Nevertheless we cannot regard this assumption of the title 'Petites Écoles' as a deliberate deception. The University

doubloison, midiacion,
monteploie et division,
et de radix estracion.
a chez vii especes savoir
doit chascun en memoire avoir
letres qui figures sont dites
et qui excellens sont ecrites.

See also Halliwell-Phillipps, *Rara Mathematica*, p. 74 *et passim*.

had already made incursions into elementary education and
the 'petites écoles,' licensed by the Precentor, had retaliated
by teaching grammar and rhetoric, which were part of the
'Trivium,' and as such properly University studies[1]. Hence
the old distinction had partly broken down. The term 'Petites
Écoles' then as applied to the Port-Royal schools merely served
to signify that they had but few pupils and were modest in aim,
and above all that they did not set out to compete either with
the University or the Jesuits.

In spite of their desire to avoid competition, the Little Schools
were hardly well-established in the rue S. Dominique d'Enfer
before they began to be regarded with a jealous eye by the other
educational institutions of Paris. There is extant a letter sent
by Angélique on February 28, 1648, to the Queen of Poland who
had at one time been in the habit of making retreats at Port-
Royal. In this letter we read that a report had been spread
abroad that at Port-Royal some children were being educated
along heretical lines by five 'fort bons jeunes hommes,' and
that they were called 'petits Frères de la Grace.' In the life
of Nicole[2] we are told that a number of Jesuits, who were called
Bagotists from their being disciples of a Father Bagot, had
established themselves in the rue d'Enfer, and spied upon the
doings of the Port-Royalists and especially on the new school
which had been started there. The solitaries evidently felt
that their work might be endangered if it were carried on in
Paris; and accordingly in 1650 some of the pupils were transferred to the vicinity of Port-Royal des Champs. A few of
them still remained in the rue S. Dominique d'Enfer under
the charge of Walon De Beaupuis. But in 1653 the Jesuits
succeeded by their calumnies in obtaining a royal order against
Port-Royal, and a police-lieutenant was sent to enquire into
the pretended disorders and to inspect the school. The

---

[1] Claude Joly, Precentor of Notre Dame and "juge des petites écoles de la
ville, faubourg et banlieue de Paris," published in 1675 a book entitled: *Avis
chrétiens et moraux pour l'instruction des enfants.* In spite however of his position
as licenser of 'petites écoles' he never mentions elementary education in his book,
but confines himself to secondary education and the education of princes.

[2] *Vie de Nicole*, p. 22.

lieutenant examined the various rooms, and asked for the names of the children and what they did. Apparently no definite step was taken as a result of this visit, but the solitaries saw that they could not hope to carry on undisturbed any teaching work in Paris. Accordingly Walon De Beaupuis with the few pupils whom he still had with him rejoined the rest of the boys and their masters in the country. The school was there divided into three chief groups, one at Les Granges, a farm on a hill overlooking the abbey of Port-Royal des Champs, one at Les Trous, the country seat of M. De Bagnols near Chevreuse, and one at Le Chesnai near Versailles, in the house of M. De Bernières. The last-named group was probably for some time the largest and contained about 20 pupils, whose average age was 10 or 12 years. When Walon De Beaupuis left Paris he organised this school on the lines hitherto followed at the rue S. Dominique d'Enfer; there were four class-rooms and a master in charge of each. Fortunately we possess a 'règlement' which was drawn up by Walon De Beaupuis at this time and which was in vogue not only at Le Chesnai, but at Les Trous and Les Granges as well; it is quoted in the *Supplément au Nécrologe.*

A detailed description of the manner in which the Le Chesnai group was organised is also given in the *Vie de Nicole.* There were four classes each in a separate room. The first consisted of three or four pupils in charge of Coustel; the second of four boys under a M. Le Bon, who afterwards became Archdeacon of Soissons. In the third room there was "a young officer who had left the army and had since been M. De Saci's secretary[1]," together with two boys, and all three were under the direction

---

[1] This probably refers not to Fontaine, who is best known as De Saci's secretary and companion in prison, but to De Séricourt. He was De Saci's elder brother; he left the army and entered Port-Royal at the age of about 27 in 1638 or 1639. He acted as copyist to the solitaries, for although the *Nécrologes*, *Letters* of Saint-Cyran and De Saci, *Mémoires* of Lancelot, Fontaine, and Du Fossé, *Rélations*, &c., were not printed till the 18th century, they all existed much earlier in MS copies prepared by certain of the solitaries and nuns. De Séricourt was one of the first of the solitaries to devote himself to this work and for this reason, probably, is called De Saci's 'secretary' in the above quotation. De Séricourt died very soon after the transference of the schools from Port-Royal de Paris to the country.

of Étienne De Bascle.   The fourth class consisted of the most
advanced pupils, of whom seven are mentioned by name.   The
group at Les Granges, a farm close to the abbey of Port-Royal
des Champs which was at this time occupied by the nuns, was
probably not so carefully organised as that at Le Chesnai; the
pupils were older than those under Walon De Beaupuis, and
their education was in the hands of Lancelot, who taught
Mathematics and Greek, together with Nicole and a master
named Contes who taught *belles-lettres*.   This group however is
of special interest to us; for in 1655 Racine, who was already
16 years of age, was entered as a pupil at Les Granges.   There
were at this time about 15 pupils in this group.   In spite of
the persecution which fell upon Port-Royal in the following
year and interrupted its educational work, Racine remained a
pupil until 1658.   As he is by far the most illustrious product
of the Port-Royal schools, it will be interesting to discover
who were his teachers during this period.   Chief of them was
Lancelot who, we know, taught Greek at Port-Royal; he has
been called by a Jesuit writer the 'chief of the Hellenist sect of
Port-Royal,' and he is the principal contributor to the *Jardin des
Racines Grecques*.   It is to Lancelot therefore that the author of
Andromaque and *Phèdre* owed his knowledge of the Greek
language.   But Racine was fortunate in that he came in contact
with two of the solitaries who did not teach regularly in the
schools but who could give him something which the ordinary
Port-Royal masters most lacked—a sound literary judgment.
First of these two solitaries is Le Maître, between whom and his
pupil there was a warm affection; we have a letter which was
written by him in 1656 to the young Racine, and which concludes:
'bonjour, mon cher fils; aimez toujours votre papa, comme il vous
aime.'   In addition to Le Maître, the doctor Hamon inspired the
future poet with a love of the beautiful in literature; and he also
seems to have been on the warmest terms with his pupil.   Although
in after life Racine wandered far from Port-Royal and in many
ways proved untrue to the spirit of its education, yet in his will
he left instructions that his body should be buried at Port-Royal
at the foot of M. Hamon's grave.   We may take this not only
as a testimony of the very real remorse which Racine felt in

later years for the acts of his early manhood and his attacks on Port-Royal, but also as a token of the love which he never lost for the kindly physician who had first taught him to recognise and to value the beauties of literature.

The group at Les Trous near Chevreuse was the least important of the three; it was under the control of Pierre Borel, a priest of the diocese of Beauvais, who had entered Port-Royal as a solitary in 1646 and subsequently, after the Peace of the Church in 1669, became 'confessor' to the nuns.   There were in addition a few quite small or only temporary groups.   We have indications for instance of a school at Sevrans or S. Severans near Livry in charge of the Abbot of Flexelles, but no very definite information about it remains to us.   Du Fossé again tells us how he was sent with four other pupils under the charge of Le Fèvre to live with M. Retard, the Curé of Magny, which was the next parish to Port-Royal des Champs.   But they had been there scarcely six months, when Le Fèvre died suddenly, and his pupils were accordingly sent to join the group at Les Granges; there they met Dr Arnauld, Le Maître and De Saci, and being already 15 or 16 years old they began to be much influenced by their friendship with these solitaries.   The schools were disorganised once more by the civil wars which broke out in 1649 and the solitaries and their pupils had to seek refuge in the castle of the Duc De Luynes at Vaumurier quite close to Port-Royal des Champs.   But in 1653 peace was restored and the number of nuns and solitaries alike increased.   The schools also flourished greatly.   The buildings at Les Granges were enlarged and an augmented number of children were received there.   Du Fossé tells us with what care and attention they were educated in Christian virtues and the studies of good learning.   "It was considered," says he, "a great advantage that, in the very place where so many persons were living retired from the world and in a state of penitence, young children should be educated in piety and good conduct and learn perfectly not only secular knowledge, but even more the true knowledge of Christianity[1]." We may indeed regard this period as the most flourishing epoch of the Little Schools of Port-Royal.   Not only were the schools

---

[1] *Mémoires*, p. 123.

full, but also all the masters who had made them famous were at this time in touch one with another and were able for a few years to work out their educational methods in peace. We read also of conferences which they held at Vaumurier, when the theories of Saint-Cyran on education were discussed and practical methods of teaching compared and criticised. It was here that the educational doctrines and practice of the Port-Royalists were tested and elaborated; so that in after years, when the schools were no longer in existence and the Port-Royal schoolmasters had leisure to write their treatises on education, they put into these books the results of actual school-room practice, tested in their own experience and compared with the experience of others.

It may be objected that the educational treatises of the solitaries do not necessarily embody the practice of the Little Schools, but merely set forth their individual views on teaching. This is, on the face of it, very improbable. Moreover there is throughout the educational writings of the Port-Royalists a remarkable unity of doctrine, which cannot be accidental and which is obviously based on the theories of Saint-Cyran slightly modified by class-room experience and by other influences to be considered in a later chapter. Continually the Port-Royal authors tell us that they have found so and so to be the case 'par expérience'; and thus we have in their treatises the matured results of many years' teaching. From our point of view, then, the closing of the schools is an advantage, since it afforded the solitaries opportunities for setting down the outlines of their school practice and the results of their experience. As Sainte-Beuve admirably says: "Les estimables maîtres usèrent du loisir forcé et de la retraite à laquelle on les condamnait, pour recueillir leur expérience et pour en communiquer au public les fruits. Port-Royal, au moment le plus voilé de son éclipse, continuait par là d'éclairer et d'enseigner. Un avantage de cette marche graduelle, c'est que ces procédés d'enseignement ne se ressentent en rien d'une théorie précipitée; ils avaient été auparavant essayés et pratiqués de longue main, et ils n'arrivaient au public que perfectionnés par l'usage[1]."

[1] Vol. III, p. 508.

According to M. Carré, the educational ideas of the Port-Royalists are scattered throughout voluminous collections in which it is somewhat difficult to discover them. This is true of the history of the schools, but it is much less the case with the Port-Royal theory of education. This is contained in great detail in Coustel's *Règles de l'éducation des Enfans*—the most valuable perhaps of all the Port-Royal educational treatises. It was published in two volumes in 1687, but is now unfortunately rare[1], and for this reason little known. M. Carré says of it: "Quoique cet ouvrage n'ait paru que bien après la ruine des Petites Écoles et qu'il ait été composé dans une vue générale, on ne peut douter qu'il ne reproduise fidèlement l'esprit de l'institution primitive et les maximes d'éducation que Coustel avait lui-même mises en pratique avec MM. De Beaupuis et Lancelot. Aucun écrit de Port-Royal ne nous fait mieux pénétrer dans la vie intime des Petites Écoles. Comme fond, c'est du pur Saint-Cyran, un peu mitigé peut-être par la pratique des enfants et l'expérience de l'enseignement[2]." If any further proof were needed that this work enshrines the actual practice of the Port-Royal schools, this is furnished by the last sentence of Walon De Beaupuis' *Règlement* for the school at Le Chesnai; it runs as follows: "It would be necessary at this point to go on to speak of the manner in which the boys were taught their lessons, and of the good and pious maxims with which we endeavoured to inspire them. But as this has been already done in the Rules for the good education of children, printed 'chez Michallet,' this repetition is hardly necessary[3]." Here is an obvious reference to Coustel's book which alone among the Port-Royal educational treatises was printed "à Paris chez Estienne Michallet rue S. Jacques, à l'Image S. Paul." The proof thus seems conclusive that Coustel does give us a clear picture of the actual practice of the Little Schools. In our description therefore of the details of the schools and the teaching in them, frequent reference will be made to Coustel's book.

[1] It is unrepresented in the British Museum, the Bodleian Library, and the collection of Port-Royal books at Sion College. The copy used by the writer was that belonging to the Musée Pédagogique, Paris.

[2] p. 89.   [3] *Suppl. au Nécr.* p. 58.

Other sources, from which our knowledge of Port-Royal school practice is drawn, are the prefaces to the various school books of Lancelot and Guyot; Le Maître's *Règles de la traduction française*, which he prepared for the benefit of the young Du Fossé; the latter's own memoirs and the short description by Georges Walon of the school organisation at Le Chesnai, which together give us a picture of the Little Schools from the pupils' standpoint; also Jacqueline Pascal's regulations for the Port-Royal girls' schools, together with the *Règlement* of Walon De Beaupuis, already referred to, and Nicole's *Traité de l'Éducation d'un Prince*. We are justified in including the last-named work in our list of treatises setting forth the Port-Royal school methods, because its general tone is precisely that of the Saint-Cyran tradition, as modified by experience and as illustrated in Coustel's *Règles*. There are passages which refer more especially to the education of those in high places, but the bulk of the treatise is devoted to the exposition of a liberal education such as would apply to any child who was destined for a professional or ecclesiastical career. Nicole himself says: "Most of the recommendations made in this book can be applied under any conditions and are of interest to all fathers who are bringing up their children."

Since, then, the educational doctrines of Port-Royal are clearly based upon the results of experience in school-room practice quite as much as upon the theories of Saint-Cyran or any other thinker, a study of them has a special value for those who are interested in teaching. In reading Locke or Rousseau or Herbert Spencer we have the brilliant lucubrations of men with gifted minds, but who have had no experience of the routine of the class-room and little first-hand knowledge of children. With the Port-Royalists it is quite different; every page of Coustel or Lancelot, every rule laid down by Walon De Beaupuis or Jacqueline Pascal, gives evidence of a thorough knowledge of actualities in the education of boys or girls. And since the great love that the solitaries had for children gave them deep insight into wise methods of teaching and of school administration, so that their schools were in most respects two centuries in advance of their contemporaries, we shall find a study of their

ideas and practice useful even to-day; for although Pestalozzi
has shown us the more excellent way, yet the Port-Royalists
preceded him in making love for children and adaptation to their
capabilities the basis of the process of education, without being
led astray into vapid sentimentality or losing sight of the practical
needs of the case.

During this period when the schools were prospering there
were added to the community Blaise Pascal and his sister
Jacqueline, both of whom—and especially the latter—were
destined to play an important part in the educational work of
Port-Royal.   Before we pass on to the final chapter of this
history of the schools, an attempt must be made to sketch
these two personalities, for then our picture-gallery of those
concerned in Port-Royal education will be, for the time being,
complete.   Of Blaise Pascal little need be said here, for
his biography has been many times written.   Both he and
his sister Jacqueline, who was his junior by two years, early
showed great talent—he in science and mathematics and she
in composing poetry.   In 1646 Blaise and Jacqueline together
with their father came into contact with Port-Royal, though
none of them actually entered the community at this date.   In
the autumn of 1647, owing to Blaise's weak health, he and his
sister went to Paris to seek medical advice; while there they
were frequent attendants at the church of Port-Royal and seem
to have been profoundly influenced by Singlin, who was at that
time director of the community.   Jacqueline at once conceived
a desire to take the veil and enter the abbey, but her father
opposed the design.   However, upon his death in 1651, she
was free and accordingly entered the convent of Port-Royal in
January 1652, where she became known as Sister Sainte-
Euphémie.   In June 1655 she was appointed assistant mistress
of the novices and given charge of the education of the girls
at Port-Royal; and at the beginning of the same year her
brother Blaise, influenced alike by a marvellous escape from
death and by a sermon of Singlin's, himself retired to Port-
Royal des Champs.

To Jacqueline we owe a detailed *Règlement*, which was

drawn up for the administration of the girls' schools and which
gives us much insight into their methods.   There has also
been preserved to us a letter written by Jacqueline to her
brother Blaise, asking for details of a new method of teaching
reading which he had invented.   We shall have to refer to
this letter again; but for the present it suggests the query: did
Pascal ever take an active part in the educational work of Port-
Royal?   There seems no proof that he did.   His health when
he entered the community was far from good and his controversial writings must soon have engrossed his attention, for the
first of his *Provincial Letters* appeared early in 1656; moreover
he is never mentioned by the Port-Royal writers as having
actually taught in their schools.   But we must not suppose
that he was without interest in education; his sister's letter to
him would be sufficient to disprove that.   We know also that
he collaborated in the production of the Port-Royal educational
treatises, as well as in the *Logic*; he probably took part in the
conferences at Vaumurier and the criticisms and suggestions of
so brilliant a mind may well have been an asset of no little
value, even though Pascal himself had never been a schoolmaster.
His life at Port-Royal was a short one[1], and most of it was spent
in intense physical suffering.   During the first part of that time
he was engaged in defending Jansenism and Port-Royal against
the Jesuits; and in his later years he devoted his time to medi-
tating upon a proposed 'magnum opus' on religion; the notes
for this work were collected after his death and published under
the title of *Pensées*.   But it appears that Pascal had had another
aim in view and might have carried it out had he lived and enjoyed good health.   This was a definitely educational work;
Nicole tells us that "one of the things on which the late M. Pascal
had the largest number of opinions was the education of a prince.
He was often heard to say that there was nothing in which he
would more gladly have taken part if that had been his business
and that he would willingly have sacrificed his life for so important a matter[2]."   While therefore Pascal does not from our
point of view take that place of chief importance among the

---

[1] January 1655 to his death in June 1662.
[2] *Essais de Morale*, Vol. II, p. 214.

Port-Royalists to which he is normally entitled, yet he does merit to be accounted one of the educationalists of the community.

Port-Royal was not allowed to carry on its teaching work for long in peace, for the storm which had menaced them in Paris now threatened to break over the schools in the country. The Society of Jesus had for long eyed Port-Royal askance. The *Augustinus* of Jansen had been condemned at Rome; Arnauld's book *De la Fréquente Communion* and his defence of the *Augustinus* had alike irritated the Jesuits; but when Arnauld was himself condemned by the Sorbonne, Pascal took up the cudgels on his behalf, and the agile but piercing sarcasm of the *Provinciales* stung the Jesuits to the quick. The letters of Pascal immediately made an immense impression; they were being read everywhere and the credit of the Society of Jesus was in imminent peril; "the Jesuits confess," says Racine in his history of Port-Royal, "that exile, imprisonment, and the most terrible tortures did not equal the pain which they felt at being mocked and deserted by everybody[1]." We are told that the Chancellor of the University was so dismayed on reading the first of the *Provincial Letters*, that he almost choked and had to be bled seven times before he recovered. The situation of the Jesuits was desperate; hitherto Port-Royal had been merely a thorn in the flesh; now she appeared as a mighty and triumphant enemy. Accordingly they at once solicited the aid of the Court, over which they had great influence[2], and a royal order, authorising the dispersion of the Port-Royal schools, was obtained. On March 30, 1656, a police-lieutenant visited the groups at Les Granges and Le Chesnai and broke them up; the solitaries were driven out and the children were sent back to their parents or to families who were willing to receive them. Du Fossé being by this time 22 years old, retired to Paris where he and De Tillemont continued their studies, living together under the care of an ecclesiastic named Du Mont. In 1657 he returned to Port-Royal des Champs with Le Maître who had obtained permission from Mazarin for them to do this.

[1] p. 63.
[2] A Jesuit (Father Annat) was at this time confessor to Louis XIV.

The dispersion of the schools in 1656 was certainly damaging to Port-Royal, but it was not complete; the groups at Les Trous and Vaumurier had not been visited and the educational work still went on in some families in a mutilated form. Some of the children went to the house of the Marquis De Guivry at Perchai and others were put under the protection of M. De Buzenval, Bishop of Beauvais. It appears that De Beaupuis still held out with some seven pupils at Le Chesnai. The final and complete extirpation of the schools was yet to come. It seems strange at first sight that the Jesuits did not pursue their advantage to its furthest; but we can discover at least two reasons why their persecution of Port-Royal was arrested for a time.

On March 24, 1656, there had occurred at the convent of Port-Royal de Paris an incident that was long remembered in the community as the ' miracle of the Holy Thorn.' It is described in great detail in a letter of Angélique, which still remains to us. There was a little girl named Marguerite Périer, ten years of age, who was being educated at the convent school. She was a niece of Pascal and was afflicted with lachrymal fistula in the left eye; the disease was of a most severe character and had made extensive and disfiguring ravages, so that the bones of the nose and palate had become carious, giving rise to a constant and offensive discharge. During the ceremony of venerating one of the thorns which had composed Our Lord's crown and which had been lent to Port-Royal by a certain M. De La Potterie, a nun pressed the holy relic to the ulcer, uttering a fervent prayer for healing. And from that very hour the patient was cured. Naturally this event, whatever be its explanation, made a great impression not only upon Port-Royal and upon Pascal, who was led by it to compose his *Pensées*, but also upon the outside world. The miracle was regarded as a manifestation of divine favour towards Port-Royal, and accordingly there was a revulsion of feeling in favour of this community, to the corresponding discredit of the Society of Jesus. The Port-Royalists found a support at Court in the queen-mother who sent her own physician to investigate the case; "probably," says Racine, "her piety was touched by the manifest protection of God towards these sisters. This wise princess began to judge more favourably of their innocence. It was no longer suggested to take away their novices and their boarders and they were left free to receive as many of them as they liked[1]." It seems that this armistice extended even to the boys' schools at Port-Royal des Champs and that some attempt was made to build them up again.

There was another incident which helped to paralyse for the time being the malignant activity of the Jesuits. In one of their 'collèges' (that of Clermont in Paris) a nephew of Mazarin, Alphonse Mancini by name, happened at this time to be an 'interne.' Now Mazarin, being an ecclesiastic, had no son who could be his heir, and he hoped to make this, his favourite nephew, the inheritor of his wealth and the successor of his position. Unfortunately there was in vogue at Clermont a custom, not unknown in certain English boarding schools, called 'la berne.' This consisted in placing a boy in a blanket, the corners of which were held by other boys, and in tossing him into the air. While the young Alphonse Mancini was undergoing this ordeal on the night of Christmas Day 1657 he fell heavily to the floor and injured his spine. In spite of all the wisdom of the king's own physician, the unfortunate boy died on January 6, 1658. Naturally it was a terrible blow to Mazarin, and in consequence of the incident the Jesuit schools fell for a time into disrepute, while Port-Royal was left undisturbed.

But the Society of Jesus soon recovered its power and at once used it to give the *coup de grâce* to Port-Royal. On March 10, 1660[2], the police-lieutenant arrived at Le Chesnai with orders to make a decisive end of the Little Schools. The two masters and seven children whom he found there were at once driven out; the few children who remained at Les Trous had already been sent back to their parents, and there remained only two sons of a M. De Bagnols (who had died in 1657) under the care of their tutor—probably Borel. As for the house at Les Granges it was already empty. The dispersion of the

[1] p. 57.
[2] See Appendix A.

boys' schools was followed by the persecution of the nuns and the destruction of the girls' schools in the following year. The solitaries also began a life of wandering and exile; Lancelot died at Quimperlé in Brittany; Nicole fled into Flanders; Dr Arnauld, 'errant, pauvre, banni, proscrit, persécuté,' ceased not till the end of his life to defend the doctrines of Jansenism and to suffer for what he believed to be the truth.

It is interesting to notice that, even after their dispersion from Port-Royal, most of the teaching solitaries continued to manifest their interest in education, not only by writing the treatises already referred to, but also by acting as private tutors, chiefly to high-born children. Lancelot undertook the tuition of the Duc De Chevreuse and afterwards of the young Princes De Conti; Coustel was appointed tutor of the nephews of Cardinal De Fürstemberg, Bishop and Prince of Strasbourg, to whom he dedicated his *Règles de l'éducation des Enfans.* Walon De Beaupuis had charge for a time of the education of the two young Périers, Pascal's nephews and brothers of the heroine of the Holy Thorn miracle. Guyot went over to the Jesuits, as has already been said; for in 1666 he dedicated one of his books to Messeigneurs De Montbaron, pupils at the Jesuit 'collège' of Clermont—"a famous school which piety has dedicated to learning and virtue." Nicole did not lose his interest in education in spite of the fact that he devoted the rest of his life to theological controversy and the writing of ethical treatises. Reference has already been made to his *Traité de l'Éducation d'un Prince,* which appears in the second volume of his *Essais de Morale,* published in 1671.

We may gather from these instances that the interest of Port-Royal was rather with the education of the 'upper' classes than with that of the people. As will presently be shown, there was no room in Saint-Cyran's educational theories for the education of the masses; such ideas were left for Comenius and the Protestant reformers to initiate. This was due not to any lack of sympathy with the poorer members of the community, but rather to a deeply-engrained religious belief that the divers orders of society are ordained of God and that any attempt fundamentally to alter them savours of impiety. Contrasted with their contemporaries, and more especially with the Jesuits, the Port-Royalists show on the whole quite a liberal spirit in this matter; but even in their case we read of a softer seat being provided for children of noble birth, and arrangements were made in the girls' schools that pupils of high rank might have a bedroom to themselves and a 'sister' to wait upon them.

Nevertheless this attitude did not necessarily imply a fatalistic contentment with the existing state of the community. Nowadays we usually seek to regenerate society from the bottom; we try to improve the mental, moral and physical condition of the masses and to soften the contrasts which separate one class from another. But in the time of Port-Royal an often-proposed solution for social and economic problems took the form of devices for regenerating society from the top by the provision of sovereigns who had been properly educated for their position. We may perhaps regard this phase of thought as being to some extent the outcome of a movement to which Richelieu and Mazarin had devoted all their energies—the establishment of an absolute monarchy in France. Be that as it may, the age of Louis XIV is marked by the appearance of a number of treatises on the education of princes, which form quite a feature of contemporary literature and of which Nicole's *Traité* is but one among many instances. As early as the thirteenth century Vincent De Beauvais had written his *De Institutione Principum* and *De Eruditione Filiorum Regalium*; the *Institutio Principis Christiani* of Erasmus appeared in 1526, and Sturm was also the author of an *Institutio Principis*. But it is in the seventeenth century that we find the largest output of treatises of this type. Péréfixe, Archbishop of Paris, and Le Mothe Le Vayer, the tutors of Louis XIV and his brother, both set down their theories in writing; so also Bossuet and Fénelon have left records of the methods which they used in teaching the Dauphin. Duguet of the Oratory wrote a huge treatise on the education of children of high rank; and Lancelot himself has left, in a letter to De Saci, a description of the manner in which he taught the Princes De Conti. Fleury and La Bruyère also devoted themselves to work of

this kind and the methods which they used can be gathered
from their writings; while, as was mentioned above, Pascal
is reported to have said that he would have sacrificed his
life, if possible, to so important a duty as the education of
the great.

The whole phenomenon is an interesting one, because it seems
to be symptomatic of a widely-prevalent idea that society needed
reform and that this could best be accomplished by the right
education of those who would one day be all-powerful in the
state. But there is as yet no conception of popular education
as a solution of contemporary problems; even at Port-Royal
education was never regarded as a right due to every member
of the community alike. Still, in these many treatises we may
trace a feeling among educated and thoughtful men that the
evils of bad and irresponsible government needed urgent reform
and that this must be accomplished somehow. Had the methods
which they advocated been successfully applied, France might
perhaps have found a less drastic solution for her social and
economic problems than the excessive reaction, with its accompanying horrors, of the Revolution.

It is high time to return to the Little Schools of Port-Royal
and their destruction in 1660. At most they had endured for
14 years and not more than three or four of these were ever
consecutively peaceful. The situation of the schools was continually being changed; the number of the pupils constantly
altering; the work of the teachers perpetually harassed or interrupted by dangers and anxieties. As far as we know, the
number of the pupils never at any time exceeded 50, and
the total who passed through the Port-Royal schools during
the whole time of their existence was not more than 250[1] at
most, and of many of these the education could only have been
partial and unsatisfactory. Can we therefore ascribe the persecution which the Society of Jesus carried on so bitterly against
the Port-Royalists solely or even chiefly to jealousy of their
educational work? By the middle of the seventeenth century

---

[1] Compayré's 1000 is by far too many (*Hist.* I, 240). See discussion of this point
later, on pp. 165 f.

there were flourishing Jesuit 'collèges' in all parts of France and they had eclipsed even the University itself. In 1651 we learn that the Collège de Clermont contained 2000 pupils and by 1675 this number had risen to 3000; as early as 1627 there were in the Jesuit schools of the province of Paris alone no less than 13,195 boys, and the educational methods of the society won the praise of Descartes and Bacon. It seems scarcely probable that an institution of this magnitude could ever have felt its existence imperilled by the Little Schools of Port-Royal, with their 40 or 50 pupils and their tuition-system of school administration which could hardly have been made permanent. The following passage from Racine expresses a widely-held theory, but it evidently needs some qualification : " The Jesuits even feared for some time that Port-Royal might deprive them of the education of youth—that is to say, that their influence might be dried up at its source....This question of the education of youth, as I have said, was one of the chief reasons which led the Jesuits to destroy Port-Royal[1]." It may perhaps be true that the Society of Jesus saw in Port-Royal a rival which might one day become formidable in the field of education; but this vague jealousy is not in itself enough to explain the relentless and malignant persecution with which the Jesuits pursued the community.

Setting aside then the explanation given by Racine, let us next hear what a modern Jesuit writer has to say on this subject. Father Rochemonteix, in his history of the La Flèche school[2], rightly points out that from Port-Royal originated the substitution of the vernacular for Latin as a teaching medium. But, instead of welcoming this movement as a desirable reform, Rochemonteix sees in it a serious educational mistake; and he quotes with approval the dictum of Joseph De Maistre : " L'enseignement de Port-Royal est la véritable époque de la décadence des bonnes lettres." Latin as a school subject is considered to be of unique importance. " La divine Providence," says Rochemonteix, "a confié à cette langue le dépôt de la foi, les livres sacrés et tous les enseignements qui émanent des Docteurs, des

[1] pp. 40—1.
[2] *Un Collège de Jésuites aux* XVIIe *et* XVIIIe *siècles*, Le Mans, 1889.

Saints Pères, des Conciles, du siège apostolique; elle est la langue du monde catholique[1]."

The Jesuit defence therefore is that by persecuting the Little Schools, they were upholding the cause of Latin, the sacred language and the one subject of supreme importance in education. There are at least two answers to this excuse. In the first place Latin, in spite of all reforms, continued to hold at Port-Royal a paramount position in the curriculum. It was chiefly in their methods of teaching this subject that the solitaries differed from the Jesuits. Again, the Society of Jesus at once recognised the value of using the vernacular in teaching—to some extent, at any rate; and they did not hesitate to follow the example set by Port-Royal. In 1650 a Latin grammar, written in both Latin and French, was published at La Flèche[2]; and this was superseded in 1664 by a Latin and French edition of the *De primis Latinae grammaticae rudimentis libellus* of Annibal Codret. The Jesuit Jouvency also in 1711 distinctly laid down in his official *Ratio discendi et docendi*: "non est negligenda tamen lingua vernacula"; and he goes on to give rules and recommendations which accord in detail with Port-Royal school practice.

The question of the use of the vernacular in teaching will be dealt with at greater length in a later chapter. But enough, perhaps, has been said at present to make it clear that the Jesuit attack on the Little Schools cannot be explained away as a sincere desire to secure for the sacred language of the Church that place of chief importance in the curriculum which it would naturally hold in the schools of a religious order. We must therefore look elsewhere for the true causes of the destruction of the Port-Royal schools.

The most obvious of these causes is to be found in the theological dispute which was being carried on between the two religious corporations. The question at issue will be considered at a later stage; but it should be here remembered that the appearance of the *Provinciales* had dealt a blow to the Society of Jesus from which it with difficulty recovered. The

---

[1] *op. cit.* p. 148.
[2] This is the *Despauterius Novus* referred to on p. 128.

doctrines of Jansen, espoused by Port-Royal, and Arnauld's book *De la Fréquente Communion* had aroused the anger of the Jesuits against whom they were directed; but it was not until the appearance of Pascal's *Provinciales* that the Jesuits saw in Port-Royal a really formidable enemy.   Moreover there was to a certain extent a personal quarrel between the Society of Jesus and the Arnauld family, which formed the backbone of Port-Royal.   Some of Dr Arnauld's ancestors had been Huguenots —a fact which in itself was enough to cast aspersions on his orthodoxy.   Besides this, his father Antoine Arnauld had been a famous advocate and had represented the University of Paris in its struggle against the Society of Jesus.   In 1593 an attempt had been made on the life of Henri IV by a certain Pierre Barrière who confessed that he had been instigated by the Jesuits. The University seized this opportunity to demand the expulsion of its rivals from France, and Antoine Arnauld was chosen to act as its counsel; "he pleaded this cause," we are told, "with such vehemence and success that the Jesuits never forgave him." When therefore the son of their old enemy produced his treatise *De la Fréquente Communion,* in which he censured the laxity of the Jesuits in almost direct terms and ascribed to them responsibility for the evil state of contemporary society, the Jesuits became possessed of a definite grievance against the Arnauld family and thus Port-Royal was dragged in; "the whole quarrel of Jansenism," says Sainte-Beuve, "can be simply defined as the quarrel between the Arnauld family and the Society of Jesus."

Other causes contributed to widen the breach; Pascal had aroused the opposition of the Jesuits in his experiments upon the vacuum, so that in his *Provinciales* he was not only defending Arnauld but also to some extent paying off old scores on his own account. The Port-Royalists had made other enemies besides the Jesuits.   Lancelot tells us that Saint-Cyran had known some unsavoury secrets concerning the life of Richelieu; and if knowledge of this kind and in connection with so powerful a man be not turned by its possessor to his own advantage, it may easily become dangerous or even fatal to him.   Perhaps it is here that the real cause of Saint-Cyran's imprisonment lies. Again the reputation of some of the friends of Port-Royal tended to compromise the society in the eyes of the outside world. "With a facility more Christian than judicious," to quote Racine's phrase, they welcomed into retreat at Port-Royal a number of disgraced courtiers or notorious ladies whose past life had not been free from blemish. They remained under the patronage of De Retz, to whose real character they apparently remained wilfully blind; "they forgave his depraved morals," says Fontaine, "in consideration of his many excellent qualities and his great anxiety to have persons of merit for his friends." Their connection with him and also with the Duc De Luynes, the Prince De Conti, the Duchesse De Longueville and others caused a report to be circulated that Port-Royal was implicated in the wars of the Fronde and was using its influence against Mazarin and the King; but we have no proof that this was so. During the disturbances the community seems to have devoted itself whole-heartedly to relieving the distress caused among the poor of the neighbourhood, but there is no evidence that Port-Royal itself took any part in this civil strife.

It is clear then that, quite apart from the existence of the schools, the Jesuits were bitterly hostile to the solitaries of Port-Royal and the community was in bad odour both at the Court and also to some extent in the world at large. When therefore there issued from Port-Royal a series of books the influence of which menaced the very existence of the Jesuits and tended hopelessly to compromise their credit as 'directors of consciences,' it was not difficult for them to set in motion the civil authorities and with their help to crush the Jansenist community. The object of their hatred was not so much the schools, of which they could never have been very greatly afraid, but the solitaries who were responsible for the books. These books had exposed Jesuit methods; they threatened to destroy the influence of the Society in the sphere of religion and education alike; and it is to the appearance of these works then that we must ultimately trace the attack which incidentally involved the downfall of the Port-Royal schools.

The boys' schools never recovered from the blow; the solitaries were dispersed and the pupils sent to their homes. The

MAP OF THE RE-
MOTER ENVIRONS
OF PORT-ROYAL
DES CHAMPS.

From a manuscript
in the possession of
M. Gazier, Professor
at the Sorbonne, and
quoted by Hallays
(p. 100), we learn that
there were two routes
by which a traveller
might reach Port-
Royal des Champs
from Paris. One
passed through Passy,
Sèvres, Montreuil,
and Voisins, and was
perhaps the most
usual one. The other
went viâ Montrouge,
Châtillon, Bièvres,
Saclay, Saint-Aubin,
Saint-Rémy, Chev-
reuse, and Saint-
Lambert—i.e. almost
parallel to the present
Orléans railway line
to Saint-Rémy les
Chevreuse, though to
the west of it.

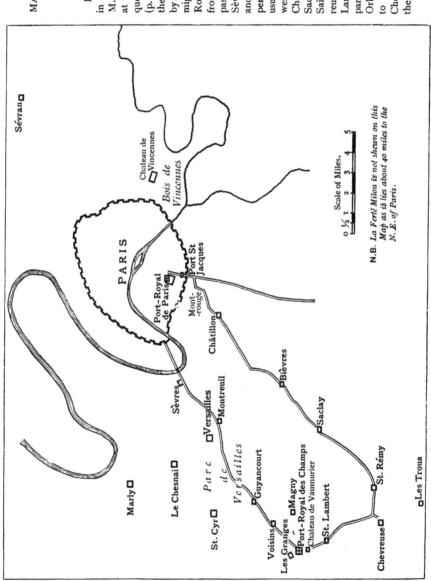

Scale of Miles.

0 ½ 1 2 3 4 5

N.B. *La Ferté Milon is not shewn on this
Map as it lies about 40 miles to the
N.E. of Paris.*

girls' schools, under the care of the sisters, were revived in 1669, at the 'Peace of the Church,' but these also were closed in 1679 by the King's orders. Yet, though the line of succession was thus broken, we can still trace a kind of recrudescence at a later date of both boys' and girls' schools alike. In 1678 Nicole had founded a girls' school at Troyes and this continued to be carried on by teaching sisters until it was finally closed by royal order in 1749.

Another Jansenist girls' school was established in Paris. Cardinal De Noailles, from whom the decree for the suppression and destruction of Port-Royal des Champs was extorted, seems to have desired to make amends when it was too late; for in 1713 he sanctioned the formation of a community of 'Sœurs de Sainte-Marthe,' who set up girls' schools, on Port-Royal lines, in the parishes of S. Séverin and S. Leu. These schools were suppressed during the Revolution, but were revived in 1801. In 1870, the sisters, being accused of Jansenism, were driven out of Paris by their archbishop and settled at Magny-les-Hameaux, a village near the site of Port-Royal des Champs. Here in 1908 M. André Hallays found the last two sisters of the order, still wearing the habit of the Port-Royal of old—a black coif and white scapulary, emblazoned with a large scarlet cross[1]. Both of these aged ladies have since died and with them have vanished the last traces of the nuns of Port-Royal and their girls' schools.

More interesting from our special point of view is the Jansenist boys' school which came into existence early in the eighteenth century[2]. A Jansenist ecclesiastic named Tabourin, whose biography is given in the *Supplément au Nécrologe*, established in 1709 a school for poor children in the parish of S. Etienne du Mont at Paris; in 1713 the school was organised

---

[1] The regular habit of the Cistercian nuns included a plain black scapulary. This had in fact been worn by the Sisters of Port-Royal previous to 1647. But in that year the Institute of the Holy Sacrament was united to Port-Royal de Paris; and, although the rule of S. Benedict was strictly retained, the white scapulary with its scarlet cross, which had characterised the nuns of the Holy Sacrament, henceforth formed part of the uniform of Port-Royal.

[2] For a detailed account of this school, together with a reprint of its *Constitutions*, see Séché, *Les Derniers Jansénistes*, Vol. II, p. 404.

and put in charge of six or seven teaching brothers. In 1721 Tabourin, who in addition to his school work had been training masters and mistresses who should teach in all parts of France and had also been distributing 'des bons livres,' was exiled owing to his Jansenist sympathies; but the schools under a priest named Adrien Potherie continued to flourish. We also read of a priest named Goury whose life is described in the Port-Royal *Nécrologe*, and who took an active part in the teaching and administration. The schools in Paris were enlarged and other Jansenist schools were set up in the provinces, at Orleans, Auxerre, Eu, and Rouen. The declining influence and final expulsion of the Jesuits in 1762 removed any fear of opposition from this quarter, and by the time that the Revolution broke out there were no less than 32 schools, and between 6000 and 7000 pupils. Moreover these institutions had a notable influence; we are told that "in less than 20 years, the schools of the faubourg S. Antoine had so softened and polished the manners of its inhabitants, that it was no longer like the same place. M. Hérault, lieutenant of police, said that the police of this district cost him 30,000 francs per year less than they cost his predecessors and that he ascribed this solely to the establishment of these schools[1]." The teaching methods were, as far as was possible under the altered conditions, those of the original Little Schools of Port-Royal; the vernacular was used, difficulties were removed from the child's path wherever practicable and the Pascal method of teaching reading was in vogue. But the great difference between Tabourin's schools and the Little Schools lies in the fact that the former were free elementary schools for poor children, whereas in the latter a more or less complete education had been given to the sons of well-to-do parents and a kind of tutorial system had been adopted. In the Tabourin schools therefore the tone of the discipline was more austere than at Port-Royal, the rod was more often used, and the school methods seem to have reverted to some extent to the barbarisms of the Middle Ages. The Revolution disturbed the work of these schools, and they were closed by order on the 9th of Thermidor in the year II; they were reopened in 1802 and obtained royal recognition

[1] Quoted by Hallays, p. 206.

in 1820. Schools were set up not only in Paris, but also, as before, in many provincial towns. Unfortunately their prosperity was affected by bad administration and, in spite of their being transformed from free-schools into middle-class fee-taking schools, they gradually declined.

There was, however, one exception; a Jansenist school founded at Saint-Lambert, a village mid-way between Milon and Port-Royal des Champs, had been endowed by a M. Silvy, who was an enthusiastic Jansenist and admirer of Port-Royal. To him the conservation of the ruins of the abbey and the collection of the contents of the present museum are largely due. This one institution survived the general decline of the Tabourin schools. It is to-day no longer directed by the Tabourin brothers or 'frères de Saint-Antoine,' as they were sometimes called, for their last superior died in 1887 and their place is now taken by 'instituteurs laïques'; but the school occupies the presbytery of the old church of Saint-Lambert of which Le Nain De Tillemont was for a time curé, and, as M. Hallays says: "quelque chose de l'esprit ancien persiste dans la vieille maison." To this day one can read the inscription on the façade of this school, telling how it was founded by M. Silvy; and it is here that we may recognise the present-day representative, in an indirect line and an altered form, of the Little Schools of Port-Royal. Even though the institution which binds them to our generation is not a direct descendant and has, perhaps, inherited only a small portion of the tradition of Saint-Cyran, yet it is not without interest to have traced the history of Port-Royal education down to our own times.

CHAPTER III

THE EDUCATIONAL THEORIES OF THE PORT-ROYALISTS

Now that we have followed the history of Port-Royal education from its birth in the mind of Saint-Cyran to its last faint
traces in modern France, we must turn aside to consider the
theological foundation upon which the whole educational doctrine of Port-Royal was based. It is not necessary to make a
detailed exposition of Jansenism, but it is at the same time
quite impossible to appreciate the educational position of the
Port-Royalists save in the light of their theological beliefs; for
the former followed more or less logically from the latter.

Saint-Cyran's theology is to be found in Jansen's *Augustinus*, a work embodying the doctrines of S. Augustine and
S. Paul. It was accused by the Jesuits of containing five
heretical propositions, which need not be specified here; but in
reply the Port-Royalists raised two points, one of 'fact' (i.e.
whether the five propositions really *were* in the *Augustinus*),
and the other of 'law' (i.e. whether the five propositions were
heretical). Port-Royal condemned the five propositions qua
'law,' but it denied their existence in the *Augustinus* qua 'fact.'
Hence the whole point at issue between the Jesuits and the
Jansenists would seem at first sight not to have been a question
of dogma, since both alike considered the five propositions
heretical; but it turned apparently on the question as to whether
the *Augustinus* contained these five heretical propositions; and
the persecution with which the Jesuits harassed the nuns of
Port-Royal after the dispersion of the solitaries and their pupils
took the form of trying to compel them to sign a statement
that Jansen's book *did* contain the heretical doctrines and was
therefore worthy of condemnation.

There were none the less definite doctrinal points at issue throughout and these were made specific in Arnauld's book *De la Fréquente Communion*. Jansenism had in fact imported into the bosom of the Roman Church the doctrines of Grace and Predestination, which formed the staple of the recently-formed heresy of Calvin; and it was not likely that such an attempt should pass unchallenged. The state of the controversy was briefly as follows :

Man is born in a state of original sin ; he is a lost creature on account of the Fall. Saint-Cyran himself says, " It is certain that the devil possesses the soul of the infant in his mother's womb. S. Augustine upheld this dogma against the Pelagians and defended it by the Church's ceremony of blowing upon the infant during the rite of baptism, in order to drive away the evil spirit....S. Augustine concludes against the heretics that since infants are continually suffèring, they must necessarily have committed some sin, which is none other than original sin simply and solely[1]." Baptism restores the lost infant to a state of innocency; but this is no safeguard for the future, since he is still liable, owing to his corrupt nature, to fall back into deadly sin. Recourse may be had to the sacrament of absolution, but for this to be effectual Saint-Cyran considered grace to be necessary; and it is impossible to rely upon grace, for the Jansenist doctrine of Predestination held that God gives this only to whomsoever He wills. In order then for a man to be saved, according to Jansenism, his own free-will avails nothing ; his only hope is in the free-gift of grace from God, whereby he is converted and becomes one of the elect. In opposition to this not very comfortable doctrine the Jesuits asserted that *sufficient* grace is given to all men, as men ; but for it to become *efficacious*, it must be deliberately chosen by the individual's free-will. The Jansenists replied that if man, in a state of original sin, is still so far free that he can at will accept the sufficient grace offered to all and so render it efficacious, he is not an absolutely lost being ; since he can of himself take the first step towards regeneration. This being so, the necessity of the supernatural gift of efficacious grace, given freely to us by the sacrifice of

[1] Fontaine, *Mémoires*, p. 190.

Christ, is done away with; for His work of redemption ceases to be of unique worth, if man can begin his own redemption. To this the Jesuits with some show of reason retorted that this did not follow; according to Jansenism Christ did not die for *all* men but for the predestined only; whereas the real truth was that God's sufficient grace was offered to *all* men, once and for all, by the sacrifice of His Son; and that the only thing needful was that man in virtue of his power of free-will should accept the free-gift of God's grace and so make it efficacious for his own salvation. This was surely a logical position and it obviated the difficulty of reconciling Predestination and Free-will which confronted the Jansenists. Thus the Jesuit doctrine so far from depreciating the unique value of Christ's death, rather emphasised it more than did the Jansenist doctrine; since it taught that Christ died not for the elect and predestined, but for the 'sins of the whole world.' It may be true that the Society of Jesus used this doctrine for making religion too easy and for compromising with the world, and that Dr Arnauld's attacks upon them were therefore justified; but to many minds the doctrine of all-pervading grace, accessible to all mankind, must have been more acceptable than the dogma that a special and (as far as man was concerned) uncontrollable grace was necessary.

The Jansenist position involved absolute contempt for human nature in itself, as well as a terrible and bitter uncertainty at times in humble and self-doubting natures. We can illustrate both these effects: Nicole in his *Essais de Morale* speaks of the world as a 'place of execution,' 'a river of blood,' 'a great hospital full of patients'; the soul is compared to 'a vast but dark chamber full of adders and serpents'; while to represent the state of original sin he says, "let us imagine a universal plague or rather accumulation of plagues, pests and malignant pustules with which a man's body may be covered." The effect of this grim doctrine of Predestination upon a timid soul may be illustrated by the fears which obsessed the saintly Angélique before her death. In spite of her long life of piety and her frequent meditations upon death, she felt during her last hours like 'a criminal at the feet of justice, awaiting the carrying out of the sentence[1].' She regarded death as a terrible uncertainty and the grim doctrines of Jansenism had no comfort to hold out to her. For if our salvation really depends not upon our own efforts but upon the seemingly capricious gift of God, then may we well have doubts as to ever attaining eternal life, in spite of a life well spent and all religious duties punctiliously fulfilled.

However, Port-Royal always remained more or less under the shadow of the doctrine of Predestination, and this fact explains its distrust of the world and its lack of appreciation of the beauties which the world has to offer. It also supplies the key to the educational position of Port-Royal; innocency is indeed given at baptism, but to ward off the attacks of the demon, grace is necessary. But, as we have seen, Jansen believed that God gives this only when and to whom He pleases. Hence the best way to ensure salvation is to conserve baptismal innocency by education—that is to say by taking every possible precaution to prevent the devil finding an entrance into the regenerated child's soul. The child is at first a non-rational animal and is restored unwittingly to man's primal state of innocency before the Fall by the salutary effect of the sacrament of baptism; but, in the words of Sainte-Beuve, "dès que cet âge de raison commence, pour que l'effet salutaire du baptême ne soit pas comme non avenu, il faut l'expliquer à mesure, le *traduire en raison* chez l'enfant; tellement que cet état de Grâce, qui lui a été acquis par un bienfait ineffable sans qu'il l'ait compris ni voulu, lui devienne un état réfléchi, senti, et pratiqué. Il faut effectuer et faire vivre en lui cette seconde naissance[2]."

In order to sum up the Jansenist position with regard to education, recourse may perhaps be had to a parallel from the science of medicine. In a case—let us say—of phthisis there are two factors to be considered: the seed and the soil; a man may have constitutionally weak lungs and so be predisposed towards consumption, but he is safe so long as he can avoid the invasion of the disease germs. Similarly, the Jansenists held that all men are born in a condition, as it were, of advanced consumption; they are in a state of original sin. But by the

---

[1] *Mémoires et Relations*, p. 266.   [2] Vol. III, p. 480.

supernatural agency of the sacrament of baptism men are de-
livered from the disease, though their constitutions still remain
unsound; that is to say: being corrupt by nature, they are of
themselves blind to the good and eagerly disposed towards all
that is evil. The disease germs are intensely active and are
trying their utmost to take root in this soil which is so congenial
to them—in other words, the devil does his utmost to lead
astray mortals whose own corrupt nature makes them only too
ready to follow him. The first object of education then is much
the same as that of modern preventive medicine—to take measures
lest the malignant germs be given a chance to invade the weak
constitution. This explains the all-important necessity, according to Port-Royal, of having complete control over the child's
environment. The second object of education, as understood
by the Jansenists, was to translate baptismal innocency into
reason; that is to say—to revert to our medical parallel—so to
develop and fortify the constitution, which was originally weak,
that it may eventually grow strong, and even, when adult life
arrives, be able to risk exposure to infection and yet be strong
enough to resist the disease. But as medical science must
always in the last resort fall back upon the Higher Powers, and
as those cases, which seem most surely on the high-road to
recovery, sometimes end fatally, so also in education God is the
ultimate arbiter. The teacher must do his utmost for the cure
of the spiritual invalids under his charge; but their fate is none
the less in the hands of God. By predestination He gives grace
to whom He will and in His own good time; and the science of
education can no more ensure the gift of grace than the science
of medicine can ensure the gift of healing.

This then in outline was the rather complicated argument
which underlay all the Port-Royal educational theories[1]. The
position seems weak, for the whole issue is confused by the
doctrine of Predestination and again, since special grace is
necessary for the teacher to carry out his work, we are once

---

[1] The bearing of Port-Royal's theology upon its educational doctrines is well
summarised in Varet's *Éducation Chrestienne des Enfans* (1669). The author,
although a Jansenist ecclesiastic as well as an educationalist, had—so far as I have
been able to discover—no direct connection with the Little Schools.

more driven back upon the arbitrary gift of God, which no man can ever be absolutely sure of possessing. Happily the practice of the Jansenists here, as in other matters, was superior to their theory; and instead of being quite logical and relapsing into paralysed inanition, they came to consider the work of education of first importance as a means of salvation. This change of attitude was probably in a large measure due to the influence of Descartes; but as this topic will be discussed in detail at a later stage[1] it is enough merely to refer to it here. Still, the Port-Royalists never ceased to realise the awful responsibility of the teacher, to whose care the eternal welfare of his pupils was committed; and they regarded all the processes of education as but means towards the great end of this life—the attainment of everlasting bliss hereafter.

Saint-Cyran's doctrine of Grace and his insistence upon the importance of personal religion as opposed to orthodox formalism brought him near to Protestantism; but at the same time he maintained definitely Catholic ideas in regard to the Sacraments. This led him to distinctly sacerdotal views on the priesthood, for which he thought a very special grace and a definite 'call' were necessary, and many of his letters are devoted to setting forth the dignity and duties of this office. In addition to this, a still further grace was essential for preaching, which Saint-Cyran regarded as the most august of all the priest's duties and even more potent in its influence than the celebration of the Mass itself. "Preaching," he says in one of his letters, "is no less terrible a mystery than the Eucharist; nay it even seems to me far more terrible, for it is by this means that souls are born or raised again into eternal life; whereas they are only nourished or rather healed by the Eucharist....Personally I would rather say a hundred Masses than preach one sermon. The altar is a solitude, but the pulpit is a public assembly where the danger of offending the Master is far greater[2]."

Now Saint-Cyran's conception of the teacher's office is closely parallel to his idea of the preacher's. Like Luther he would say: "I am convinced that, next to preaching, this (the

---

[1] See pp. 209 ff. [2] Quoted by Sainte-Beuve, Vol. I, p. 449.

office of a schoolmaster) is the most useful and greatly the best
labour in the world; and in fact I am sometimes in doubt which
of the positions is the more honourable." Another parallel is
furnished by the Jesuit Jouvency; "Too often," he says, "the
preacher sows the word of God in vain because his discourse is
wasted on the closed ears of his audience....The Christian
master, on the contrary, can continually impress the same
saving doctrines upon the same disciples." All these three
thinkers, who though very different yet had something akin,
realised the inestimable importance of the spoken word and the
subtle power of personal influences in the development of a soul
and its direction towards God. The teacher's office, according
to Saint-Cyran, is to watch over the child's soul which is by
nature fallen and inclined towards evil rather than good. He
must make it fit to repel the assaults of the devil, or, if possible,
give the evil one no opportunity of assailing the child; and this
function implies an immense and solemn responsibility. It also
implies a vivid realisation of the superlative importance of
education to the individual. Lancelot tells us that according
to Saint-Cyran "next to that love of which it is said 'maiorem
hâc dilectionem nemo habet, &c.,' which disposes us to die for
our brethren, comes the love of those who devote themselves to
educating children in a Christian manner;...and at death one of
the greatest consolations we can have is that of having contributed to the good education of some child[1]." In another
passage Saint-Cyran is reported as saying: "The guidance of
the humblest soul is a more important thing than the government of a whole world." He could not understand how people
could be content to look upon the teacher's office as 'le dernier
emploi de la nature,' while the position of master of the stables
in a prince's house was held in the highest esteem[2]. This

---

[1] *Mémoires de S.-C.* Vol. II, p. 334.

[2] Erasmus and Ascham put this even more strongly: cf. "Deligunt cui committunt curandum equum et filium cuivis committunt," *Christian Marriage* (1526)—no
pagination; "And it is a pity that commonly more care is had, yea, and that amongst
very wise men, to find out rather a cunning man for their horse than a cunning man
for their children....God, that sitteth in heaven, laugheth their choice to scorn and
rewardeth their liberality as it should; for He suffereth them to have tame and
well-ordered horse, but wild and unfortunate children," *Scholemaster*, p. 23.

realisation of the dignity and responsibility of the teacher's office permeated Port-Royal; Fontaine says of De Saci: "He believed there was no occupation equal to this (i.e. teaching), nor more worthy of a Christian, when it was done out of sheer love"; Lancelot speaks of the "importance of this profession and the vigilance which must be applied to it[1]." Quotations of this character from Port-Royalist writers might be multiplied indefinitely.

The teacher's duty of preserving baptismal innocency in his pupil, of defending him against his own corrupt nature and the attacks of the evil one, demands a very special sustaining grace, comparable to that required by the preacher. Thus the teacher must himself be predestined, for God gives grace only to His Elect. "The Apostle," says Saint-Cyran in one of his letters, "enumerates the gifts of the Holy Spirit and says that they are divided among the faithful and that no one possesses them all. But I can assure you that the gift of instructing and educating children is one of the rarest and we can say of it what S. Gregory says of the ministry, that it is a 'tempest of the spirit[2].'" This implies that a definite 'call' must be realised by those who aspire to become teachers; they must be fitted for the office by a special gift of grace. Their duty is to regenerate the individual by means of education; but before they can do this they must be regenerate themselves. They must therefore be assured, as far as this is possible, of their own predestination in order to be able to work out the salvation of their pupils.

This implied not only selection of the teachers, but also even of the children, according as they seemed to show signs of grace. Saint-Cyran complains that parents do not realise the vital importance of education for their children; but at the same time he would not undertake their education merely in order to relieve their parents of them; that would mean "turning a profession worthy of angels and an occupation entirely of love into sheer servility." Accordingly we find De Saci recommending with great emphasis that only those children should be received as pupils whose parents were 'honnêtes gens'; for there seems

---

[1] *Mémoires*, p. 390.   [2] *Suppl. au Nécr.* p. 48.

to have been a shrewd underlying suspicion that the gift of
grace sometimes runs in families. But if expectations were
deceived and a child who had been accepted turned out to be
devoid of grace, the Port-Royalists humbly and reverently
acknowledged the finger of the inscrutable God and continued
to do their best. "The judgments of God," says one of them,
"are always incomprehensible; but they are never more terrible
than when He allows to be destroyed at their very beginning,
works of piety which might have contributed to the salvation
of many souls[1]." The best commentary on this is furnished by
Saint-Cyran himself in a striking phrase: "Il y a cette consolation dans les travaux que l'on prend pour Dieu, qu'il n'en
demande pas de nous le succès, mais le travail[2]." The doctrine
of Predestination did indeed seem to throw some light on the
mystery of innate differences; two children might be born from
the same stock and follow the same education, and yet to one
the gift of grace might be granted, though it were denied to the
other. Fontaine, speaking of Catherine Arnauld, says: "How
many a time did she tremble to see with her own eyes the
terrible judgments of God, Who permitted so many inequalities
among her children—some of them mounting like eagles towards Heaven...others preferring to creep along the ground."
Truly, as Sainte-Beuve aptly remarks, "the child is the book
of Grace, open at the article on Predestination, at its most
obscure passage[3]."

None the less, in spite of their Jansenist doctrines, the Port-
Royalists were never content to abandon their efforts and
indulge in the mere fatalism to which their theological ideas
might eventually have led them; the Little Schools furnish
the best proof of this. However, if it was felt that a pupil was
not fulfilling expectations, that his moral character showed no
signs of indwelling grace, and that his own corrupt nature had
definitely assumed control of him, he was straightway expelled
from the Port-Royal schools, lest he should corrupt his companions. In one of his letters Saint-Cyran lays it down: "If
children were found to be unteachable and not amenable to the

---

[1] Sainte-Marthe, quoted by Sainte-Beuve, Vol. III, p. 487.
[2] Fontaine, *Mémoires*, p. 195.   [3] Vol. III, p. 491.

discipline under which I wished them to live in this house, it was in my power to expel them without their parents being entitled to find fault[1]." We have several instances of this measure being carried into effect; a child named Saint-Ange was turned out of Port-Royal for fear he should exert an undesirable influence upon the son of D'Andilly, the 'petit Jules' to whom reference has already been made. We also read of Saint-Cyran going one day to buy a pair of stockings and seeing in the shop a little boy of promising appearance. Learning that he was to be sent to a Jesuit 'collège,' Saint-Cyran persuaded his father, the stocking-seller, to allow the boy to be brought up with Saint-Cyran's own nephew. But after a while it was found that the experiment was not likely to succeed, and the embryo hosier was sent back in disgrace to his father and so perhaps entered a Jesuit school after all.

Saint-Cyran's original aim in starting the educational work of Port-Royal was to provide recruits for Holy Orders. In this he was, perhaps, influenced by the example of De Bérulle of the Oratory and Vincent de Paul, both of whom had recently founded seminaries. "I had conceived the design," Saint-Cyran tells us, "of building a house which should be a kind of seminary for the Church, in order there to preserve the innocence of children, without which I always recognised that they could with difficulty become good clergy; my object was to construct it for six children only, whom I would have selected from the whole city of Paris, according as it had pleased God to make me meet with them[2]." Looking round upon the state of the Church in his days, Saint-Cyran felt that it was full of priests who were unworthy of their office and had no 'call' or special grace for their ministrations. He quotes with approval the dictum of S. Francis of Sales, that out of ten thousand priests who make profession hardly one is worthy of being chosen; and when we remember Saint-Cyran's theological views on the subject of Grace, we can realise that the unworthiness of the ministry would appear a scandal of unparalleled enormity in his

[1] *Suppl. au Nécr.* (1735), p. 47.
[2] *Suppl. au Nécr.* (1735), p. 46.

eyes. The aim of education then at Port-Royal was and continued to be moral and religious; it sought to regenerate the
individual and the Church alike. The Jesuits have often been
reproached for making their education a means of fostering their
personal or political aims, but the Port-Royalists ever showed
a complete and single-hearted devotion to the welfare of their
pupils and to their ideas of the truth; and for these they were
willing to sacrifice security, comfort, and all that the world holds
most dear.

As a result of this, mere knowledge always held a subordinate place in the Little Schools of Port-Royal; the Jesuits
might aim at turning out the largest possible number of good
Latinists, but Port-Royal's first concern was to produce heirs of
eternal life. Indeed intellectual gifts were often regarded as
a weak place in the spiritual armour through which the demon
might easily wound the soul of their possessor. Lancelot tells
of a child of eight, who had manifested great love for all kinds
of knowledge; he had even composed for his own amusement
several little treatises, but had never shown any evil propensities.
Nevertheless, it was thought that such promise might degenerate
into intellectual pride or an ambitious aspiration to high ecclesiastical office; and when therefore Saint-Cyran was consulted
with regard to this child he "decided off-hand that it was by
no means necessary to set him to study, and this was carried
out absolutely. He distrusted these intellectual prodigies, which
one is tempted to address by the name of demon." The Abbot
added that "sometimes out of a hundred children, not one ought
to be put to study[1]." "He could not bear that knowledge and
study should be given the chief place in the education of children,
as is done now-a-days[2]. He looked upon this as one of the most
serious faults that could be committed in this holy occupation;
he pointed out that not only did it prove distasteful to the pupils
who were backward and cause the others to be vain, but it
recoiled eventually still more on the State and the Church,
burdening the Bride of Christ with a number of people whom
she had never called and the State with a crowd of lazy people

---

[1] Lancelot, *Mémoires de S.-C.* Vol. II, p. 195.
[2] This evidently refers specially to the Jesuit 'collèges.'

who thought they were superior to everybody since they knew a little Latin, and who considered that they would be dishonoured if they followed their father's profession. For this reason he said that though one were placed in complete charge of a large number of children, only a few of them should be put to study, namely those alone in whom had been noticed great docility and submission and some signs of a well-assured virtue and piety[1]." In another place Lancelot says that Saint-Cyran "remarked that generally speaking knowledge did more harm than good to the young. And he once made me attentively consider this saying of S. Gregory Nazianzen, who said that the sciences had entered the Church 'like the flies in Egypt, to cause a plague[2].'" Among the solitaries there was none of that somewhat exaggerated estimate of the value of mere knowledge which characterised some of their contemporaries among the Protestant reformers (e.g. Comenius), and which initiated the demand for education as a right due to all men of whatever degree.

Intellectual education then at Port-Royal tended to be sacrificed to moral education, and the attitude of the solitaries towards secular knowledge, literature and art was usually one of distrust. Owing perhaps to the influence of Dr Arnauld and Pascal this attitude may have changed slightly as time went on; but in the Port-Royal of Saint-Cyran, with which the schools are most closely concerned, this austerity was but rarely relaxed, and then chiefly by such solitaries as Hamon and Le Maître, who took no regular part in the teaching work of the community.

Since the world was essentially corrupt and evil in the eyes of Port-Royal, secular knowledge could not be good in itself; it was admissible only with a religious aim in view. "There is nothing I hate more," exclaims Saint-Cyran, "than those seekers after truth who are not truly devoted to God and who are not led solely by love of Him in their researches." Coustel also draws a distinction between the education which the heathen in classical times gave their children, and that which Christians ought to give. "Since the former," he says, "had only the world

1 Lancelot, *Mémoires de S.-C.* Vol. II, p. 338.
2 *op. cit.* p. 195.

in view, they devoted themselves to making their children acceptable through the sciences and literature. But this is not the case with Christians; their goal is heaven, for which the sciences are far less necessary than a good character[1]."

The logical outcome of such an attitude would have been to leave secular studies entirely alone and to confine the curriculum to the reading of religious treatises. This was actually put into practice in the girls' schools of Port-Royal; but fortunately here as in other matters the solitaries did not carry their ideas to the strict logical conclusion and their practice was far superior to their theory. None the less, profane literature was continually eyed with distrust and it was recognised that the greatest vigilance must be exercised in using it for school purposes. Saint-Cyran used to perform the exorcisms of the Church over the works of classical authors previous to reading them; and these were always expurgated with the utmost rigour before being used in the Little Schools. One day Saint-Cyran visited the school and, 'with his usual pleasant air and benevolent manner,' said to the children: "Well, and what are you doing? For you must not waste time and that which you do not fill up the devil will take for himself." He was shown a Virgil, which the class was studying. "You see those beautiful verses?" was his comment. "Virgil in making them procured his own damnation because he composed them in a spirit of vanity and for the sake of glory. But as for you, you must win salvation in learning them, because you must do it in a spirit of obedience and with the desire of becoming capable of serving God[2]."

Saint-Cyran's attitude was that of all whole-hearted Jansenists. According to their doctrine, one of the chief sins which entered the world through the Fall was that which they stigmatised as 'concupiscence.' Two phases of this were described as 'libido sciendi' and 'libido excellendi,' which together covered all kinds of literary knowledge and the appreciation of *belles-lettres*, as well as the investigation of nature. This onslaught on secular studies was stoutly resisted by the Jesuits and notably by Father Bouhours, who has left us in his *Entretiens d'Ariste et d'Eugène*

[1] Vol. I, p. 165.
[2] Lancelot, *Mémoires de S.-C.* Vol. II, pp. 332—3.

a vigorous criticism of the style of many of the Port-Royal writers.

The original Jansenist conception of classical and secular knowledge was in marked contrast to the spirit of the Renaissance. This movement had been a reaction against the idea that education is a discipline which prepares the way for the life to come and that its means must be entirely determined by this end. It had stimulated a joy in this transitory life and in the things of this present world; it had promoted the study of the recovered classics for their own sake. But the Renaissance educators had continually found some difficulty in reconciling their attitude towards secular knowledge with a due regard for the claims of religion. Thus to some extent the Renaissance had tended to become anti-Christian; and it was sometimes levelled as a reproach even against the Jesuits that they had cared more for intellectual than religious education. This is true only to a limited extent; the Society of Jesus sought to compromise between the rival claims of religious and classical learning by regarding the classics as 'Christi praecones.' They appreciated the beauties of Greek and Roman literature and made the power of writing good Latin prose the proximate aim of their schools. But the ultimate end of their education was the subordination of the individual to the Church; and their teaching was not disinterested and undertaken solely for the advantage of the pupil, but rather to the benefit of the Society. Hence although, as Sainte-Beuve tells us, they might inscribe above their schools 'DOMINO MUSISQUE SACRUM,' yet their aims were not so simple as would appear at first sight; although in their appreciation of the classics they may have been far truer to the spirit of the Renaissance than was Port-Royal, yet they were much further removed from that spirit than the solitaries in so far as the Renaissance was an attempt to reconstitute the individual as a free being and deliver him from the dominion of a theological despotism. It was indeed the object of Port-Royal to make children think for themselves and so develop them into responsible beings; and in this respect they were whole-hearted Cartesians. Compayré well brings this out in a passage where he is contrasting the educational methods of the Jesuits with those of the Jansenists. "The gentlemen of Port-Royal," he says, "desired that the child should think and reflect as far as he was capable of this. That is why they set before him exercises graded to his young intelligence and busied him with things that he understood and were within his reach. The spirit of Descartes—that is to say of the first French philosopher who, before Pascal, had said plainly that man's dignity consists solely in his power of thought—the spirit of Descartes had penetrated the schools of Port-Royal[1]."

This desire, then, to develop the individual to the utmost of his powers, to make him a reasonable and responsible being, permeates Port-Royal, and in this respect shows the greatest possible contrast with the methods of the Society of Jesus. The educational aim of the latter was to subject the pupil's mind to authority, but at Port-Royal there was ever a spirit of freedom. Guyot sums up education as 'precision of mind and rectitude of will'; Nicole defines the aim of instruction as 'the carrying of the mind to the extreme point that it is capable of attaining'; Coustel understands by education the 'cultivation of the soul's two chief faculties, namely intellect and will; intellect by making the child learn good literature and will by moulding him in virtue.' By the time we reach Port-Royal we have already left behind the conception of education which regards it merely as the filling of an empty vessel; we see that education is rather the development of a complex organism and that the ultimate aim of the process is to ensure that, by the time the soul becomes self-guiding and responsible, it will function in a desirable way because its powers have been rightly stimulated and developed. For much of this Port-Royal is indebted to Descartes who all along tends to modify the strictly logical outcome of Saint-Cyran's theological education.

Though this elevated conception of education was held at Port-Royal it remains true that purely intellectual education was at a discount there and that any hankering after knowledge for its own sake was considerably discouraged. This hardly squares with the solitaries' theories as to the means of the educative process, but the explanation lies in the fact that

[1] Vol. I, p. 248.

development of character always took precedence of the acquisition of mere information. Reference has already been made to the little boy of eight who showed great intellectual promise and who was incontinently forbidden to study. Instances of this kind might be multiplied. Jacqueline Pascal, as has already been said, gave early signs of some considerable poetic talent. At the age of 12 she composed a sonnet in honour of the pregnancy of the Queen (not a very suitable subject for a little girl); it was shown to this princess and the youthful authoress was granted an audience. After this Jacqueline frequently visited the Court and her verses won considerable renown. In 1640—she was then 15—she won a prize offered by a society at Rouen for a poem on the Immaculate Conception— another somewhat unusual subject for so young a poetess; but what interests us most is that it was Corneille who had advised Jacqueline to compete and that he himself thanked the adjudicators on behalf of the authoress. When therefore she came into contact with Port-Royal, Jacqueline had already won a certain amount of fame as a writer of verse, and it might have been expected that such a gift would be encouraged there, for it was at any rate not exactly a desire for secular knowledge. But even a natural aptitude for poetic composition appears to have been distrusted at Port-Royal; it was evidently felt that this might afford a loophole for the entering in of the evil one. Accordingly, when Jacqueline, desiring to translate some Latin hymns into French verse, applied to Singlin for advice, the following answer was given through the mediation of Agnès, Angélique's sister: "Yours is a talent of which God will in no wise demand an account from you, since humility and silence constitute the lot of our sex....You ought to hate this talent and the others which are perhaps the reason why the world holds you back; for it wishes to reap that which it has sown[1]."

A still more notable instance of the manner in which Port-Royal treated genius is afforded by Racine. In order to realise himself he had to a large extent to become untrue to the spirit of his upbringing. He owed his knowledge of Greek and the use of religious subjects for his plays to his Port-Royal education;

[1] MS Letters in Bibliothèque Nationale, quoted by Sainte-Beuve, Vol. II, p. 485.

but the development of his strong natural love for the beauties
of literature was largely an accident; it was not the outcome of
his contact with the regular masters in the Little Schools, but, as
has been pointed out, of his chance connection with Le Maître
and more particularly with the 'roi-mage,' Hamon.

The attitude of Port-Royal towards the drama was indeed
exceptionally austere; classical literature was regarded as a
valuable instrument if used aright, though otherwise fraught
with danger, but the theatre was looked upon as a definite and
serious evil.   The Port-Royal educationalists are unanimous on
this point; Coustel wrote a tract entitled *Sentimens de l'Église
et des Saints Pères sur la Comédie et les Comédiens* (1694),
the attitude of which may be inferred from the title; in his
Règles de l'éducation des Enfans he has a long chapter[1] on the
same subject, and quotes S. Chrysostom to support his dictum
that children should not visit the theatre; Lancelot gave up the
education of the young Princes De Conti rather than take them
to see a play; Arnauld condemns the practice in the Jesuit
schools of allowing the children to act; Pascal regards comedy
as a great danger to those who aim at living the Christian life;
Nicole, as usual, expresses himself intemperately on the subject;
he refers to dramatic authors and novelists as 'public poisoners
not of the bodies, but of the souls of the faithful—which is the
worst kind of homicide.'   This was the expression which caused
the final breach between Racine and Port-Royal.   Racine replied
to the tirade in a letter which is still extant and which paid back
Nicole in his own coin.   The tone of the letter is bitterly sarcastic
and the sympathies of any modern reader are at once enlisted
on the side of Racine.   Nevertheless at a later date he was
reconciled to Port-Royal and seems to have deeply regretted
the attack which he had made on his Alma Mater.

Not only were the pupils of Port-Royal forbidden to visit
the theatre, but they were also not allowed to read novels or
any books 'in which the passions of young people are inflamed.'
There is a well-known story of how the young Racine was once
surprised in reading a romance entitled *Les Amours de Théagène
et de Chariclée*.   Port-Royal is not the only type of school

[1] Vol. II, ch. ix.

where such literature is considered undesirable, and the book was promptly thrown into the fire. However the young delinquent managed to procure a second copy, which shared the fate of the first, and then a third, which he committed to memory. This done, he presented the book to Lancelot with the words: "You can burn this one as you did the two others." Let us hope that this was made one of those rare occasions on which the rod was brought into use at Port-Royal.

As to the other forms of art Port-Royal was equally severe; instrumental music was almost wholly neglected and there was no organ in the chapel of the community. The church services were sung to simple modes; but we have evidence that plainsong chanting formed part of the curriculum in the girls' schools and it is barely possible that this was the case in the boys' schools also. The convent was noted for its singing; Racine says: "The grave and touching manner in which the praises of God were chanted at Port-Royal won admiration." A Franciscan father also tells us that the nuns used the ordinary Roman plainsong according to the Paris use, since they belonged to this diocese; but they never indulged in trills or runs which might mar the solemn beauty of the music or show off the vocal powers of any of the singers. We have no definite proof that the boys actually took part in the sung services of the church; yet it seems probable that even if definite instruction in singing were not given, opportunity was afforded to pupils who possessed gifts in this particular direction to employ them to the glory of God. At any rate it stands on record that De Tillemont who was a pupil at Port-Royal from the age of ten and who afterwards became a solitary there, had a passion for church music 'qu'il avait appris de lui-même dès sa plus tendre jeunesse'; he had also a knowledge of theoretical music and was able to compose.

This repugnance to the beautiful things of this present life extended to architecture and church decoration. Even Hamon speaks of the difficulty of worshipping in a 'too beautiful' church. Agnès, at one time Abbess of Port-Royal, says: "The more one takes from the senses, the more one gives to the spirit. All pleasure taken in visible objects in so far diminishes the life of grace." Hence, no flowers on the altar and no curious needlework

on the priestly vestments. The following is a description of
the chapel at Port-Royal des Champs given us by some nuns
who made a pilgrimage to it in 1697, but it will hold for the
time during which the Little Schools were in existence for it is
borne out in detail by a contemporary print[1]: "Gold and costly
ornaments which often constitute the beauty of a church and
attract people to it are unknown here; the altar has a retable
of simple carpenter's work and a painting of the Last Supper.
Moreover it has only one step up to it, which is not the usual
custom. Two big wooden contrivances fixed to the retable serve
as candlesticks. No tabernacle is to be seen, but there is a
hanging vessel, the cover of which is enriched with silver; its
lower surface, on which the Holy Sacrament is exposed, is also
embroidered with gold. These are the only richly embellished
ornaments which they have; the chasubles and other vestments are
not even adorned with gold[2]." Saint-Cyran himself had approxi-
mated even nearer to a puritan distrust of beautiful things in
connection with religion; he directly condemns beauty of church
furniture and vestments and desires them to be plain or even ugly[3].

The only form of art that appears to have been allowed any
entrance at Port-Royal was that of painting. The solitaries
numbered among their friends an artist named Philippe De
Champagne who was permitted to adorn the otherwise austere
chapel at Port-Royal des Champs with some of his paintings.
His style is described by Sainte-Beuve as 'simple, sérieuse,
solide, fervente, avec l'éclat intérieur de plus.' Many of his
works remain to us; in the Louvre there is a portrait of
Richelieu by him and a picture of Christ in His shroud; there
is also an interesting representation of the miraculous healing
at Port-Royal of the painter's lame daughter, who had taken
the veil there under the name of Sister Sainte-Suzanne. De
Champagne painted the portraits of many of the solitaries; that
of Saint-Cyran, a reproduction of which constitutes the frontispiece to this volume, is at present in the Musée at Grenoble.

---

[1] No. 4, 'gravé chez Cochin.' There is a copy in the Sion College Collection.
[2] Quoted by Hallays, pp. 103—104.
[3] It should be noted that absence of ornament in churches and on vestments was
characteristic of the Cistercian order to which Port-Royal belonged.

Still, in spite of the fact that the solitaries numbered among them a painter of some merit and that his art was evidently held in honour at Port-Royal, there is no evidence at all that any form of painting or drawing was ever taught in the schools.

Some of the foregoing remarks upon the estimate set by the Port-Royalists upon art and literature may seem only indirectly to be concerned with an exposition of their educational work. But if any excuse be needed, recourse must be had to that already urged in extenuation of a rather detailed consideration of the principal masters in the Little Schools. In order to arrive at a just estimation of the educational work of any establishment it is not enough to look merely at the curriculum ; we must know the kind of men who teach there, and the out-of-school influences brought to bear on the pupils. For this second reason, Port-Royal's attitude towards aesthetics in its various manifestations has been dealt with at this stage of the discussion.

The explanation of Port-Royal's distrust of art and even to some extent of literature lies in its theological position. Every possible precaution must be taken to prevent the devil being allowed the smallest opportunity of infecting the child's soul ; no risks are permissible, for since in the eyes of Port-Royal, as has been already explained, the child was like a man with a weak constitution who is exposed to the influence of a highly infectious disease, every avenue must be closed by which there is even the smallest chance for the attack of the malignant germs. For this reason the masters were carefully selected ; undesirable pupils were expelled lest they should corrupt their companions ; reading both in and out of school was rigorously regulated ; and even the subtler influences of art and music were so controlled as to give no possible occasion for stumbling. Coustel puts the position of Port-Royal in a quotation from S. Chrysostom who " compares the soul of a child to a golden city in the midst of which the King of Heaven desires to place His residence ; and he compares the schoolmaster to the governor whose duty it is to watch over its preservation. He says that its citizens are the thoughts which go in and out by the three chief gates, the eyes, the ears, and the mouth. He wishes the council to take every precaution and to do its duty by setting trusty guards at these three gates, through which death may enter the soul[1]." Sainte-Marthe also says: "In the Little Schools an attempt was made to remove from the presence of the children all objects which might harm them. Care was taken that they should never hear or see anything which would wound their modesty and purity, which is so delicate at that age....But though it is good that children should never leave this happy state of simplicity which preserves Christian innocence in them, yet it is desirable that they should grow in wisdom and intellect, so that they may not be blind to what is good nor imprudent when evil is to be avoided. Hence an attempt was made to teach them anything which could contribute to advance them in virtue[2]."

The logical outcome of such ideas was a constant and complete surveillance of the children by the masters. The pupils of Port-Royal were never allowed out of sight for an instant, even during their games; such at any rate was the rule of the community, though we have indications that it may have been slightly mitigated in practice. "The devotion we have for children is useless," says Lancelot, "if we relax to the smallest degree the constant vigilance which we should exercise over them, for this is of vital importance. And we deceive ourselves when we think we have well fortified the citadel on every side, if we leave a single gate open at which the enemy may enter[3]." In the *Supplément au Nécrologe* we have another striking statement by Walon De Beaupuis which exactly expresses the ideas of the solitaries on this subject: "It was in order to be able to acquit themselves of their obligations that they used to watch continually over this little flock, never losing sight of it and regarding it as a precious trust of which God would one day require of them a terrible account; so that they could say with Jacob: Noctu diuque (sic) aestu urebar et gelu, fugiebatque somnus ex oculis meis[4]."

A corollary of this constant supervision was the regulation that a child would be accepted as a pupil at Port-Royal only on

[1] Vol. I, p. 166.
[2] *Suppl. au Nécr.* (1735), p. 50.
[3] Quoted by Carré, p. xix.
[4] *Suppl. au Nécr.* (1735), p. 50.

condition that the community were allowed to have complete charge of him. The family had to cede its rights absolutely to the school. The Duchesse De Guise on one occasion made overtures to Saint-Cyran for the education at Port-Royal of her son, who was destined for the Church; when however she learnt that this would involve her abandoning the care of the boy entirely to the solitaries, she drew back and the negotiations fell through. For Saint-Cyran was not the man to relax regulations which he had made in the interests of the morals of his pupils, to oblige a lady of title. In the girls' schools we learn that the pupils were allowed to see their relations once every three months for half an hour at most.

The severity of this regulation is at once explicable when we remember Port-Royal's views on the 'world' and on the necessity of guarding against its infection. But the ideas of the solitaries were perhaps not so exaggerated by their theological doctrines as might at first sight appear. The French Court at this time was a hotbed of vice and extravagance of every kind, and its brilliance was equalled only by its scandalous immorality. Now the majority of the Port-Royal pupils were drawn from the so-called 'upper classes,' and their families would therefore be more or less brought into contact with this welter of debauchery and corruption. Little wonder is it then that the solitaries in their stern and determined reaction against contemporary vice insisted that they should be given undivided control of the children for whose eternal welfare they made themselves responsible. The brilliance of the French Court had also contributed to the weakening of religious beliefs; and against this as well Port-Royal made a stand. "The world's great heresy," says Nicole, "is no longer Calvinism or Lutheranism, but Atheism and there are all kinds of atheists." This again afforded an additional reason for complete and unrelaxing control of the pupils at Port-Royal.

In order to turn the charge of their pupils to the best possible advantage, a compromise between the 'collège' system of the Jesuits and individual tuition was adopted. The question is discussed by Coustel. Education in the pupil's own home ensures good breeding and a proper attention to health, but it makes systematic work difficult, complete control is impossible, and evil influences are often rife. The boarding school system of the Society of Jesus fosters scholarship and encourages the formation of useful friendships; but the individual pupil usually receives too little attention and there are often serious moral dangers entailed. There is a third possible alternative, namely education in a religious community; this is admirable for training morals but tends to leave the other sides of the character undeveloped. Port-Royal then very wisely sought to combine the advantages of all three and so to ensure the three elements of a good education as they are given by Coustel, viz. (i) training of the intellect; (ii) development of moral character; (iii) instruction in the good manners of polite society.

The system which the solitaries adopted had already been adumbrated by Erasmus in his *Treatise on Christian Marriage*. "Plerisque placet media quaedam ratio, ut apud unum praeceptorem quinque sexve pueri instituantur; ita nec sodalitas deerit aetati, cui convenit alacritas; neque non sufficiet singulis cura praeceptoris; et facile vitabitur corruptio quam affert multitudo[1]." We have already seen how these recommendations of Erasmus were carried into effect when the school was first established in the rue S. Dominique d'Enfer. The school occupied a separate building not far from the Abbey of Port-Royal de Paris; there were four masters, each of whom had charge of five or six pupils in a separate room. In this manner the master was able to give each pupil individual attention and difficulties of discipline were reduced to a minimum. It is possible that when the numbers of the Port-Royal schools increased, the size of these classes may have been slightly augmented; but this can only have been to a very small extent, since it is probable that the boys' schools never contained more than 50 pupils at any time and we have evidence of solitaries other than the four original masters assisting in the work of teaching from time to time. This being the case, it is evident that the Port-Royal system could never have been carried out on any large scale; it would have proved far

---

[1] In the 1526 edition there is no pagination, but the quotation occurs 16 pages from the end of the treatise.

too expensive for ordinary use, and the recruiting of an adequate supply of suitable masters would have presented insuperable difficulties. This is evidently the reason why the Jansenist schools of the Abbé Tabourin which succeeded the Port-Royal schools, were able to follow their illustrious predecessors to an only limited extent. So far as teaching methods went, Tabourin was free to adopt many of those in vogue at Port-Royal; but he could not imitate in a school with large classes measures of discipline and administration which were suitable only for small groups of pupils under a master. The real reason why the Port-Royal system succeeded is to be found in the very short life of the schools and in the fact that their troubled existence greatly limited the scope of their activity.

We have yet to ask whether the pupils in these small groups were divided according to ability or age, and whether the masters taught all the form subjects to each group or acted as specialists. There appears to have been no hard and fast rule in this matter. Each class seems to have been more or less in charge of one and the same master and the pupils of an equal ability seem to have been united as a rule. But at the same time there were a few lessons in which groups were united and it is certain that masters who had specialised on definite school subjects were given the duty of teaching these as far as possible to all classes alike. It also appears that any solitary at Port-Royal who had a marked aptitude for any particular branch of knowledge was pressed into the service of the schools. Thus Dr Arnauld, De Saci, Le Maître, and Hamon, though not regular masters in the schools, all took part at times in the teaching. It would also seem that a similar task was imposed even upon visitors who were eminent for their learning. For instance, the *Nécrologe* tells us of an ecclesiastic named Jean Bourgeois, a Doctor of the Sorbonne, who stayed upon several occasions at Port-Royal and subsequently from 1669 to 1679 became confessor to the nuns of the community. His chief interest for us is that he is reported to have taught the young Du Fossé philosophy. We may then conclude that although the form-master system was generally in vogue at Port-Royal, yet this did not altogether preclude specialist teaching, particularly

in the case of older and more advanced pupils. This combination of the form-master and the specialist system, together
with the ease with which classes could be united or separated,
is due to the very small numbers both of the whole school and
of the classes; it ensured thorough instruction by competent
masters and at the same time a large amount of individual
attention for each pupil.

Although Port-Royal seems to have given its chief attention
to guarding against malign influences which might harm the
child's soul, yet it at the same time appreciated the value of
good positive influences, and laid great stress upon the salutary
effects of a suitable environment. The solitaries also appear to
have preferred to teach their pupils in the country when practicable rather than at Paris. Du Fossé tells us of the school at
Sevran that 'the place was extremely pleasant owing to its
gardens, its streams and the surrounding walks, which were very
beautiful'; again, the calm and beauty of Port-Royal des Champs
are still apparent in spite of the fact that the Abbey itself is now
a desolate waste. But too much emphasis must not be laid on
this point; for the chief reason why the Port-Royalists preferred
the country was obviously that the dangers of the 'world' were
less to be feared there than in a city.

In order to ensure that none but desirable influences should
be brought to bear on the immature soul, great care was taken
at Port-Royal that the servants with whom the children might
come in contact should be beyond reproach. It is evident that
this was at the time a real danger and especially for children of
high rank who were educated at home by a tutor. Locke makes
several references to the evil. Lancelot, when undertaking the
education of the young Princes De Conti, congratulates himself
on the rigorous care with which the servants were selected in
their family. Of the Princesse De Conti, their mother, he says:
"The care which she gives to choosing the persons who have
the honour to be near her children is far beyond expression....
I will say merely that for personal attendants she has only
taken such as have been already formed and tested in the house
and of whom she is quite sure; as to footmen, I have more

than once seen her give more care to appointing one for their Highnesses...than many bishops show in giving a priest to the Church[1]." Similarly at Port-Royal itself great care was taken that only such servants should be appointed as were 'fort sages et fort réglés'; thus, since the children would have none but good examples set them on every side, alike by the masters and by the domestic servants, it was hoped that 'they might be under the happy necessity of acting only according to the actions which they saw.'

The views of Port-Royal on the importance of environment and example may be summed up in a passage from Guyot, where he is, true to the spirit of the community, pointing out the far greater importance of moral than of intellectual education. " The lesson of the heart (i.e. of morals)," says he, "is a lesson of example; that of the intellect a book-lesson; actions instruct the heart, just as words instruct the intellect; the heart learns through the eyes, the intellect through the ears; we must work, meditate, and study in order to teach the intellect, but we must act and live well in order to teach the heart. And since everything is often full of evil actions, evil words, evil sentiments, evil examples, in short an evil life, be it in the parents, the servants, the friends, the masters, or any of the persons who have access to the young, we must not be surprised if their heart is more instructed in evil by that which they see than their intellect by that which they hear....This shows us with what circumspection and caution we should behave ourselves in regard to the young, and what care we should take neither to do nor say anything in their presence which might harm them or cause them to stumble[2]."

This position naturally involved a complete condemnation of travel as an educational agency. It was a custom, then as now, for those who could afford it to supplement the education of their sons by sending them abroad to see the world. Rabelais, Montaigne, and Locke all recommend it. But since this brings a number of new and uncontrollable influences to bear upon the young mind and since the world is in itself corrupt, travelling was forbidden by Port-Royal as an educational instrument.

[1] *Suppl. au Nécr.* (1735), p. 167.
[2] Preface to Guyot's translation of *Ad Familiares*—no pagination.

According to De Saci to travel merely consists in seeing 'the devil dressed up in all kinds of fashions—German, English, Italian; but it is always the same devil, crudelis ubique[1].' Curiously enough Coustel allows an exception in the general condemnation of travelling for educational purposes, in favour of children of high rank.   But in order that travel may be of value to them he makes the following provisos: "(1) That they have a good knowledge of the map, the history and even the language of the country they propose to visit. (2) That they have a good guide who is not content to show them the situation and the strength of the towns through which they pass, or even the beauty of the churches and palaces, but also the people of merit and learning. (3) That he should point out to them carefully what is most worthy of note in the laws, manners and customs; and in a word the good and bad qualities of the nations. (4) Lastly, that he should teach them that it is not in their faults that these nations should be imitated, but in their good and commendable qualities.   Thus, for instance, one must not go to Italy in order to become licentious, to Germany in order to learn excessive drinking, to Spain in order to increase one's pride; but one should rather try to learn from the Italians their temperance and prudence; from the Germans courage and patriotism; from the Spanish steadfastness; otherwise travel is of little use[2]."   For Port-Royal it is all a question of the influences brought to bear on the child; if in travel matters can be so arranged that the good influences are preserved and the bad avoided, then this may be allowed as an educational medium. But since under ordinary circumstances it is extremely difficult to engineer matters thus, the normal attitude of Port-Royal towards travel remained uncompromisingly hostile.

The most important element in the educative environment which surrounded the child in the Little Schools of Port-Royal was obviously the character of the masters who taught there. Reference has already been made to the high estimation in which their office was held by the community and to the special gifts from On High which were regarded as necessary before

[1] Fontaine, *Mémoires*, p. 396.   [2] Vol. I, p. 247.

a man could take upon himself the solemn and responsible duty of educating children. We must now look more closely at the requirements which Port-Royal exacted from its teachers and the recommendations in regard to the teaching profession laid down in the treatises of the Jansenist educational theorists.

Nicole has given us an enumeration of the qualities required in the tutor who is to have charge of the education of a prince; but since princes are ultimately very much like ordinary mortals, we may well take the picture he draws as the ideal schoolmaster according to the Port-Royalists; especially as this picture is reproduced in many of its details by others of the solitaries who wrote on education. The teacher must not be merely a man who is free from vices and has a knowledge of literature, history, or mathematics; mere information indeed is a good or a bad thing solely according to the use which is made of it; we must therefore demand something more of the schoolmaster than academic attainments. What this essential something is, Nicole finds difficult to define in a single word; "my meaning," he says, "cannot be better made clear than by saying that it is that quality which leads a man always to blame what is blameworthy and to praise what is praiseworthy, to despise that which is despicable and to appreciate what is lofty, to judge everything wisely and fairly, to set forth his judgments in a pleasant manner, accommodated to those whom he is addressing; in short, on every subject to turn the mind of his pupil towards the truth[1]." In a similar strain Coustel points out that ability to train the intellect should be a secondary consideration in choosing a master; his premier qualification should be his power to influence aright the moral character of his children. Thus in the detailed enumeration of the qualities requisite in a schoolmaster Coustel puts first irreproachable character; second in importance comes knowledge; then scholarly judgment and good literary taste, method in teaching, prudence, experience, authority over his pupils, and lastly knowledge of the amenities of polite society.

It is interesting to notice that Coustel advocates the professional training of teachers. With consummate common sense

[1] *Essais de Morale*, Vol. II, p. 258.

he says: "On this subject it may be remarked that it is somewhat astounding that in this profession one acts in an entirely different manner from that in which one acts in all other arts. For example, a man who has never been on the sea does not venture to take the tiller of a ship in his hands and ply the trade of a pilot. If a man knows nothing of the different temperaments of the various kinds of diseases, and of the doses to be prescribed, he does not undertake to play the *rôle* of physician. Teaching is the only occupation in which men take upon themselves to become a master without having first served their apprenticeship; and they often tamper with the instruction and education of others, at a time when it is rather they themselves who are in need of instruction and education[1]." These wise words were written nearly 250 years ago, but even yet their wisdom is not always appreciated. In many schools in England we are still in the darkness of the Middle Ages in this respect; but our elementary schools and many of our secondary girls' schools have set a praiseworthy example and it is to be hoped that before long professional training may be exacted from all teachers of every kind, just as it is demanded of all medical practitioners.

Although professional training for masters formed a definite article in Port-Royal's educational creed, yet the value of experience was not overlooked; Coustel emphasises this in the case of those who have to educate children of high degree 'on whom it is difficult to make one's apprenticeship.' But it was none the less the case that at Port-Royal a preference seems to have been felt for young masters. Saint-Cyran desires 'a man of 20 or 25 years of age, knowing that older men are usually unsuitable for teaching languages to children[2].' It is a little difficult to see why a man of 20 should *ceteris paribus* be considered a better teacher of Latin than a man of 30 or even 40; it would appear that the opposite might be, to say the least, equally true. But it must be remembered that at Port-Royal the smallness of the classes made difficulties of form management almost non-existent, and that the teaching methods used were to a certain extent stereotyped. In 1646 then, when the Little Schools were first organised and established in the rue

---

[1] Vol. I, p. 135.   [2] *Suppl. au Nécr.* (1735), p. 47.

S. Dominique d'Enfer, we find that the respective ages of the chief masters were as follows: Nicole 21; Coustel 25; Walon De Beaupuis 25; Lancelot 31; the date of Guyot's birth is unknown, but since the period of his literary activity was from 1666 to 1678, he was probably quite a young man in 1646. In the girls' schools Jacqueline Pascal was put in charge of the education of the children at the age of 29. At the same time, too much stress must not be laid on the preference of Port-Royal for young teachers. Saint-Cyran had attracted to himself a number of young men in whom his personality and his doctrines had kindled enthusiasm; it was natural therefore that he should look to them to carry out his ideas on the subject of education, which he regarded as so vitally important. But there is no evidence that as they grew older they were replaced by younger men, nor that, if the schools had survived, these masters would not have continued to teach in them to the end of their days.

CHAPTER IV

GENERAL TEACHING METHODS

WE have by this time studied in some detail the general atmosphere in which the pupil was educated at Port-Royal, and we have looked at the type of master to whom he was entrusted. We have now to consider the various points of general school method which characterise the process of education as carried on by the solitaries; that done, we shall the more easily be able to examine the particular methods which they adopted in teaching the various subjects of the curriculum.

As has been seen, the bedrock upon which the Port-Royalists founded all their teaching was affection for their pupils. Coustel gives as one of the 'excellent maxims' which a master must employ in regard to his class: "Avoir le cœur tout plein de charité pour eux." "It is certain," he says, "that nothing is so useful, both to master and children, as this honourable and charitable behaviour; because it is an infallible means for the master to make himself loved and so to lead his children to study and right conduct. For since the heart is the spring of all the actions, when you are once the master of it, you can straightway do whatever you please. 'If you would be loved, love first of all,' says Seneca[1]." And Coustel goes on to exhort the schoolmaster to follow the example of our Lord who loved little children and blessed them. Saint-Cyran in like manner lays stress on the dignity of childhood and on the respect due to it, since Christ has exalted humility and "by taking it upon Himself rendered it worthy of our high esteem." Sainte-Beuve has implied that Saint-Cyran's love for humanity is not spontaneous but arises out of his theological position and his love for God; M. Carré also takes up a similar view with regard to

[1] Vol. I, p. 171.

Saint-Cyran's affection for children. But with all due deference to these authorities, the writer is inclined to feel that Saint-Cyran had a very strong natural love for children which was not wholly coloured by theological dogmas or religious enthusiasms. Reference has already been made to the ardent expressions in which he gives utterance to his love for the young; and his zeal in the cause of education, his games with the children in prison, and his letters to his grand-niece all show the sincerity of his words. But perhaps the best instance of the triumph of the natural man over the theologian is to be found in an anecdote of Saint-Cyran given by Lancelot; the Abbot is represented as sending a present of sweets to a little girl and at the same time salving his conscience as a Jansenist theologian by saying to a bystander: "In no wise accustom children to the pleasures of the world, which make them lose the taste for those of God[1]." What a charming inconsistency! Lancelot, who is in everything a true disciple of Saint-Cyran, says in a letter to De Saci that the master should feel the 'love of a father' for his pupils; "a master who is not of this frame of mind will never do anything. If on the contrary he *does* adopt this attitude, he will soon feel that grace is no less powerful in operation than nature; and this love will inspire him to find more ways of being useful to his pupils than all the advice that could be given him[2]." Thus we see that, though Port-Royal advocated professional training for the future teacher, it realised that this was vain unless the root of the matter—a natural love for boys and sympathy with them—were already in him.

The aim of education according to the Port-Royalists is the building-up of character, and towards this all formative influences are directed; since instruction is only one of these influences, it must never usurp a position as the goal of the educative process. We may thus truly describe all Port-Royal education as a distinctly *moral* education based upon affection for the pupils. But the solitaries, being practical schoolmasters, knew well that any kind of direct moral instruction often arouses contrariance in the pupil and so defeats its own end. Hence they deprecated set lessons on morality and preferred to inculcate it as much as

[1] *Mémoires de S.-C.* Vol. II, p. 338.   [2] *Suppl. au Nécr.* (1735), p. 163.

possible indirectly, by digressions and asides in the ordinary
form work and still more by the example and subtle personal
influence of all those with whom the children were brought into
contact.   Virtue is a tender blossom and if it be too closely
analysed and dissected, its charm may easily be destroyed and
its fragrance lost.   Nicole therefore wisely says of moral instruction: "though this study should be the chief and most
often given...it should none the less be imparted in a manner
suitable to the age and ability of the pupils, so that not only
they may not be burdened with it, but even that they may not
notice it.   If possible they should know all the precepts of
morality without scarcely knowing that there is such a thing,
nor that one ever had the design of instructing them in it[1]."
De Saci also considers formal moral lectures to be of very little
good to a child, unless they are somewhat rare, short, and
appropriate to his age, and unless they appear to arise more by
accident than from a deliberate intention to admonish or to catch
him.   Even in regard to the girls' schools, where the curriculum
consisted almost entirely of the reading of theological books and
the performance of religious exercises, the Abbess Agnès could
say: "There are some truths that should rather be felt than
learnt."

Indirect moral instruction was given in various ways at
Port-Royal.   Attendance at the services of the church and at
sermons was obviously one of the most important; but in
reading the educational treatises of this austere religious community, one is continually impressed by the obviously earnest
desire not to overdo the devotional exercises of the pupils and
so to render them meaningless.   There were of course daily
morning and evening prayers and the elder boys at Le Chesnai
at any rate used to go to Prime.   But there was no attempt to
enforce attendance at Mass every day; this was exacted only
upon festivals, and even then only from those who were thought
worthy to go.   At all times the offices of the Church were
regarded as exercises of the deepest solemnity and as privileges
accorded to those who took part in them; and thus any misbehaviour by pupils during them was visited with severity.

[1] *Essais de Morale*, Vol. II, p. 266.

We also learn that while Du Fossé was a pupil in the rue
S. Dominique d'Enfer (his age being then about 11 or 12) he
was taken every Sunday to hear either M. Singlin preach at
Port-Royal de Paris or an Oratorian father named Desmares
whose eloquence in the pulpit had made him famous throughout
Paris. In the girls' schools devotions and attendance at religious
services played a much larger part than in the Little Schools;
though even here attendance at the divine offices was not
insisted upon, but rather regarded in the light of a favour to be
merited by good behaviour.

Another medium through which Port Royal sought to train
the character of its pupils was the teaching of the ordinary form
subjects. It began in the lowest forms with the writing and
reading lessons. As 'copies,' texts from Scripture or sententious
maxims were set which the children might commit to memory,
while at the same time they learnt to write; "for one must
never neglect, where it is possible, to combine several advantages." Similarly the reading book was carefully chosen with
the same end in view; "one of the most valuable rules," says
Nicole, "that can be followed in the education of children is
always to combine different advantages and to take care that
the books which they are made to read should serve also for
forming their mind, judgment, and character." So also in the
Logic of Port-Royal the authors sought to combine moral and
intellectual instruction by choosing ethical maxims for many of
the examples which illustrate logical rules; e.g. as an instance
of the syllogism in Camestres we have: "All those who are
followers of Jesus Christ crucify the flesh; All those who live an
effeminate and voluptuous life do not crucify the flesh; Therefore none such are followers of Jesus Christ[1]"; or again for an
example of Barbara we are given: "Everyone who is the slave
of his passions is unhappy; Every vicious man is the slave of his
passions; Therefore every vicious man is unhappy[2]."

But the chief source of moral instruction was the texts read
in class. Coustel lays it down that the schoolmaster "should
husband with care whatever he finds in his authors—even in
profane authors. For instance, what a wealth of excellent

[1] Baynes' trans. p. 198.   [2] *op. cit.* p. 213.

maxims is there in Cicero, in Horace, and in Seneca, which can
serve not merely to instruct a young man in manners and in the
duties of civil life, but also to attract him towards virtue and
draw him away from vice, provided that his master is clever
enough to develop them a little and give them the requisite
turn....I know quite well that it is not here that we must look
for the essential and fundamental truths of our religion. But it
is good always to utilise the occasions to which these authors
give rise for saying things to our pupils which may prove
advantageous to them[1]."

Since there is often much in a classical author which is not
suitable for a young child to read, the texts used at Port-Royal
were expurgated with the most meticulous care. De Saci is
responsible for the editing of many of the books used in the
Little Schools; he translated and expurgated the *Fables* of
Phaedrus, and the *Andria, Adelphi*, and *Phormio* of Terence
"qu'il avait rendues très honnêtes en y changeant fort peu de
chose." He also co-operated with Lancelot and Nicole in
preparing a carefully selected *Epigrammatum Delectus*, containing, besides the epigrams, moral maxims drawn from
Plautus, Terence and Horace. De Saci is indeed the expur-
gator *par excellence* at Port-Royal; "How he used to groan,"
says Fontaine, "to see things in Latin authors which did not
accord with Christian purity! But owing to the fact that the
persons of piety and enlightenment who had had charge of him
in his youth had made him undertake the reading-through of
these books (since the source of latinity is to be found in them,
and as it is sometimes necessary to defend the Church, it would
be a pity if the defenders of the truth had not such strong and
well-polished weapons as their adversaries[2]), he found himself,
against his own inclinations, compelled to consent that children
should also be permitted to read these authors. But with what
precautions was his permission given! What care he took to
ensure that these tender souls might draw from these authors

[1] Vol. i, pp. 185—6.

[2] This refers ostensibly to the dispute between Catholicism and the new-formed
Calvinistic and Lutheran heresies; and it probably also covers the quarrel between
the Jansenists and the Jesuits. These latter were noted for their Latin style.

what was advantageous as regards linguistic, without being spoiled by what was evil and liable to corrupt their morals! Has not his love given him ingenuity for discovering how to render pure what was most impure? Did he not take from these masters of lewdness the venom with which they poison tender souls and has he not contrived that Terence may be good Latin without being obscene; that Horace may be profitable without being harmful by his horrible foulness; and that Martial may innocently stimulate children's minds by selections from his epigrams, without immersing them in his disgusting filth[1]?" Similarly Nicole exclaims: "ibi vero cohorrui fateor, ad tot spurcitiarum aspectum," and says of Martial and Catullus, "quos iam diu aeterna oblivione sepultos et vindicibus flammis expiatos decebat"; however, he justifies his share in preparing the *Epigrammatum Delectus* by reminding us: "sed enim ut in viperis non omnia noxia, quaedam etiam ad salutem accommodata, sic non ubique illi virulenti sunt, aliquando etiam innoxie festivi; interque tot venena videre est pulcherrimos flores, et clarissimarum sententiarum fructus[2]." None the less it is a little strange to find Martial and Terence in use at Port-Royal, even though they had been rigorously expurgated. Terence indeed is quoted in the *Ratio Studiorum* of the Jesuits as an example of an author who is beyond hope of expurgation and must therefore not be read—"si omnino purgari non poterunt, quemadmodum Terentius, potius non legantur[3]." Louis Racine tells us that in the copies of Plato and Plutarch which his father had used at Port-Royal and which he had left to his son, all the passages to which any exception could possibly be taken were carefully crossed out and rendered illegible. This custom also seems not to have been confined to the schools, but to have been usual with the solitaries themselves. In the Horace which belonged to Dr Arnauld all immoral passages were completely effaced with a red pencil; and Pascal treated in a similar manner

---

[1] Fontaine, *Mémoires*, pp. 393—4.

[2] Preface to *Epigr. Delect.* § 1.

[3] *Ratio*, p. 20. Later Terence seems to have been admitted, for he appears in Jouvency's catalogue of Latin authors, though with the proviso " non legatur, nisi repurgatus."

all the remarks in his copy of Montaigne which might have given offence.

Moral lessons were imparted as far as possible indirectly and when opportunity offered in digressions from the texts which were being read and explained in class. Coustel wisely remarks: "Digressions on these occasions are not to be feared, because they lead to something more useful than what was originally proposed. Besides, this method makes the greater impression upon children, the less they are prepared for it[1]." In Coustel's recommendations there is implicit the whole question of the value of indirect suggestion in moral education which has not been rendered explicit until our own times[2].

Another method was the noting and collection of passages of a high ethical value in the authors which were being read; to quote Coustel again: "When one comes across some beautiful moral maxim or some fine examples which may serve to render virtue lovable and vice hateful, a halt should be made in order to turn the light upon them and to set them off, if possible, with some noble passages taken from Scripture or one of the Fathers."

It would appear that direct moral lessons were rarely given at Port-Royal and then only when there was a suitable and natural occasion and usually by the 'director,' who held an ecclesiastical office, rather than by the ordinary form-master. Saint-Cyran, when he visited the schools, used to bless the children and teach them to make the sign of the cross; "and when they were able to understand it, he always used to say something good to them, which was like a seed of truth which he sowed, as he passed and in the sight of God, that it might spring up in good time[3]." Lancelot, however, tells us that: "he was careful to point out that, in order to educate children well, 'il fallait plus prier que crier,' and one should speak more about them to God, than to them about God. For he did not like long discourses to be addressed to them on piety nor for them to be tired out with admonitions. He desired that they should be spoken to only upon the occasions and opportunities which God

[1] Vol. II, p. 86.   [2] Especially in Keatinge's *Suggestion in Education*.
[3] Lancelot, *Mémoires de S.-C.* Vol. II, p. 332.

brings into being[1]." Here again the practice of the Port-Royalists was far in advance of that of their contemporaries; it is not yet universally recognised that set moral lessons tend to defeat their own end. A comparison of the children's literature of 60 years ago with that of to-day will illustrate the advance which has been made; but our modern ideas were anticipated more than 250 years ago by Saint-Cyran. Even yet we have with us those who in the ethical training of children would rely solely on the direct moral lesson; and nowhere has it greater vogue than in France.

The affection which inspired the teaching methods of the Port-Royalists gave rise to an infinite patience and perseverance on the part of the masters. Their writings are full of recommendations to this effect. Saint-Cyran "desired us to bear long with their faults and weaknesses, that by so doing we might induce God to have mercy on ours.... He added that we should show still greater love and compassion for those who are seen to be especially feeble and backward—those whom original sin has wounded with unusual severity[2]." De Saci emphasises the necessity of hoping the best for our pupils and bearing with their faults. Coustel says that the master must ever be ready to help his boys and "to endure with great patience the innumerable little faults which age corrects"; he also enjoins special care and affection for pupils who are physically weak and quotes S. Bernard's comparison of the conduct of mothers "who lavish special caresses on those of their children who are the most feeble[3]." So also Du Fossé tells us how Le Fèvre by his tact and patience won the respect and obedience of an ill-mannered and intractable boy named De Bohebert, and so turned him from 'a wolf into a lamb.' Indeed the patience and perseverance which invariably marked the attitude of the solitaries towards their pupils is worthy of our special attention. The resident assistant-master of to-day who has a reasonable amount of house-duty to perform, be he never so enthusiastic about his profession and ardent in his love for boys, none the less at times

[1] op. cit. Vol. II, p. 337. [2] Lancelot, Mémoires de S.-C. Vol. II, pp. 334—5.
[3] Vol. II, p. 170.

longs for the end of the term and for a change in his environment. But at Port-Royal the solitaries were never, day or night
and from one year's end to another, out of touch with their
pupils; their supervision was constant, and, where patience was
required for a stubborn or backward pupil, it could never be
relaxed. Surely then the self-discipline of these men and their
absolute devotion of every faculty to the education of the boys
entrusted to them, are worthy of our deepest admiration. Moreover, if their pupils committed faults, the solitaries, instead of
blaming them, were far more prone to blame themselves, as
being responsible to God for those under their care. Hence we
read of the Port-Royal masters doing penances on their pupils'
behalf; Saint-Cyran in Lancelot's *Mémoires* says that often
"we ought to punish and chasten ourselves on their account,
partly because we should always beware of participating in
their faults either by our hastiness or our negligence, and partly
because this duty is an obligation binding upon all those who
are put in charge of the education of others[1]." The whole
history of education cannot show a more true and unreserved
devotion to children. The Port-Royalists are worthy of being
classed with Pestalozzi in this respect; but they excel the Swiss
reformer, in that they are absolutely free from that somewhat
hysterical sentimentalism which at times obscures his argument
and wearies his readers.

The Port-Royal educationalists had anticipated Pestalozzi in
yet another particular; they had already recognised the necessity
of child-study in education and of grading school work according
to the mental capacity of the pupils. We are thus already on
the threshold of the application of genetic psychology to teaching
methods. Coustel lays down as the first principle of successful
teaching that the master should study the individual psychology
of his pupils and adapt his methods accordingly; "it is un-
questionable that they should not all be treated in the same
manner. If a physician cannot prescribe remedies suitable for
the healing of the body, without knowing its various temperaments, and if a farmer ought not to set about sowing a field
without knowing the quality of its soil, then beyond doubt a

[1] Vol. II, p. 336.

schoolmaster should also know the different kinds of intellect which he has to educate[1]." Coustel goes on to enumerate the various types of child mind and the manner in which each should be treated, quite in the style of an up-to-date American educational psychologist. It must be remembered that the study of the individual child and the accommodation of teaching methods to his particular needs were far easier in the small groups of pupils at Port-Royal, than in our modern classes which range in numbers from 20 to as many as 60.

Two corollaries follow from this gradation of school-work according to individual needs. In the first place the master must adapt himself to the child's intellectual feebleness. "We can properly know these little souls," says De Saci, "only by bringing ourselves to their level[2]." So also Coustel recommends to the schoolmaster a maxim laid down by Quintilian: "Imitate the action of a grown-up person who is walking with a little child; he restrains his ardour and moderates the length of his paces so as not to cause the child trouble[3]." Similarly the master should go slowly and make sure that each step in the lesson is well understood before advancing any further; in this respect children are like bottles with narrow mouths into which the wine of knowledge must be poured slowly, drop by drop, if none of it is to be spilled and lost.

The second corollary is that all unnecessary difficulties and obstructions should be removed from the path of the learner. The most important manifestation of this theory of the Port-Royalists, in their educational practice, was their adoption of the vernacular as the medium through which early education should be given—a practice almost wholly at variance with contemporary methods. Since this point will be treated later in greater detail, it is sufficient merely to refer to it at this stage. It is none the less a distinctive feature of Port-Royal that the masters taxed their ingenuity to find out the shortest and easiest teaching methods; and these are preserved to us in the various educational treatises of the solitaries and also in the school-books which they produced. "We must remember our own childhood,"

---

[1] Vol. II, pp. 73—4.   [2] Fontaine, *Mémoires*, p. 392.
[3] Vol. II, p. 59.

says Guyot, "and the difficulties which we ourselves had in the acquirement of knowledge. So shall we accommodate ourselves to the feebleness of our pupils and never cause them the least difficulty over and above that from which we cannot possibly excuse them[1]." This attitude led Port-Royal to anticipate Froebel in some of his kindergarten methods in the education of quite young children. Coustel would have us "contrive that study appear to them as a kind of diversion or game, rather than as a troublesome and wearying occupation. This is obviously why the ancients have represented the Muses with a very cheerful and lively air...disporting themselves each in a different way[2]." An instance of how these playful methods may be introduced is in another context furnished by Coustel himself: "Nouns are either substantive or adjective. The nouns substantive may be compared to persons of noble rank who nearly always go attended by their train and their suite. The adjectives are like the attendants who are obliged to follow their masters wherever they go and who serve to make them appear with the greater magnificence and pomp. And so if the substantive is masculine or nominative or singular or plural, the adjective has to follow suit[3]." One cannot help feeling that we have in this illustration one of those small touches which reveal in Coustel the practical schoolmaster, who writes with a knowledge of children and with much personal experience of teaching methods; it reminds one of D'Arcy Thompson and one looks in vain for anything of this nature in the theorisings of Rousseau and those other writers upon teaching whose fame rests upon their powers of imagination rather than upon their personal knowledge of the practical points at issue.

Not only did the Port-Royalists endeavour wherever they could to remove difficulties from the path of the learner, and to render instruction as pleasant as might be, but they also recognised the value of a varied curriculum, which might prevent the child from becoming wearied during the course of instruction. This

---

[1] Preface to Trans. of *Ad Familiares*, no pagination.

[2] Vol. II, p. 57. Cf. Ascham, *Scholemaster*, p. 62, "The muses, besides learning, were also ladies of dancing, mirth, and minstrelsy."

[3] Vol. II, pp. 83—4.

was especially prescribed in the case of the younger children ; " As far as possible," says Coustel, " their little exercises must be diversified, and they must be made to pass as it were imperceptibly from one to another, without their perceiving that to do this is to study. Thus they must be set now to read, now to recite some fine passages from the authors with which they are acquainted, now to relate a history, or occasionally to speak of geography. For variety is pleasant and it is far easier for them to do many things in succession than the same thing for a long time[1]." Here again Port-Royal has anticipated one of the fundamental principles of modern kindergarten teaching. But while school-work was to be made agreeable and varied whenever this could be done, the solitaries had no sympathy with 'soft paedagogics.' Children must be accustomed by degrees to application "which is indispensable for study"; and in regard to those who will not make this effort Coustel quotes with approval the words of S. Augustine: " They must be compelled to do it. I had no liking for study in my youth, and I had a strange dislike for the strictness with which I was forced to apply myself to it. However, my teachers did not stop at my inclinations and my laziness, but always urged me on ; and they did well, since the aversion which I had for all kinds of work would have prevented me from learning anything, had they not compelled me to it[2]."

It is evident then that Port-Royal sought to combine the education of interest with the education of effort. Coustel's *Règles de l'éducation des Enfans*, which, more than any other book, sets forth in detail the education given by the solitaries, was published in 1687 ; and in 1692 appeared Locke's *Essay on Education*, in which the disciplinary conception of education appears to the almost complete exclusion of the idea of education as a natural and pleasurable process. For the development of this latter conception, the world had to wait till the appearance of the writings of Rousseau and of those whom he inspired. As Monroe points out, " the period of reconciliation of the two conceptions...is practically that of the present generation[3]." Yet 250 years ago in a small and almost forgotten French school

---

[1] Vol. II, p. 60.   [2] Vol. II, p. 64.   [3] p. 752.

the problem was being faced and solved. On the one hand the Port-Royalists would have had little sympathy with the narrow classical grind, the extensive use of corporal punishments, and the often-abused fagging system which characterised English public schools during the seventeenth, eighteenth, and first half of the nineteenth centuries. Nor on the other hand would they have approved of the natural and negative education advocated by Rousseau; that would have offered endless opportunities for evil to infect the child's soul. Thus, when once allowance has been made for the monastic character of the Port-Royal schools and the theological atmosphere which pervaded them, one is continually impressed by the strikingly modern appearance which they present.

There is yet one more respect in which the Little Schools anticipated Pestalozzi and the present-day elementary school methods which owe so much to him. The solitaries recognised that the education of young children should be carried on through *Realien*, by means of object lessons and pictures, wherever practicable. Port-Royal had already foreshadowed Pestalozzi's doctrine of *Anschauung*, and, had he, like Rousseau, been acquainted with the writings of the solitaries, we should be tempted to infer that he had borrowed from them in this particular. Almost all the Port-Royal writers on education lay great stress on knowledge of objects; their advice is ever 'ipsis consuescere rebus.' De Saci reminds us that "as a rule children are capable of instruction only through the senses." Nicole says: "Since the child's intelligence is always very dependent upon his senses, it is necessary, as far as possible, to connect with the senses the information which is given them, and to make it enter not merely by the hearing but also by the sight[1]." For this reason Nicole recommends 'practical' geography—i.e. that learnt from nature and not from a book; pictures of Roman antiquities and portraits of historical characters should be shown to the children, and for pictures and descriptions of unknown animals recourse should be had to the *Natural History* of Aldrovandus of Bologna. Nicole, like Rabelais, would even recommend for children the study of anatomy. Guyot is

---

[1] *Essais de Morale*, Vol. II, p. 279.

another exponent at Port-Royal of the *Anschauung* method; he lays it down that "care must be taken in exercising pupils in speaking or writing that they do it with clearness and precision...and with clear and definite knowledge of things.... For this reason they should usually be set to write about things of which they know most[1]." In this particular the Port-Royalists may possibly have been inspired by Comenius; but in any case they have surely something to teach the modern world. Miss Hodgson wisely comments: "If a list of 'subjects for composition,' set in one week in all the schools of England could be collected, no additional proof could be needed that we are at present very far from acting on Guyot's advice that children should 'write about things of which they know most[2].'" Coustel as the chief exponent of the Port-Royal educational theory has also much to say on the education of children by means of concrete objects. He, like Nicole, advocates object lessons, and the use of pictures and illustrated books, such as those of Lipsius. He also remarks: "Children should be given suitable liberty of asking for enlightenment on all matters which they do not understand[3]."

We might have expected that this stress upon education through *Realien* might have led the Port-Royalists, like Locke and Rousseau, to advocate manual training as an element in the complete education. It is true that many of the solitaries busied themselves on the estate at Port-Royal des Champs; Fontaine tells us that two hours in the morning and two hours in the afternoon were devoted by them to manual work. Le Maître and De Séricourt used to cultivate the garden, gather the harvest, and busy themselves with the haymaking. D'Andilly superintended the fruit-growing and the fame of his pears extended beyond Port-Royal to the Court, whither they were frequently sent as presents for the Queen or Mazarin. D'Andilly also is responsible for the draining of the pond and the marsh from which Port-Royal probably took its name and which had always rendered it so unhealthy. Besoigne again tells us that the solitaries "repaired part of the buildings which had fallen

---

[1] Trans. of *Epp. ad Atticum* (1668), Preface.
[2] *Studies in French Education*, p. 67.   [3] Vol. II, p. 99.

into ruin, and raised those which were too low or sunken[1]." We thus have abundant evidence that manual labour was held in high honour among the solitaries and was diligently practised by them; and it is therefore a little strange that nowhere in their educational treatises is any reference made to it as a desirable element in the education of children. In the girls' schools the pupils were taught to do needlework and to make 'gants d'estame'; but we have no evidence of anything of a corresponding nature for the boys.

Passing reference has already been made to the discipline of the Little Schools of Port-Royal; a more detailed study is now demanded of the punishments which were in vogue there. In this matter again Port-Royal had anticipated the best modern practice, and compared with the measures customary in contemporary schools, the practices of the solitaries possess an added glory. When we remember that in the seventeenth century education was ordinarily regarded as the process of forcing uninteresting matter upon the child's mind by clumsy methods and through the medium of an almost unknown language, we can understand that the results would have been negligible, had not the schoolmasters of the day made free and constant use of the birch, for the purpose of goading on the unfortunate pupils to their demoralising task. Both the content and the method of their education are summed up with admirable precision in the old rhyme: "Qui, quae, quod. Fetch me the rod"; or in Laurie's more elegant phrase: "grammar and flagellation, twin-brothers[2]." The barbarism of contemporary methods had already been censured by Comenius and Montaigne; Locke also, who had been at Westminster School during the reign of the notorious Dr Busby—a contemporary of Port-Royal—believes that "*caeteris paribus*, those children who have been most chastised seldom make the best men[3]"; and in spite of his disciplinary conception of education he vigorously condemns severity in punishments, except in the most extreme cases. Unfortunately in England the inordinate use of the cane, so

---

[1] Vol. I, p. 208.   [2] *Educational Opinion*, p. 29.
[3] *Thoughts on Education*, § 43.

degrading to pupil and master alike, has too long held sway; and it is in some measure to this that we may perhaps attribute the fact that in this country the schoolmaster is not held in the honour that he receives from the general public in France and Germany, and which the dignity and importance of his profession would warrant. Port-Royal recognised that affection and not fear is the best basis for all teaching methods. The system which relies on corporal punishment is at its best typified by Kipling's *Famous Men* who "daily beat on us with rods, for the love they bore us." But the Port-Royalists showed a more excellent way, although it was more easily applicable to their small groups of pupils than to forms or classes of the usual size; and while they wisely did not entirely abolish the cane, they used it only in the most extreme cases and then after much prayer and meditation.

The solitaries are unanimous in their attitude towards punishments. Saint-Cyran besought those who had charge of a little boy at Port-Royal "to treat him kindly, but none the less to use the rod when he is obstinate or repeats his faults." Lancelot also tells us how he was unwilling "that recourse should be had to the rod, except for serious faults and that only after having used all other punishments, one after another[1]." De Saci again recommends the master to be slow to punish and Coustel recognises the futility of roughness and ill-temper in teaching: "As heavy rains merely run over the surface of the ground without soaking into it and making it fertile, so rough words make no impression upon the mind into which they do not enter[2]." But though Coustel recognises the value of mildness, he also, like Saint-Cyran, realises that the rod has its uses: "Although it is desirable that we should always be able to treat children with the greatest gentleness, yet there are none the less some...for whose advantage it is that we should appear somewhat severe[3]"; and Coustel goes on to quote with approval from Ecclesiastes and the Book of Proverbs those well-worn texts in which the value of the rod as an educational medium is set forth.

In another part of his treatise Coustel gives a detailed *résumé*

---

[1] *Mémoires de S.-C.* Vol. II, p. 335.   [2] Vol. I, p. 170.
[3] Vol. I, p. 182.

of the Port-Royal educational theories with regard to punishments; they may be summarised as follows: Some faults are
not serious and should be left for age to correct; the more serious
ones should be at first reprimanded. With great wisdom Coustel
points out that a reprimand must take into account the temperament of the offender; "a gentle and timid disposition must be
dealt with differently from one that is haughty and arrogant[1]."
Violent abuse should never accompany any punishment, but
there is a righteous and restrained anger which if rarely and
rightly used is of the highest value. If warnings and reprimands
are of no avail, Saint-Cyran advises us to deprive the offender of
"something that he likes, or of his play or even of his 'goûter'
or part of his dinner and not to have recourse to the rod except
as a last resource and for serious faults[2]." What these 'serious
faults' were, we can gather both from Saint-Cyran himself and
from Coustel; they appear to have been repeated and wilful
disobedience, 'malices noires,' lying, and bad behaviour during
the church services. Curiously enough these last two offences
were regarded as worthy of the same punishment. There was a
wholesome horror of untruths in the Little Schools and it was
common to boys' and girls' schools alike. Du Fossé reports
that the Port-Royal masters "inspired us above all with the fear
of God, an aversion from sin, and a very great horror of falsehoods....I can also declare that I have never known people who
were more sincere and with whom it was more necessary to live
straightforwardly. For they were enemies of every kind of
insincerity and had deeply-graven on their hearts that declara-
tion of Scripture which assigns to the lake burning with fire and
brimstone all liars together with the accursed, the murderers,
etc.[3]" So also Jacqueline Pascal tells us that special watch for
the vice of telling falsehoods, which is 'fort ordinaire aux petits
enfants,' was kept upon the little girls, and special means were
taken to help them overcome it. Saint-Cyran reserved the rod
for those children "who were given to lying and bursting into
laughter on the most serious occasions. He was not willing that
they should be forgiven for faults committed in church[4]." In a

[1] Vol. II, p. 120.　　　　　[2] Lancelot, *Mémoires de S.-C.* Vol. II, p. 335.
[3] p. 49.　　　　　　　　　[4] Lancelot, *Mémoires de S.-C.* Vol. II, p. 336.

similar strain Jacqueline Pascal writes: "I cannot forbear from saying here that reverence for the church can never too much be impressed upon children, especially during the Holy Mass, and that faults committed there must be punished most severely[1]." We have here a somewhat remarkable lapse from the sanity and sympathetic knowledge of child nature which normally characterises Port-Royal's educational theory—at any rate, so far as the boys' schools are concerned. It does not seem to have occurred to the solitaries that bad behaviour in church may well be a sign not of possession by the evil one, but of a nervous and highly-strung temperament, the superfluous activity of which may possibly be easily worked off along other quite desirable channels. But this is a relatively small point; and, all things considered, it is remarkable that the religious enthusiasms of the Port-Royalists did not more often lead them astray.

When all other means have failed and when at last recourse is had to the cane, just as the wise surgeon has at last recourse to the red-hot iron, there are still rules to be observed and Coustel specifies them: The master's motive must be a sincere desire for the child's good; he must never use the cane in a spirit of revenge. He must always pray to God for guidance before finally deciding on the use of the cane. If he feels his anger rising he should, if possible, put off the punishment until he is in a calmer mood. But should the caning seem to have made the offender rather worse than better, the pupil must be regarded as a penance imposed by God upon the master for his sins; such a penance must be endured with prayer and patience in the hope that God in His own good time will soften the child's heart.

We are reminded here of an educational organon upon which Port-Royal laid great stress, but which would be deemed quite unsuitable for insertion in a modern treatise upon teaching methods. As the teaching in the Little Schools was in the hands of the solitaries who lived a life of religious asceticism and of fervent religious devotion, it is but natural that to them prayer was an educational instrument of the first importance. It is recommended with unvarying consistency by all the chief writers

[1] *Constitutions de P-R.* p. 438.

on education at Port-Royal. We find it first in Saint-Cyran, alike in his letters and in the *Mémoires* of Fontaine and Lancelot. 'Watch and pray' must ever be the schoolmaster's motto—watch that the evil one may have no chance to infect the child's regenerated soul; and pray both for the child and for the success of the work of education. The three chief factors in the moral education of the Little Schools are specified by Saint-Cyran as "separation from the world, good examples, and prayer"; and of these the last was relied upon no less confidently than the other two. In another context Saint-Cyran reduces the essentials of educational method to this simple prescription: "To speak little, to endure much, and to pray still more." Prayer, as has already been pointed out, was especially recommended when it is necessary to have recourse to any serious punishment; Saint-Cyran "used to say that to use the cane without first of all having prayed much was to act like a Jew and to ignore the fact that everything depends on the benediction of God....He added that at times we ought even to punish and chastise ourselves on their account[1]." So again De Saci says that the schoolmaster must never forget to ally prayer with his work and daily 'offer' his boys to God; for "except the Lord build the house, they labour in vain that build it." Coustel as usual treats the subject in detail; among the 'excellent maxims' for the use of the schoolmaster in the education of his children we find specified: "Prier beaucoup pour eux." Since his work can prosper only in so far as God blesses it, he "should endeavour to obtain from Him, by his prayers, all the benefits which he desires and which his own unworthiness prevents him from receiving[2]." The master then must rely on help from Above not only in the moral education of his boys, but no less also in their intellectual instruction. If he has success, he must humbly ascribe all the praise to God, remembering the words of the Psalmist: "Not unto us, O Lord, not unto us, but unto Thy name give glory." If he fail, he must not lose heart, but still trust in God and have recourse to prayer, believing that in His good time he will reap the fruit of all his labour; "The words which Christ spoke when sending forth the Apostles to preach the gospel: 'In what place

---

[1] Lancelot, *Mémoires de S.-C.* Vol. II, p. 336.   [2] Vol. I, p. 189.

soever ye enter into an house, there abide till ye depart from that place'—these words should be applied to the humblest duty which one is called upon to perform, and especially that of the good education of children[1]." Similarly in the Rules for the girls' schools, drawn up by Jacqueline Pascal, great stress is laid upon the necessity and efficacy of prayer alike for the mistresses and the pupils. In fact there is no matter upon which the educational writers of Port-Royal are more heartily in agreement.

We may seem here to be somewhat far removed from that modern spirit which so often breathes in the Port-Royal writers; but, whatever be our religious opinions, we must perforce admire these schoolmasters who took their profession so seriously, who loved their boys so thoroughly and bore with them so patiently, and who recognised so humbly the eternal truth that, though Paul planted and Apollos watered, it is God Who giveth the increase.

As is the case with many contemporary educators[2], great attention was given by the Port-Royalists to the subject of manners. It must be remembered that their pupils were drawn mainly from the wealthy and governing classes, and that therefore the usages of polite society would naturally form part of the curriculum, in spite of the distrust with which the outside world was regarded by the solitaries. As in the writings of Montaigne and Locke, so in those of the Port-Royalists, we seem often to be watching the education of the 'gentleman'; though it is true that at Port-Royal this process was continually obscured by the more important process of saving the child's soul. The inculcation of good manners was wisely seen by the solitaries to depend in the first instance on the teacher's own demeanour; the Port-Royalists do not go so far as does the Abbé Fleury in demanding that the schoolmaster should be of handsome appearance, but Coustel recommends the teacher to be minutely

[1] Vol. I, p. 197.

[2] E.g. the Jesuit Jouvency, p. 91, *Magistris scholarum inferiorum S. J. de ratione discendi et docendi*, 1711. Cf. also Comenius' *Tract on Manners*—see Keatinge, p. 80.

watchful of his own conduct since children are 'lynx-eyed' to
notice the smallest and most insignificant things.   The rules for
good manners, as laid down by Coustel for the special benefit of
the pupils, are divided into how they should behave (*a*) during
conversations; and (*b*) at table.   Under each heading a very
large number of maxims are given and no good purpose would
be served by reproducing them all here; the following will,
however, serve to illustrate the stress laid by Port-Royal upon
'gentlemanliness'—that virtue which has so well been defined
as 'sympathy with the self-respect of others': When taking part
in conversations, listen more than you speak; be thoughtful and
circumspect; accommodate what you say to those whom you
are addressing; don't interrupt; don't boast; always try to find
excuses for the faults of others; don't flatter; never be afraid to
retract an opinion if you are brought to see that it is wrong.
Coustel also lays down rules for jesting; it must be subtle; it
must never be directed at personal deformities or afflictions or
misfortunes; it must be discreet and moderate.   It is pleasant
to find that in the austere atmosphere of Port-Royal there was
no puritanical horror of innocent joking.   Of the twenty-odd
rules for behaviour at table, the following are perhaps the most
interesting: Sit upright and don't inconvenience your neighbours;
don't show eagerness to be served; never forget to say 'thank
you'; don't cram your mouth nor inflate your cheeks "as if you
were blowing the fire"; don't eat too fast; don't drink too much
or boast of your capacity—" a barrel has a much greater capacity
than the largest stomach"; and last but not least wise: "The
custom of forcing others to drink the healths which have been
proposed, to the prejudice of their own, is neither honest nor
praiseworthy; a man must be a glutton and unmannerly to
do so[1]."

These rules possess much of the banality and tediousness of
all didactics on the subject of etiquette; but they serve to show
the care which was exercised in order that in every department
of life the pupils at Port-Royal might take heed to their ways,
lest there should arise the very smallest occasion of stumbling.
The solitaries were not content to regulate the conduct of their

[1] Vol. I, p. 346.

pupils towards adults, but politeness one to another was also inculcated. They were encouraged "to prefer one another in honour" and the *tutoiement* was absolutely forbidden. The children were addressed as 'Messieurs' not only by the masters (a not unusual custom even to-day in France), but also by one another. Thus we find Du Fossé referring to his dearest companions, when they were children at Port-Royal, as 'Monsieur' or 'Le Sieur.' Saint-Cyran again says to Le Maître: "I must thank you for the kindness with which you have undertaken the education of little Monsieur D'Andilly[1]." Yet we must recognise that here, as elsewhere, the Port-Royalists were careful not to insist too rigidly upon their regulations; for this same 'Monsieur D'Andilly' (i.e. De Villeneuve) is elsewhere referred to as 'le petit Jules' and we have a letter from Le Maître to Racine, who was at the time 16 years old, addressed "Pour le petit Racine, à Port-Royal."

The feature of the Port-Royal schools which has hitherto received most attention is their dislike of rivalry and emulation among the pupils. It was perhaps to prevent this that the above-mentioned regulations for the conduct of the children one towards another were introduced. The explanation is doubtless that rivalry was thought to encourage evil passions, and to give corrupt nature a chance of re-asserting herself at the expense of baptismal innocency. Stress was however laid on the value of emulating one's past achievements; "children must be encouraged to do better and better, because if they are not continually advancing along the road to virtue, they are losing ground; on this subject remember the proverb: 'however good be the horse there is always need of the spur[2].'" Rousseau tells us in his *Confessions* that he was acquainted with the works of the Port-Royalists; and it is perhaps just possible that he owes to them his well-known theory of encouraging the pupil to emulate not others but himself.

At the same time, the practice of the Port-Royal schools in respect to emulation seems to have been greatly misrepresented by modern commentators. M. Carré says: "Ce même souci du

[1] Fontaine, *Mémoires*, p. 191.   [2] Coustel, *Règles*, Vol. x, pp. 183—4.

salut primant tout, avait fait bannir l'émulation des écoles de Port-Royal. Point de ces concours si chers aux Jésuites et à l'Université elle-même; point de ces luttes dans lesquelles on cherche à briller plus que les autres[1]." So also M. Compayré tells us: "À Port-Royal on supprimait de parti pris l'émulation, de crainte d'éveiller l'amour-propre[2]." But although it is clear that emulation between pupils was regarded as a danger and as needing careful regulation, the only evidence that it was absolutely forbidden at Port-Royal seems to be contained in a phrase in Pascal's *Pensées* : "Les Enfants de Port-Royal auxquels on ne donne point cet aiguillon d'envie et de gloire, tombent dans la nonchalance." It must be remembered that Pascal had never taught in the Little Schools ; and the prevalence to-day of the view that emulation was forbidden at Port-Royal is probably due to the fact that his *Pensées* are still widely read and that this passage is consequently known among scholars, of whom few are acquainted with Du Fossé's *Mémoires* or Coustel's *Règles*.

Now we have definite proof both from Du Fossé, a pupil at Port-Royal for 14 years, and from Coustel, one of the masters who taught in the Little Schools during the whole period of their existence, that emulation among the pupils *was* permitted within limits. First let us consider what Du Fossé says, and, as we are here concerned in combating a wide-spread heresy, perhaps somewhat lengthy quotations are excusable: "Since our class was composed of those who were the most advanced in their studies, we used to challenge one another (faire des défis d'émulation), as to who could recite a large number of lines from Virgil without making a mistake. And Le Sieur De Villeneuve's memory verily used to run away from us; for I can remember hearing him recite whole books of Virgil without scarcely making a mistake. However, this method of practising used to inspire us with ardour to do well and to make progress and equal the others. We had also a sort of intellectual game or a kind of little warfare in which each of us used to make the most wonderful efforts to surpass the others and to gain the victory over his comrades, not by blows of the sword, but of the tongue. For we used to form into two parties and the

[1] Introd. p. xviii.   [2] Vol. I, p. 270.

cleverest in each party used to compose Latin verses spon-
taneously, with which they carried on the attack or the defence.
When this game led to sharp words and degenerated into a
heated quarrel, the masters, who continually kept a watch on
what was going on, used to be obliged to calm our minds and
break up the two parties which were displaying too much ardour.
...It was Monsieur Des Champs who used particularly to excel
in this kind of combat, for he had a subtle and lively wit and a
keen appreciation of poetry[1]." We have here abundant evidence
that emulation *was* in vogue at Port-Royal; the 'petite guerre'
described above reminds us forcibly of the Roman and Cartha-
ginian camps of the contemporary Jesuit schools, where, however,
the spirit of emulation may often have been carried to a
demoralising degree. It was not until rivalry had ceased to be
a desirable stimulus to work and was likely to become a moral
danger that the Port-Royalists, like any other wise schoolmasters,
stepped in and forbade it[2]. Thus Coustel, while not forbidding
emulation, says: "When attempting to introduce emulation,
great care must be taken to avoid arousing in children envy for
the good qualities which they notice in their companions and
which they themselves lack[3]." If further proof is needed to
show Port-Royal's true attitude towards rivalry as a stimulus to
study we may quote the very explicit recommendations of
Coustel: "They must be stimulated to work and given emulation by offering now and then a prize for those who do best[4]."
So also Dr Arnauld in his *Règlement des Études* lays it down
that places should be taken in class every fortnight or every
month; and also that prizes should be given, on the strength of
moral character as well as general diligence, every six months
or year. We may therefore conclude that even though Saint-
Cyran in his educational theory may have desired emulation to
be abolished from the school, yet in practice this was never
carried out at Port-Royal; for this we have the testimony of
pupil and master alike. As a matter of fact the recommendation
of the *Ratio Studiorum*: "Honesta aemulatio quae magnum
ad studia incitamentum est fovenda[5]," might as justly be applied

[1] p. 92.　　　[2] Compare also the incident described on page 19.
[3] Vol. II, p. 112.　　[4] Vol. II, p. 63.　　[5] p. 126

to the school-practice of the Port-Royalists as to that of the Jesuits. But none the less, rivalry between pupils, like the reading of classical literature, was regarded as something which needed the most careful watching, since it might so easily become a great danger to the child's soul. Pascal has over-estimated in this respect the practice of the schools of which he probably knew comparatively little; and owing to the popularity of his works, this error has been repeated far and wide. But the Port-Royal schoolmasters here as elsewhere knew the child mind more thoroughly than their commentators and historians have sometimes realised.

CHAPTER V

HAVING now dealt with the more important characteristics of the school-environment at Port-Royal and the chief features of the general teaching methods adopted by the solitaries, it would be natural to consider the particular methods applied by them to the teaching of each subject in the curriculum. But before proceeding to this, it will be well to point out a principle which underlies all the particular methods of Port-Royal and in which the solitaries seem once more to have anticipated Pestalozzi and our modern educational theorists.

At Port-Royal it was seen that successful teaching must as far as possible explain the unknown by the known. The immediate result of this was the adoption of the vernacular as the medium for teaching and learning. This was an innovation of the highest importance and it was in a very real sense an innovation. In 1612 the University had threatened to suspend from his office a professor of philosophy who had ventured to lecture in French instead of in Latin. Students were compelled by a statute of François I, renewed in 1600 by Henri IV, to speak in Latin not only in class but also during recreations. That the Latin employed on these latter occasions was probably anything but classical we may gather not only from the well-known caricature of Rabelais, but also from examples given by Mathurin Cordier—'Noli crachare super me'; 'Ego transibo me de te'; 'Diabolus te possit inferre.' In the Jesuit 'collèges' the mother-tongue was forbidden not only in the class-room, but even in conversations between the pupils themselves. Two excerpts from the *Ratio Studiorum* which illustrate this may be quoted: "Latine loquendi usus severe in primis custodiatur, ita ut in omnibus quae ad scholam pertinent, nunquam liceat uti patrio sermone; eamque ob rem latine perpetuo magister loquatur[1]." "Domi linguae latinae usum inter scholasticos diligenter conservandum curet Rector; ab hac autem latine loquendi lege non eximantur, nisi vacationum dies et recreationis horae[2]." The motto of the Jesuit school was "Lege; scribe; loquere," and in each case the reference is to the Latin language. Again the *Linguae Latinae Exercitatio* of the Spaniard Vives, which, although originally published in 1539, seems to have been a favourite school-book throughout the sixteenth and seventeenth centuries, purports to be a "first book of practice in speaking the Latin language." It provides material also for conversing in Latin both in and out of school. Sturm in his gymnasium at Strassburg devoted a nine years' course to the acquirement of Latin and the ability to use this language correctly and easily; no attention whatever was given to the vernacular. In the Protestant school at Goldberg, under the care of Trotzendorf, everyone—including even the servants—spoke Latin; and the extraordinary care with which Montaigne in his youth was taught to speak Latin to the exclusion of his native French, is well known to every reader of the *Essays.* Even Comenius in one place[3] lays it down that all conversation out of school must be carried on in Latin, though this doubtless refers only to older boys who had been introduced to this language through the vernacular. Similarly in English schools the mother-tongue was normally as much forbidden as in the Jesuit 'colleges.' In an appendix to the Latin grammar written by William Lily of S. Paul's School—a text-book which held sway in English schools till well into the nineteenth century—we read:

Et quoties loqueris, memor esto loquare (?) Latine,
Et scopulos veluti barbara verba fuge.

Again Brinsley's *Ludus Literarius* (1612) gives us a conversation between Spondeus, who represents the ordinary school practitioner of the time, and Philoponus, who is Brinsley himself, the school reformer. *À propos* of the difficulty of making boys converse in Latin, Spondeus says, "But this I have had too much experience of, that without great severity they will not

[1] p. 121.   [2] p. 27.   [3] *Opera Didactica Omnia*, p. 784.

be brought unto; but they will speake English and one will winke at another, if they be out of the Master's hearing[1]." Philoponus in his reply refers to the contemporary custom of appointing 'custodes' who keep a watch on what is said and smite with the 'ferula' those who talk English; he points out the abuses to which this is liable, and suggests that the use of Latin should be confined to the formal exercises of the school-room. Similarly John Dury, author of the *Reformed School* (1649?), lays it down for the pupils that after the first year "their speech shall be wholly Latin."

We have evidence then that alike in France, Germany and England it was customary to use Latin as the medium of instruction from quite the lowest forms upwards and that often it was imposed upon children even as a conversational language.

It must be remembered that up to the end of the sixteenth century and even later, Latin held a position very unlike that which it occupies to-day; it was the language of all learned books and all learned men, and was thus the key to every branch of knowledge; it also formed a means of communication among educated persons of every European country, and achieved an end at which we are now aiming by means of Esperanto and similar contrivances. Sturm writing in the middle of the sixteenth century says: "Romanus sermo per omnes nationes et populos et regna commeat neque usquam gentium venias ubi non Latinum hospitem invenias qui viam proficiscenti monstret. Adeo linguam hanc hospitalem esse voluit Deus quam late terrarum orbis patet, hominibus[2]." This helps to explain the appearance of the numerous 'colloquies' or Latin conversation books. It is clear then that the acquirement and exercise at school of the power to converse in Latin was a matter of the highest importance, and that it cannot be fairly judged by present-day standards. So long as Latin remained exclusively the language of the learned, vernacular languages perforce remained unsettled and unstandardised. But by the seventeenth century the old conditions were rapidly passing

[1] p. 219.
[2] Quoted by Laurie, *Educational Opinion*, p. 144, note.

away and Latin was fast becoming a 'dead' language. Dante
and Boccaccio in the fourteenth century had helped to crystal-
lise their native Italian into a literary form, and by so doing
had incurred the contempt of the extreme humanists[1]; France
had to wait another 200 years before Rabelais and Montaigne
laid the foundations of French prose. It is however true that
by the time that the Port-Royal schools came into existence,
Latin had to a great extent lost its crude utilitarian value; it
was even no longer regarded as the only language in which
a learned work might be written. Ramus had published his
Dialectic in French as early as 1555, and the appearance of
Descartes' treatises in the same language clinched the matter;
it was no longer the medium of conversation for the learned—
"de mille personnes," says Coustel, "il n'y en aura pas quatre
qui au sortir du collège se trouveront dans la nécessité de parler
ou d'écrire en latin[2]."

Such then being the case, it is all the more remarkable that
even in the seventeenth century Latin should have remained the
medium of instruction in the three chief countries in Europe.
As a matter of fact, that it should ever have held this place
at all in the elementary education of quite young children
seems excessively perverse. The process of instruction must
often have been one of 'ignotum per ignotius'; the hapless
child was made to learn by heart rules of the 'propria quae
maribus' order, before he had enough knowledge of Latin
to know the meaning of what he said. The result was an
enormous waste of time and an absolutely unnecessary increase
of the difficulties placed in the child's way during the early years
of his school career.

The Port-Royalists were not the first to remark this. It had
been recognised perhaps in some small measure as early as the
first half of the fifteenth century by Vittorino Da Feltre; but we
find it fully developed in the educational theories of Ratke
(1571—1635). He says in his *Memorial* to the Imperial Diet:

---

[1] Cf. 'Quos tu mihi Dantes, quos Petrarcas, quos Boccatios?...Nam quid est in
illis quod aut admirandum, aut laudandum, cuiquam videri debeat?' L. Aretinus,
Dialogue, p. 60.

[2] Vol. II, p. 185.

"Now the right practice and course of Nature is that the dear youth should first learn to read, write, and speak correctly and readily their inherited mother-tongue (which in our case is German), and thereby they can the better understand and comprehend what they learn in other tongues. For this purpose the German Bible may be used with special profit." Again in the *Elucidation* of his *Memorial*, Ratke advocates the establishment of a school in which all the teaching should be in High German.

Ratke's ideas had but little permanent result in practice, but they are important because they influenced Comenius. The latter laid down as one of the principles of the method of teaching that "Nature proceeds from the more easy to the more difficult"; hence the teacher must speak the same vernacular as the boy; all explanations must be given in it and every grammar and lexicon adapted to the mother-tongue by which the new is to be learned. Similarly Comenius prescribes eight or ten years for learning the vernacular—the whole of infancy and part of boyhood; whereas Latin "may be despatched in two years." The Port-Royalists were hardly so innovating as Comenius with regard to the learning of Latin, but it will be interesting to consider whether they were in any measure influenced by him in their adoption of the vernacular as the ordinary medium of instruction.

Comenius had published his most important school-book, the *Janua Linguarum*, in 1631. The *Janua* is described on its title-page as "Janua linguae Latinae reserata, rerum et linguarum structuram exhibens." It is in fact a pansophic description of common objects of every kind, which is set forth in Latin and thus affords at the same time opportunity for learning the grammar of this language. The book is really one of a series; it is to be followed by the *Atrium*—"rerum et linguarum ornamenta exhibens," and preceded by the *Vestibulum*, a primer of simple sentences. In this last-named work the Latin phrases and their German equivalents are given in parallel columns; and this was the case also in the first edition of the *Janua*, but in its second and later editions the vernacular was omitted. We find references to the *Janua* in Nicole's

Traité de l'Éducation d'un Prince and in Lancelot's Preface to his *Jardin des Racines Grecques*; but in both cases the solitaries criticise adversely Comenius' method of teaching languages.   It was probably an entirely Latin copy of the *Janua* which was known to them; but we have no evidence that any of the Port-Royalists had ever consulted the *Great Didactic* which contains Comenius' general educational theory and in which the value of the vernacular as a teaching medium is especially emphasised. Moreover, the *Great Didactic* was originally published in 1630 in the author's native Czech, and it did not appear in a Latin version until the Amsterdam edition of 1657. The *Janua* on the other hand appeared in Latin in 1631, and the second edition (Latin only) in 1650; the work achieved an immediate and widespread success ; it was translated into no less than fourteen modern languages besides Latin and Greek, and became one of the most famous school-books of its day.   Lancelot tells us that he used it for his pupils, but did not find it of great value.

While then the *Janua* was obviously known and used at Port-Royal, the *Great Didactic*, which did not appear in Latin until three years before the final suppression of the Little Schools, does not seem in any measure to have influenced the teaching methods employed in them ; and therefore we may conclude that the adoption of the vernacular at Port-Royal was not due to the recommendations of Comenius. We may, however, trace elsewhere the course taken by Port-Royal in its adoption of the vernacular in teaching. In the schools of the Oratory, the French language had already been employed to a certain extent[1]; but a revolution such as this could not be effected at a single blow, for we find that the Oratorians used the vernacular only in the lower classes ; in the higher, Latin was still obligatory ; "in rhetoricae et humanitatis classibus latine, in ceteris vernacule."   Similarly an Oratorian father named De Condren published in 1642 a *Method* of learning Latin through the medium of French, and his book was thus the precursor of Lancelot's famous *Nouvelles Méthodes*.

---

[1] It appears from the Preface to Malebranche's *Recherche de la Vérité* that the Oratory was following the example of Port-Royal in this reform. This is not altogether borne out by the evidence of dates.

Both the Oratory and Port-Royal were inspired from the same source in their adoption of the vernacular; they were both influenced by Descartes. The solitaries were whole-hearted Cartesians in their desire for clearness and the formation of the judgment, and in their attempt to teach children only what they could understand. As far as human knowledge was concerned, the Port-Royalists gave reason its fullest play and aimed at the development of all the faculties of the mind to their furthest extent. It was this spirit of Cartesianism which led to their production of the *Logic*, and their opposition to the *a priori* and deductive reasoning which characterised the Middle Ages.

The adoption of the vernacular by the Port-Royalists is but symptomatic of their whole attitude towards education. In this reform they were not without their forerunners, both known and unknown to them; but, quite apart from the example of other educational innovators, they would have been led to this reform not only by their fundamental desire to develop the child's mind to its utmost in every direction and to render him a responsible and logical being, but also by their warm-hearted attempt to remove all unnecessary obstacles from the path of the learner, and so render education pleasant and expeditious.

The use of the vernacular was recommended at Port-Royal especially in connection with the teaching of reading. The contemporary custom was to make children begin to spell from Latin books, of which they could not as yet understand a single word, the reason given for this singular procedure being that Latin was pronounced more nearly as it is written than French. But as the Abbé Fleury soundly comments: "In my opinion the pleasure which a child would have in understanding what he read and in seeing the usefulness of his work would cause him to make quite as much progress." So also Coustel remarks: "It is better, in teaching children to read, to use French rather than Latin books; for, since they understand their native language, they will comprehend with much less difficulty what they read in this language than in one of which they have not as yet the slightest idea. In fact it is

B.   8 a general rule that, as far as possible, everything should be made easy for children.   A facilioribus ad difficiliora, a notis ad ignota semper procedendum est[1]."   Guyot develops the same thought at much greater length in the preface to his edition of Cicero's *Letters* (1668): " It is a very serious fault to begin teaching children to read in Latin, as is usually done, instead of in French."   This not only discourages the pupils and early engrains in them a hatred for study, but it also wastes three or four years and so exhausts the master's patience and enthusiasm. The difficulties of the learner are still worse than those of the teacher; hence "we should accommodate ourselves to the feeble-ness of our pupils and never give them more trouble than that which is absolutely indispensable."   Guyot goes on to combat the disciplinary conception of education; he would rather, if it be possible, make school-work "more pleasant than play and games."   This is obviously impracticable so long as spelling is taught in meaningless Latin; hence we should start with familiar vernacular words, taken at first in detachment from any context and referring to concrete objects well known to the children. Guyot gives as instances: "du pain; un lit; une chambre."

But there remains an initial difficulty in the teaching of reading which is not obviated by using the vernacular.   This difficulty, to quote the *Grammaire générale*, is that "though each letter has its name, it is pronounced when alone differently from when it is joined with other letters.   For example if we make a child put together 'f r y,' we make him pronounce 'eff, ar, wy' (in French 'ef, er, i grec'); which does not fail to con-fuse him when he wishes to join these three sounds together to produce the sound of the syllable 'fry[2]."

In order to remedy this confusion, a method of teaching to read was in use at Port-Royal which is explained by Guyot, Coustel, and also in the *Grammaire générale* for which Lancelot is partly responsible—that is to say by three of the original masters.   The consonants were taught to the children not by their names, but by their value in pronunciation; and either an *e* mute was added or else one of the ordinary vowels; for, as Guyot points out, the consonants are so named because they

---

[1] Vol. II, pp. 22—3.   [2] p. 23.

have no sound of themselves, but need the addition of a vowel to become voiced. Even this, however, though excellent for a language like German or Welsh, still presents difficulties in French or English, where the same sounds may be represented by different letters or collections of letters, and these latter in turn stand for different sounds in different words. The only remedy is to make the unit of spelling the syllable and not the letter. The child must be taught that 'bon' spells not 'bé, o, enne,' but, to adopt modern phonetic spelling, 'bɔ̃'; that 'jamais' spells not 'jé, a, êm, a, i, êsse,' but 'ʒa-mɛ'; that 'disaient' spells not 'dé, i, êsse, a, i, é, enne, té,' but 'di-zɛ.' This syllabic or phonetic method of reading is ascribed by the Port-Royalists to Pascal and he must have invented it very soon after going into retreat; from which we may infer that he evinced an interest in the teaching from the first, and would perhaps have taken part in it had not other matters monopolised his attention. He retired from the world at the beginning of 1655; in October of the same year his sister Jacqueline, who in the previous June had been put in charge of the girls' school at Port-Royal des Champs, wrote to him asking for details of his "method for learning to read by be, ce, de, &c., in which it is not necessary for the children to know the names of the letters." There is extant also a letter written to Angélique De S. Jean, who was afterwards Abbess of Port-Royal, by her uncle Dr Arnauld, while he was in hiding owing to the disturbance caused at the Sorbonne by his treatise *De la Fréquente Communion.* It is dated January 31, 1656, and in it Dr Arnauld says: "You will laugh at my reason for writing to you. There is a little boy here, about 12 years old, who doesn't know how to read; I should like to see if he could learn to do so by M. Pascal's method." This act of kindness amid many cares and anxieties reminds one forcibly of Saint-Cyran, who when in captivity taught the children of the prison-governor and played with them. Perhaps Arnauld was more akin to the Port-Royal of Saint-Cyran than Sainte-Beuve and other writers seem to suggest; though it is not unlikely that his letter was inspired by curiosity to see how Pascal's method would work, as well as by affectionate interest in the 'little boy, about 12 years old.' None the less he must

8—2

have had a sincere appreciation of the importance of education, for we owe several educational treatises either partly or wholly to him; and in the *Grammaire générale* in which he and Lancelot co-operated, the Pascal method of reading is adopted in its entirety.

In the teaching of reading then, the Port-Royalists not only were in advance of contemporary practice in the substitution of vernacular for Latin words, but they even anticipated the most modern methods in regard to the teaching of spelling and pro-nunciation; and it is probably true that there are in this country to-day schools in which their methods might be with advantage adopted. From Miss Plaisted's *Early Education of Children*, which embodies the best practice of present-day elementary schools in England, France, Germany and America, and is the work of an experienced and sympathetic Infants' head-mistress, may be quoted the following principles with regard to the teaching of reading which were explicitly set forth 250 years ago by the Port-Royalists: (*a*) the words used should refer to concrete objects well known to the children[1]; (*b*) the reading lesson should be a delight and not a trial to them[2]; (*c*) the sound or value of letters should be taught rather than their conventional names[3]; (*d*) children should be drilled in the immediate recognition of the sound of syllables[4]; (*e*) polysyllabic words should be divided up into their component syllables as an aid to spelling[5].

In one particular the practice of Port-Royal was far in advance of that of the average modern English public school— in the stress laid upon the art of reading aloud with correctness and expression. Coustel, after referring to the syllabic method of teaching children to read, goes on to say: "First of all they must be made to read very slowly until age and practice have given them the power of reading more quickly and without mistakes. In thinking to bring our pupils on we often set them back by hurrying them too much; for by hesitating at every word they grow accustomed to repeat them in a manner which grates upon one's ear and is altogether hateful. They

---

[1] p. 223.   [2] p. 231.   [3] p. 243.

[4] p. 244.   [5] p. 256.

must be made to pronounce each word distinctly and in an intelligible tone of voice, without stammering, and without speaking either at the back of the throat or between the teeth; for these and similar small faults, if at first neglected, soon become incorrigible. To make their reading pleasant, they must be accustomed to observe the stops and pauses necessary for the sense, and to avoid monotony as far as possible; they must likewise be accustomed to show, by raising or lowering the voice, that they understand the sense of what they read— especially when this is verse, in which the rhythm should always be marked[1]." Guyot likewise recommends that "children should read little at a time and often, in a loud and clear voice, for this will exercise the voice and chest and afford opportunity for teaching them to pronounce well, by giving the accent necessary for marking the different tones appropriate to the subject-matter, and for correcting the false cadences or inflections of voice into which they fall. Thus they will be accustomed to fineness of ear, to the arrangement of the words, and the harmony of the sentences; besides this, by reading little at a time and often, their attention will not be fatigued[2]."

This attention to expressive reading was not confined to the boys' schools. The Franciscan father Comblat, who visited the girls' schools of Port-Royal in 1678 and whose praise of the singing there has already been quoted, says of the reading of their prayers: "She who read spoke so correctly and distinctly, and at the same time so unaffectedly, that not a single word was lost nor a single phrase misunderstood; and she said everything in a tone so clear and at the same time so touching that one could not help but listen, so persuasively did she read." We may conclude then that the value of clear and expressive reading as an element in a literary education was thoroughly recognised at Port-Royal; and that the religious exercises and offices at which the pupils were present were not performed in the mechanical and perfunctory style in which the church services are read in too many public school and college chapels of the present day.

[1] Vol. II, pp. 20—1.
[2] Preface to *Nouveau Recueil des lettres de Cicéron*.

Learning to read naturally involves learning to write; and on this subject again the Port-Royalists had something to say. But since learning to write must ever be at bottom a process of imitation which can never be simplified, the recommendations of the solitaries do not contain anything very striking. A fairly large handwriting was desired, in which the letters should be well formed and rounded, and properly proportioned one to another. To ensure this, great stress was laid on the proper method of holding the pen; to quote Guyot: "They must not be allowed to write by themselves at first, but under the eye of their teacher, until they have acquired a good habit of holding the pen; that done, they should often pass the dry pen over the lines of their copy, in order that the muscles, nerves, and the whole hand may acquire the knack and movement necessary for good writing[1]." Even the most modern educational psychologist, with his explanations of habit in terms of brain-paths and the plasticity of neural matter, cannot improve upon these recommendations laid down by Guyot. To facilitate the process of learning to write, use was made of 'transparents,' i.e. pages on which were printed either black parallel lines or else the actual words to be copied; over this was placed a sheet of writing paper through which the black lines or words were plainly visible, and could thus assist the writer. It must be remembered that paper in the seventeenth century had not the opacity of the glazed writing paper of to-day; but if some fairly large and black type be placed behind the blank fly-leaf of a printed book of this period, the letters will usually be found to be clearly visible through the superimposed sheet. We learn also from a letter of Fontaine's that the question of pens was not overlooked; metal nibs were used in preference to goose-quills, as the former "do not waste the pupil's time (i.e. by needing continually to be recut) and spare them many petty worries" (e.g. sputtering and making blots).

The Port-Royalists were not content to employ their vernacular French merely as the medium of instruction; they also thought it worthy of study for its own sake. There is in the

---

[1] Preface to *Nouveau Recueil*.

pages of Coustel a striking plea for the study of the French language which is worth while reproducing, though it must of necessity lose much in the translation: we can the better appreciate its force when we remember that French as a subject of study was utterly neglected by the Jesuits and the University—that is to say in the secondary and higher education of the time. "Considering the point of perfection which our language has reached," says Coustel, "it surely deserves that we should cultivate it a little. As a matter of fact, it has never been so rich in its expressions, so noble in its phrases, so precise and so pregnant in its epithets, so subtle in its turns and circumlocutions, so majestic in its motions, so brilliant in its metaphors, and finally so natural and so altogether magnificent and lofty in its verse, as it is at present. It would then be shameful for children to be barbarians in their own country and for them to talk French like Allobroges or Germans, while all the nations are striving, one against the other, to learn all the beauties of this language and to perfect themselves in it[1]." It must be remembered that the Little Schools flourished, and that Coustel wrote his treatise, during the reign of Louis XIV, the brilliancy of whose Court had dazzled all Europe; France became the arbiter of taste, and French was adopted as the Court language of the civilised world. This had been made possible by the foundation of the Academy by Richelieu in 1637. The prime function of this institution was to regulate the French language and to render it "not only elegant, but also capable of treating all the arts and all the sciences." There followed an age of great literary activity; under the patronage of Louis XIV and Mazarin, the French drama produced its three most illustrious representatives— Corneille, Molière, and Racine. Coustel's eulogy of the beauties of his native tongue, therefore, is hardly exaggerated, especially in regard to French poetry. The prose of the Port-Royalists themselves sometimes wearies the reader and perplexes the translator by the cumbrousness of its sentences. But we must remember that, in spite of their desire to give French her rightful place in the curriculum, the solitaries had been educated

---

[1] Vol. II, p. 53.

on the old, exclusively Latin plan, and must therefore have found some difficulty in expressing themselves in good French prose. But they had no sympathy with the Latinised French which still seems to have been current in some quarters at the time, and they would have ridiculed it as did Rabelais 150 years before them.

Nevertheless the style of the solitaries is of unequal merit, and one may be allowed to digress shortly on this point, since it indirectly concerns the teaching of French in their schools. Their style is very adversely criticised by a Jesuit father named Bouhours, who censures the length of their sentences, the strangeness of their phrases, and the want of taste and moderation in many of their expressions. But he is hardly an impartial critic, and he devotes his attention chiefly to a translation of the *Imitatio Christi*, prepared by Le Maître. The least successful stylist of the solitaries whose works became famous is perhaps Nicole; he has been described as "the coldest, the greyest, the most leaden, the most insupportable of the bores of that great and tedious house." Bossuet has left a note on his reading, dated 1669, in which he says: "Some books of MM. de Port-Royal, good to read because gravity and grandeur are found in them; but their style has little variety. Without variety there is no pleasure." Nicole seems at one period to have considered it inconsistent with Christian humility to be anxious about one's style; his concern is with the subject-matter and, so long as that be a truth of vital importance, he disdains to give care to the garb in which it is presented. So again De Saci in his translation of the Bible purposely adopted a bald style that he might keep as closely as possible to the original; he did not dare, so he tells us, to try to elucidate and set forth in clear French passages which the Holy Spirit had given in obscure or inelegant Greek or Hebrew.

But the attitude of Nicole and De Saci was not that of some of the other solitaries; it was certainly not the attitude of Dr Arnauld and, above all, not that of Pascal. We are told that Balzac, in a conversation one day with D'Andilly, remarked with astonishment that so young a man as the Doctor could write his treatise *De la Fréquente Communion* in so polished and mature a style; whereat D'Andilly replied that 'he simply used the language of his family.' And since no less than 22 members of this family entered Port-Royal and perhaps half of that number were in some way connected with the Little Schools, we may infer that they exerted no small influence in making Port-Royal appreciate the value of a good French prose style. But of chief importance was the work of Pascal; before him French prose had been unstandardised and too often tended to be turgid and involved, and copied slavishly from classical models. As has been observed by an English authority upon French Renaissance literature: "It is not too much to say that France did not possess a common literary language till far into the seventeenth century. Till then, every prose writer at least, even Rabelais, even Montaigne, shows traces of the *patois* of his own province[1]." But it is partly owing to the efforts of the Port-Royalists that this common literary language was forged; and above all, it was Pascal who made it 'what it has ever since remained, a pattern of absolutely unencumbered expressiveness.' In a similar strain Sainte-Beuve remarks: "At that moment the question at issue was to fix the French language in its complete originality, to try and free it from the Latin forms and figures of speech with which the sixteenth century had clothed it....The unique work of the epoch of Louis XIV is to have entirely given up speaking Latin in French; and in this beautiful language, so clear, so forcible, which became current in 1664, not a trace of a confused or involved style is to be noticed. Port-Royal contributed to this with all its powers[2]."

A society containing Dr Arnauld and Pascal could not long have remained indifferent to the value and the charms of a good literary style. In spite, then, of Nicole with his occasional lack of literary taste and his contempt for the beauties of style— especially in his later works—we can hardly argue from a particular premiss to a universal conclusion; and therefore M. Cadet's statement that "at Port-Royal it was thought derogatory to Christian humility to pay attention to style[3]" seems to need considerable qualification. We have indeed

[1] Tilley, *Lit. of the Fr. Renaissance*, p. 31.   [2] Vol. III, p. 516.
[3] p. 34.

evidence that the inculcation of a good French prose style
formed an essential part of the educational theory and practice of the Little Schools.   Coustel, after treating of the manner
in which Latin authors should be read, goes on to say : " It is
not enough to read carefully good authors, to make judicious
extracts from them, and, if desired, to learn their most beautiful
passages by heart, if, with all that, one does not thereby fit
oneself for making use of them, when opportunity offers, by
means of translation ; this indeed it is which makes passages
in Latin and Greek books, which are beautiful and striking,
appear as such in our own language also.   It may be said that
this is the sum total of the advantages to be derived from study.
For of a thousand people who leave college, not four will find
it necessary to speak or write Latin.   But everyone should be
able to make himself understood in French ; and he, who in
good society is unable to do this, is put to shame.   Children
must therefore be especially practised in the art of translation,
because the concentration needed for weighing all the phrases,
and discovering the meaning of a Latin author, exercises both
their intellect and their judgment at the same time, and makes
them appreciate the beauty of the French as much as that of
the Latin[1]."   In another place, Coustel specifies 'travailler à se
former un bon style' as one of the means for educating 'des
personnes qui aspirent à une solide instruction'; the rules he
lays down for acquiring a good style are: (*a*) imitate the best
characteristics of the best models; (*b*) write as often as possible;
(*c*) cultivate a lively imagination, a good memory, and a sound
judgment ; (*d*) aim at clearness ; (*e*) never despair of equalling
your models.

It is clear from these quotations that M. Cadet's sweeping
statement is quite untrue as far as Coustel is concerned ; and
many of the observations of Coustel are likewise to be found in
Arnauld's *Règlement des Études*.   Similarly, Le Maître's *Règles
de la traduction française*, which were composed for the benefit
of the young Du Fossé and which are preserved for us in Fontaine's *Mémoires*, are in reality a short summary of rules for
writing good French ; and Guyot, in the preface to his edition

[1] Vol. II, p. 185.

of Cicero's *Letters to Atticus* (1668), lays great stress on the importance of the child acquiring a good French style before aiming at a good Latin style; he goes so far as to give a list of French books which he recommends as models. Even Nicole himself is so far inconsistent with some of his later expressions as to say that the child should learn by heart the most beautiful passages from ancient authors; "things learnt by heart impress themselves better on the memory and serve as moulds and forms which the thoughts take when they wish to express themselves. Consequently those who have good and excellent moulds must necessarily express themselves in a noble and lofty manner[1]." He elsewhere compares these 'moulds' or 'forms' of thought to the characters in which a book is printed, and which may be barbarous and Gothic or Roman and beautiful, quite apart from the subject-matter.

We may then be justified in concluding that as far as the schools were concerned, at any rate, and in many cases outside of them, the acquirement of a good French style was considered by Port-Royal to be one of the most important objects of education; in marked contrast to the ideas of the Jesuits, it was regarded as of equal value with a polished Latin style. The instruments by which it was to be obtained were conceived to be, firstly, the careful reading of good French authors and, secondly, translation from Latin authors. This second means was rightly seen to be of the greatest value, but it was not of the nature of those uncouth Latinised expressions, which are sometimes in our schools dignified with the name of 'translation.' Port-Royal would never have tolerated construing of the type pilloried by Mr Paton in an article on the teaching of Latin: "With which things being moved the Treviran knights, of whose valour there is among the Gauls a unique reputation, who had come for the sake of help being sent by their state to Caesar...[2]," and so forth. Coustel expressly states that a translation must be elegant, "so that it could be said that if the author, on whom one was at work, had written in our language, the translation would be what he would have written[3]."

[1] *Essais de Morale*, Vol. II, p. 296.
[2] *Aims and Methods of Teaching* (Spencer), p. 61.   [3] Vol. II, p. 196.

To foster the acquisition of a good French style, Port-Royal also included in its curriculum composition in the vernacular. This was an innovation of the highest importance, for French composition was unknown alike at the University and among the Jesuits. Guyot says that "children may begin to write in French before they write in Latin, by setting them to compose short dialogues, narratives or stories, little descriptions or short letters, and leaving them to choose the subjects out of their reading; so that they may not be accustomed to write obscurely and to be satisfied with what they do not understand; for this makes them lose the power of distinguishing light from darkness, and makes them take the false for the true, the doubtful for the certain and in short, evil for good[1]." We may note here again in passing that much of the Pestalozzian doctrine of *Anschauung* is already anticipated in this passage.

After a thorough grounding in the vernacular the pupil at Port-Royal began to learn Latin. Although the solitaries realised, to an extent unknown among their contemporaries, the value of the study of French, yet they did not for that reason belittle the study of Latin. At the same time they recognised the difficulties which inevitably beset a child in learning his first foreign language, and they saw that many other quite avoidable difficulties had been added to these by contemporary practice. It was their peculiar glory to have endeavoured as far as possible to remove these obstacles and to ensure that the pupil might attain to the most thorough knowledge and appreciation of the Latin language with the minimum of trouble and without wasting any time.

Latin language and literature were recognised at Port-Royal as humanising instruments *par excellence*; the judgment, according to Coustel, is man's principal faculty; and this can best be developed by exercising it in the careful and thoughtful reading of authors. "Our aim," says Arnauld in his *Règlement des Études*, "should be so to regulate the curriculum in our schools, that it would be practically impossible for pupils, who had spent the usual length of time there, not to understand

---

[1] Translation of *Ad Familiares*, Preface.

Latin easily, and not to have read the greater part of the so-called classical authors; and that those who had greater intellectual gifts, should write this language in a refined and lofty style, reproducing the flavour of antiquity[1]." Where this course is not followed, abuses may abound; Arnauld specifies the following: (*a*) the offices of State and Church are filled with ignorant men; (*b*) having no pleasure in literature, they have recourse to ignoble pleasures; (*c*) when they are obliged to write Latin, they use a barbarous style; (*d*) this fact tends to prejudice their efforts if they have to write in defence of the Catholic verities. It will be remembered that De Saci, in a passage already quoted, had pointed out the value of a good Latin style for those who had to compose controversial treatises and combat heresy. Nicole in his *Traité de l'Éducation d'un Prince* specifies the advantages of learning Latin as follows: (*a*) it may be used as a medium of conversation between cultured men of different nationalities; (*b*) it is the language of the Church; (*c*) in it all learned works are written.

Port-Royal, then, recognised Latin as one of the most important elements in the curriculum; not only did it humanise the mind, and develop the judgment, and cultivate the power of expression in the vernacular as well as in Latin, but it also had an immediate and practical value as an accomplishment expected in polite and learned society alike and as a weapon for the defence of Holy Church. But the solitaries were far from being content with the contemporary methods of teaching children this language and they accordingly devoted themselves to reforming these. In order to appreciate the problem which presented itself to them, let us consider in outline contemporary practices with regard to the teaching of Latin.

Since the child in his earliest school years was made to learn spelling from a Latin book, it is but natural that the rules of Latin Grammar were also written in Latin. This method was in vogue in our own country until within modern times—in some cases until the Public Schools Commission of 1861. D'Arcy Thompson gives a vivid description of his experience

[1] *Œuvres*, Vol. XLI, p. 86.

of the King Edward VI Latin grammar which was used during
his schooldays at Christ's Hospital; "The day after my entry
into this colossal institution," he says, "a Latin grammar was
placed into my hands....It gave all imaginable rules and all
imaginable exceptions...the rules for gender and quantity remained in the old Latin; and the Latin was communicated in
a hideously discordant rhythm....String upon string of jangling
unmusical lines could we repeat with a singular rapidity; understanding nothing; asking no questions[1]."   This was perhaps
typical of the state of things in an English public or grammar
school until the middle of last century; the strong common-
sense which underlay Pestalozzi's vague and incoherent ideas
has only just penetrated some of these strongholds of con-
servatism.   Perhaps there was more excuse for the schools of
the seventeenth century for they still sat in darkness.   They
too had their representative of those "grammars in which they
used to pretend to teach literary Latin by means of barbarous
Latin[2]."   It was a work composed in the early sixteenth century
by a Fleming named Van Pauteren (1460—1520).   His name
is usually Gallicised into Despautère or Latinised into Despauterius.   He had been a teacher at Louvain and had written
a Latin grammar in which the rules were reduced to verse; it
was hoped that by this means committing them to memory
would be facilitated.   But to judge by the following extracts,
we may well doubt if this purpose was in any way fulfilled:

> Ns aut rs, s demens, tis dabis apte;
> Dis vult glans, nefrens; capitis lens et folium frons,
> Libraque cum pendo, et quod cor faciet tibi nomen;
> Untis habento quiens et iens, legens (? legem) ambio spernit[3].

Or again:

> Vult xi ctumque cio, facit et iacit ecit et actum;
> Elicio per ui dat itum; fratres mage xi ctum[4].

Or again:

> Compositum quandoque dabit sibi prepos1ture
> Casum. Quo circa quartum sextumque dat exit;
> Sepe quidem docti repetunt bene preposituram[5].

---

[1] *Day-dreams of a Schoolmaster*, pp. 3, 4.
[2] Compayré, *Hist. de l'Éduc.* Vol. 1, p. 248.
[3] p. xxxii.   [4] p. lxvi.   [5] p. lxxxvii.

This almost incomprehensible doggerel is perhaps even less a stimulus to the learning of Latin Grammar than the 'as in prae-senti perfectum format in avi' of the King Edward VI *Latinae Grammaticae Rudimenta*. Can we then be surprised that Guyot should exclaim: "Everything is unpleasant for children in the land of Van Pauteren; all his rules are like a dark and thorny forest, in which for five or six years they have to grope their way, not knowing when or where all these winding paths will end; pricking themselves, running into or stumbling over everything that they meet, without hope of ever enjoying the light of day[1]"? So again Coustel says: "Some people make out that we should make use of the Latin rules of Van Pauteren for teaching children the genders, declensions, &c. They give as their reason that, because their ancestors learnt them, this ancient custom has the force of a law binding on their conscience. As if one should have other aims in the education of children than their assistance and progress in study! Now to my mind the use of Van Pauteren neither helps them, nor renders easy the learning of rules; it is a difficult book, written in Latin, and often even unintelligible in certain places....Those who before us have laboured to make rules for us, are not our masters to compel us to follow them; they are merely our guides and we are obliged to walk in their steps only so far as we find this advantageous[2]."

Van Pauteren's book appeared in 1510 and seems to have held the place of pre-eminence among school-books on the Continent for nearly two centuries. Ramus had made an attempt to dislodge it, but in vain; we find that new or revised editions of the work appeared at frequent intervals in the six-teenth and seventeenth centuries. Coustel tells us that "the book has undergone repeated corrections and numerous altera-tions," and he makes special reference to a *Despauterius Renovatus* edited by Dupleix. The work was in vogue as a school-book even as late as the early eighteenth century; there is extant a cash account of a boy named Filley De La Barre who was a pupil at the Jesuit college of Clermont (Louis-le-Grand) from 1716 to 1722 and in it figure two copies of Van Pauteren's grammar one costing 12 sous and the other 15 sous. As typical

---

[1] Trans. of *Epp. ad Atticum*, Preface.　　　[2] Vol. II, pp. 29, 31.

of the book in its best form during the existence of the Little
Schools, we may take the *Despauterius Novus,* edited by a Jesuit
father named Paiot and published at La Flèche in 1650. In this
work we have the original versified grammar rules, but to them
are appended explanations in French; after each section of the
grammar also there is a mass of miscellaneous information, quite
in the manner of Comenius, given both in Latin and French, and
illustrating in a more or less vague manner the preceding rules.
For instance the gender rules are followed by excursus on famous
men and women, cosmography, uranography, etherography, hy-
drography and geography; the declensions afford an occasion
for treating of classical mythology and customs, of the true God,
and for a melodramatic description of the various forms of
torture in different countries and ages. All this was none the
less a distinct advance upon the older practice, and it shows
that even among the Jesuits an attempt was being made to
render study less disagreeable and more varied and interesting.

The chief objection to Van Pauteren and books of this type
was their Grammar rules in bad Latin jingles. The most successful attempt that had been made, previous to the Port-
Royalists, to supersede these was that of Comenius. In 1631
he had published his *Janua Linguarum,* the success of which
was immediate and widely felt. As has been mentioned before,
it was translated into fourteen different modern languages and
apparently did much eventually to banish Van Pauteren from
the schools. The *Janua* contained a list of one thousand Latin
sentences, comprising eight thousand different words, with their
German equivalents. The subject-matter dealt as far as possible
with things known to the pupil and endeavoured to touch upon
all departments of human knowledge; for Comenius it must be
remembered was an encyclopaedist—the exponent of pansophia.

The *Janua* was well known at Port-Royal, and, though in
many ways it illustrated the educational doctrines of the solitaries, it was judged by them to contain several defects and was
therefore not adopted for use in the Little Schools. Nicole
remarks that: "The French, the Dutch, the Germans and the
Italians have idolised a certain book called *Janua Linguarum*
which comprises all the Latin words used in continuous discourse;

and they have imagined that by making children learn this book first they would soon get to know the Latin language, without the need of reading so many authors[1]." Nicole goes on to point out that Comenius leaves the question of teaching Grammar, which after all is the greatest difficulty in elementary Latin, still unsolved. "The ideas of those who will have nothing to do with Grammar are but the ideas of lazy people who want to avoid the trouble of explaining it; and the children, far from being helped, are burdened with an infinitely greater number of rules, since they are deprived of a light which would facilitate their understanding of books, and are obliged to learn a hundred times what it would have been enough to learn once[2]." Nicole here is perhaps a little unjust to Comenius and had he known the *Great Didactic* would probably have been more temperate in his language; still he recognises that the *Janua*, if unsuitable as a school-book, may well be of great use to the master.

A more interesting criticism of Comenius' *Janua* is that of Lancelot; he calls it "a work estimable in itself, but not sufficiently proportioned to the title it bears and the intention of its author. It not only requires an extraordinary memory to learn it, of which few children are capable; but also I can assert, after having personally made several experiments, that scarcely any are able to retain it because it is long and difficult; and since the words are never repeated, the beginning is forgotten before the end is reached. Thus children feel a constant dislike for it, because they always find themselves, as it were, in a new country where nothing is recognisable. The book is full of all kinds of unusual and difficult words and the first chapters are of no help for those which follow, nor are these for the last, since there is no word in one which is found in the others....What might be called the Gate to Languages ought to be a short and easy method for leading as quickly as possible to the reading of the best books; the object being to learn not only the words that we do not know, but also what is most noteworthy in the turn of phrase and of greatest purity of expression, which is beyond doubt the most difficult and most important part of every language[3]."

---

[1] *Essais de Morale*, Vol. II, p. 289.   [2] *op. cit.* Vol. II, p. 292.
[3] *Jardin des Racines grecques*, Preface to 2nd ed. pp. ii—iii.

Lancelot recognised then, what the best language teachers of to-day advocate, that the reading of authors as soon as possible should be the object to be aimed at.   To achieve this he rejects on the one hand the long and tedious Grammar rules in Latin verse of Van Pauteren, and on the other the vocabularies and phrase-lists of Comenius, which tend to burden the memory and still leave Grammar to be learnt more or less inductively, thus involving a huge waste of time.

To replace Van Pauteren and the *Janua* alike, Lancelot published in 1644 the first of Port-Royal's school-books, the *Nouvelle Méthode pour apprendre facilement et en peu de temps la Langue latine.*   This work is in its essentials an abridgment of Van Pauteren's grammar, translated into French verse.   In his 'avis au lecteur' Lancelot says: "Holding firm to the common-sense principle that children should be given the rules of the Latin language in French, which is the only language known to them...I thought that if I were to assist their minds by making things clear and intelligible, it would be necessary at the same time to put these rules into little French verses; by so doing they would not be at liberty to change the words, being constrained by the fixed number of syllables composing them and by the recurrence of the rhyme which makes everything easier and more pleasant[1]."   As an instance of Lancelot's work the following excerpts may be quoted:

Des Noms en NS, et en RS.

Ceux en NS comme en RS,
Auront TIS en perdant leur S.
Mais Glans, Nefrens, Lens, Lende ont DIS,
Et Libripens, libripendis,
Joins-y Frons feuille, et ceux de Cor,
Qui prennent un D après OR[2].

Des Verbes en CIO.

Fácio fait feci, factum,
Et jácio, jeci, jactum ;
ITUM, UI, Elicio :
Les autres pris de Lácio
EXI, ECTUM, posséderont ;
Ceux de Spécio les suivront[3].

[1] p. 19.   [2] p. 111.   [3] p. 231.

These two extracts are Lancelot's equivalents for the first two passages from Van Pauteren quoted on page 126.

It is obvious that though Lancelot's grammar, being in French, was at least intelligible to the child and in so far was an improvement on Van Pauteren's, yet it was not without its disadvantages. The rhymes were too often mere 'chevilles,' and not Racine himself could have turned the rules of Latin Grammar into poetry. Thus Rousseau who during his stay at Les Charmettes applied himself to study Lancelot's *Méthode latine*, says: "Ces vers ostrogoths me faisaient mal au cœur et ne pouvaient entrer dans mon oreille[1]." It may also be questioned whether a pupil who had learnt these versified Grammar rules by heart was even then prepared in the best way; it would have been enough to know the rules, to be able to quote an example for each, and to apply them when reading authors. However, Lancelot does realise the value of using the rules learnt as soon as possible in reading Latin texts; and he quotes with approval Ramus' maxim "Few rules and much practice." Moreover, as M. Egger points out, "The barbarous quatrains that Lancelot mixes with the rules in prose in his *Méthodes* have quite gone out of fashion now. But then it was something to employ the French language instead of Latin; it was something to have set out the declensions and conjugations at greater length; to have facilitated the effort of memory necessary for pupils in learning the vocabulary of a dead language by the choice of the most useful words[2]." In one particular Lancelot merits our special commendation and the careful notice of many modern writers of Latin grammars; he would spare the child the minutiae of Grammar. "I have been careful," says he, "to avoid some observations that seemed to me not very useful, remembering the excellent saying of Quintilian that it is part of the science of a really skilful grammarian to know that there are some things that are not worth knowing[3]." And yet it is not so very long ago that the present writer was being taught that *amussis* and *cannabis* make their accusative in -*im*, and that *acinaces* and

[1] *Confessions*, p. 211.
[2] *De l'Hellénisme en France*, Vol. II, p. 60.
[3] Preface to *Méthode latine*, p. 7.

glis are masculine. Surely we have something yet to learn even from Lancelot's uncouth French verses.

As soon as the pupil at Port-Royal could read and while he was still engaged in learning his Latin Grammar, he was introduced by means of French translations or 'versions,' to the Latin authors which he would one day read in the original. These 'versions' had a double object; in the first place they were expected to teach the child to speak and write the vernacular with ease and in a pure and pleasant style; and secondly they would familiarise him with the subjects which he would study later on in the Latin texts and so render them more easily translated. The most important translations of the classics which issued from Port-Royal are those of Cicero's *Letters* and of Plautus' *Captivi*, prepared by Guyot; to De Saci also we owe a rendering of three comedies of Terence and of the fables of Phaedrus. It must be confessed that these translations are not of any great value; in their desire to attain an elegant style which might serve as a model for their pupils, the Port-Royal translators took liberties with the text and did not shun having recourse to the most elaborate paraphrases; for example: "Postumia tua me convenit et Servius noster" is rendered by Guyot, "Madame votre femme m'ayant fait l'honneur de me venir voir avec Monsieur votre fils." So also the names Trebatius and Pomponius appear as M. De Trébace and M. De Pomponne—the latter being the name of D'Andilly's third son. A modern Jesuit author—Father Daniel —says of these translations: "Quelles traductions! On ne les appellera pas de belles infidèles, car, en travestissant l'antiquité, elles ne sont que ridicules." But Daniel's book[1] has been well described as "un ouvrage de polémique plus que de science," and his opinions of Port-Royal and all its works are obviously biassed. None the less it remains true that the translations prepared by the solitaries were considered to be of the highest elegance at the time when they appeared; and they are still worthy of our respect, in that they were part of a great and whole-hearted attempt to give the vernacular that place of honour in the school curriculum which is its due.

[1] *Les Jésuites instituteurs de la jeunesse française*, Paris, 1880.

It appears to have been customary in the time of the Port-Royalists to make the child begin Latin prose composition, as soon as he had learnt the Grammar rules. Coustel tells us: "When children know the most important rules of syntax it is usual to make them compose in Latin; this is commonly called 'writing themes[1].'" He goes on to point out the disadvantages of this contemporary method; in teaching children modern foreign languages we do not set them to write compositions until they have read some authors and studied their language and noted their expressions. Coustel recommends that this method should be applied to the teaching of Latin; prose composition should not be attempted until a good vocabulary has been acquired by reading the best authors. "To act otherwise and to set children to do composition before they have gained a few necessary ideas as to how to express themselves in Latin, what is this but to accustom them to a jargon which is neither French nor Latin, and to make them learn a pitiable rigmarole which they will have the greatest difficulty imaginable in unlearning afterwards[2]?" In the same strain Arnauld in his *Règlement des Études* lays it down that the reading of authors should take an earlier place in the curriculum and that prose composition should not be introduced until a much later stage.

Translation then must follow as soon as possible the learning of Grammar; in this way the elementary steps in Latin are rendered easier and more interesting, and there is also opportunity for the early application of Grammar rules learnt to actual examples found in the Latin writers themselves. The reading and translation of authors were seen to ensure various advantages which are detailed by Coustel; in the first place they stimulate judgment and independent thinking; and secondly they inculcate an appreciation of the beauties of style and of expression, and help to form a good literary taste. To these we may add another important advantage to be derived from translation, to which reference has already been made—the value of Latin translation in teaching the vernacular. "Children must be especially practised in translation," says Coustel, "because the attention which they are obliged to give to weighing all the

[1] Vol. II, pp. 50—1.   [2] Vol. II, p. 52.

expressions and finding out the sense of a Latin author, exercises at once their intellect and their judgment, and makes them learn the beauty of French as much as that of Latin[1]."

Since Latin translation was recognised by the Port-Royalists as an educational instrument of so great importance, we find in several of their educational treatises detailed rules with which it must comply. The fullest and most important are those given by Coustel in his *Règles de l'éducation des Enfans* and by Le Maître in his essay on translation into French, written for the benefit of the young Du Fossé; since they cover virtually the same ground we can easily combine their more important features. The chief rules for Latin translation in the Little Schools, then, are as follows: (*a*) the spirit and style of the original must as far as possible be preserved; (*b*) the distinction between the beauties of prose style and poetry must be reproduced in translation; (*c*) the translation should not be slavishly literal but elegant and should read like the work of a French author; (*d*) the translation must be clear; if necessary expand the original, or if its sentences are too long, split them up; (*e*) nothing should appear in the translation for which a sufficient reason cannot be given; (*f*) avoid jingles which jar on the ear. Two centuries and a half have not impaired the excellence of these rules and they might well be adopted as a standard in every class-room to-day where translation from any foreign language is carried on.

In one particular Port-Royal seems to have gone too far; there was apparently an exaggerated attempt in the Little Schools to avoid an exact and literal translation, and to reproduce the meaning of an author in up-to-date and polished French. Guyot illustrates this point of view: "It suffices if I make Cicero think nothing but what he actually did think; but it is not necessary to make him speak as he actually did speak —that is to say to make him talk Latin in French terms; it is essential that my readers should be able, thanks to my translation, to enter into his meaning, although ignorance of his language bars their way to it[2]." We can judge how this theory of translation resulted in practice by reading some of Guyot's

---

[1] Vol. II, p. 185.   [2] Trans. of *Epp. ad Atticum*, Preface.

own renderings of Cicero's *Letters*, from which a quotation has already been given.   By way of criticism it may be said that in the case of children who are just beginning to read Latin authors, it is very desirable to keep as close as possible to the original. Doubtless, a bald and absolutely literal translation is not desirable; but with low forms free translation may often serve to cover inexactitudes or even 'howlers' of the worst type.   It is because the Port-Royalists were so anxious to make the power to write good French one of the first results of their curriculum, and because they realised the value of Latin translation in teaching the vernacular, that in this particular they came somewhat short of the strong common-sense and sound knowledge of school practice that normally characterises their methods.

When some small advance had been made in the reading of authors, the pupil at Port-Royal was encouraged to make extempore translations *vivâ voce*.   This must have entailed great effort on the part of the learner, but it is obviously of immense value in developing power of expression and in increasing ability to read Latin quickly and easily.   The importance of the speaking voice was particularly emphasised in connection with 'versions' and translations.   Guyot points out that Latin as a spoken language was in his day dying, if not already dead; and he thinks it would be a great advantage if these Latin authors could be in some manner "resuscitated and reanimated with our spirit, voice and action, that they may teach us in a vivid and natural manner.   This may be done by translating their works *vivâ voce* to the children, or by reading the translation (i.e. a 'version') to them, in this way serving them as a living and animated interpreter who speaks to them in their own tongue, as the dead would speak to them in theirs if they were still living....Thus, in order to bring out the natural signification of the movements of the soul which accompanies the artificial signification of the thoughts, the teacher must brighten the lesson by his tone of voice and his gestures in reading to them, first in French and then in Latin, with all the appropriate inflections and accents[1]."   Thus, although there was

---

[1] Trans. of *Epp. ad Atticum*, Preface.

no desire at Port-Royal to impose Latin as a medium of conversation, as was commonly done in contemporary schools, an
attempt was obviously made to render the reading of Latin
authors vivid and actual; the pupil was made to feel that the
Romans had been a real people who had naturally expressed
their thoughts in this language.   The child at Port-Royal could
never have been in the same condition as Tom Tulliver, who
"had no distinct idea how there came to be such a thing as
Latin on this earth" and to whom it was inconceivable "that
there ever existed a people who bought and sold sheep and oxen
and transacted the every-day affairs of life, through the medium
of this language[1]."

Mention has already been made of some of the Latin authors
read in the Port-Royal schools; the following is a fairly complete
list of the classical books used at Port-Royal collected from
references made by Coustel, Guyot, Nicole, Lancelot, and Dr
Arnauld; it must be understood that in most cases selections
only were permitted and that all texts were rigorously expur-
gated: Phaedrus; Cornelius Nepos; Florus; Eutropius; Livy;
Cicero; Sallust; Caesar; Tacitus; Quintilian; Quintus Curtius;
Justinus; Pliny (*Letters*);   Pliny the Naturalist;   Valerius
Maximus; Velleius Paterculus; Suetonius; Seneca; Plautus;
Terence;   Virgil (especially the *II, IV,* and *VI Aeneid* and
IV Georgic);   Horace;   Ovid;   Catullus;   Lucan;   Martial;
Juvenal; Propertius; Tibullus; Persius; Statius; Claudian;
Ausonius; Prudentius; Sulpicius Severus; Homer; Herodotus;
Xenophon; Thucydides; Plutarch; Aristotle; Euripides; Sopho-
cles; Aristophanes; Pindar; Anacreon; Menander; Demosthenes;
Isocrates; Lucian; Aesop; Josephus.   To these might be added
a few more modern Latin writers such as certain of the Fathers,
Erasmus (*Colloquies*), Grotius, Buchanan, &c.   It will be gathered
from this list that a very wide field was open to the pupil at
Port-Royal and, since an attempt seems to have been made in
the higher classes to read as much as possible and to give
less time than was usual at that period to the cultivation of
Latin prose, we may infer that a wide and varied classical
education was imparted.   The above list contains most of the

---

[1] George Eliot, quoted by Adams, *Herbartian Psychology*, p. 271.

authors commonly read on the classical side of a modern secondary school with the noticeable exceptions of Aeschylus and
Plato[1]; and in addition some examples of silver Latin which
might not nowadays be regarded with a favourable eye. But
since the prime concern of the Little Schools, when once the
elementary stage was past, was with the subject matter rather
than the language, we can see that their typical pupil must have
possessed a range of interests far wider than could have been
imparted by the scholastic and linguistic education of the Jesuit
schools or the University.

Coustel gives us detailed information as to the method of procedure in explaining a Latin author; and this is amplified by
Arnauld in his *Règlement des Études.* Before an author is begun,
the master should give the class a general introduction to it; if,
for instance, Virgil is to be read, the story of the siege of Troy
should be outlined. Grammar, Syntax, the structure of sentences,
and the exact meaning of words must not be neglected; indeed
in the three lower classes these will be of greatest importance.
But an attempt must always be made to rise above the words
to the subject matter, and when the higher classes are reached
this will be the chief concern, though beauties of style will of
course be carefully noted. An excellent usage practised in the
Port-Royal schools and still commonly adopted in French
'lycées' was that of the 'compte rendu.' After having read
a passage of prose or poetry the pupil is required to reproduce
in his own words in the foreign language the meaning of what he
has read. This is an exercise of the very highest value, and it
deserves to be more widely adopted in English schools than is
apparently the case at present. Another point emphasised by
Port-Royal writers, when treating of the reading of authors, is
the learning by heart of select passages. Coustel, Nicole, and
Arnauld are at one in saying that whole books should not be
committed to memory, but only those passages which are most
striking because of the beauty of their expression or of their
thought. We are told that Nicole allowed the whole of the

---

[1] Racine is said by his son to have read Plato at Port-Royal, but this author
is not included in any of the lists given in the various educational treatises of the
solitaries.

II and *VI Aeneid* and most of the *IV* to be learnt by heart; but in other authors only the 'purple patches' were prescribed. Nicole himself prepared an *Epigrammatum Delectus* from the works of various Latin poets and appended thereto a *Dissertatio de vera Pulchritudine et adumbrata.* The work appears to have become immediately popular as a school-book and that even beyond the borders of France; the copy of the 1686 edition of this work preserved in the British Museum bears on the title page the legend "In usum Scholae Etonensis." The object of the *Epigrammatum Delectus* was to provide a number of short Latin verses which might easily be committed to memory and might at once teach Latin and provide moral maxims suitable to those of tender years. It was thus realised that one of the greatest aids to writing a good style and to engendering a love of beautiful literature was to permeate the child's mind with the finest passages from the authors he read; and in order that they might become a κτῆμα ἐς ἀεί, Coustel recommends that they should be frequently revised until they become firmly ingrained in the pupil's mind.

To assist this process common-place books or collections of striking passages were prepared by the pupils either under the direction of the masters, or even, in the case of those who were older, on their own initiative. Nicole, as we are told by a writer whose identity is unknown, used to mark those passages in classical authors which he considered beautiful with a big B, while those which were of transcendent beauty were distinguished by a BB. We can gather from Coustel that the elder pupils at Port-Royal were encouraged to adopt some similar method and to copy out these remarkable passages into a notebook, which might thus soon become a 'bibliothèque portative.' In this way, as Seneca points out, they must imitate the bees who fly from one flower to another and gather the honey. For the guidance of the pupil in making his collection, Coustel lays down certain rules of which the following are the most important: (*a*) there must be some underlying principle; e.g. is the collection to be one of beautiful expressions or of beautiful thoughts; is it to be of service to a humanist or a historian; (*b*) only the very best things must be admitted and they must be well arranged; (c) the collection must be committed to memory and often re-read and revised[1]. M. Carré says that some specimens from the collection of 'purple patches' made by Racine while at Port-Royal have been preserved for us in his *Œuvres Complètes*[2]; a careful search among several different editions of Racine's complete works has not revealed these. It is perhaps the case that M. Carré whose work, in spite of its value, contains many inaccuracies, is referring to the extracts with appreciative comments made by Racine from Homer's *Odyssey* and the *Odes* of Pindar. These passages and the accompanying notes are given in any complete edition of Racine's works; they were not, however, prepared at Port-Royal but in 1662, after the destruction of the Little Schools, when Racine was studying for Holy Orders at Uzès.

When the pupil by much reading and committing to memory many fine passages had at last attained to some appreciation of a good Latin prose style, he was at last permitted to compose in this language for himself and to write 'themes.' M. Carré tells us: "It seems that at no time during the school course did the pupil at Port-Royal write 'compositions' in the modern sense of the term—that is to say, the exact and literal translation of a piece of French into Latin[3]." This is perhaps not entirely correct; at any rate, we have in Arnauld's *Règlement des Études* a recommendation that the master should himself translate into French some passage from a classical author and then give it to his class to be put back again by them into the original. In this manner the contrast is emphasised between the style of the author and that of the pupil. It will be remembered that a somewhat similar method of teaching Latin prose composition had been recommended by Roger Ascham.

However, we can gather from Arnauld and still more clearly from Coustel, who chief among the solitaries represents the practice of the Little Schools, that extemporaneous composition was much preferred at Port-Royal to the translation of set passages. Often this took the form of reproducing the substance of what had been read in a classical author, either as a *vivâ voce* 'compte rendu,' or in a more carefully prepared written-out

[1] p. 165.　　[2] p. xxix.　　[3] p. xxvi.

composition.   Sometimes the boys were made to put Latin verses
into good Latin prose or to expand some outlined theme.   At
other times some simple subject was given for them to develop;
Coustel gives as instances: to describe a journey, a conversation
with a friend, or a visit; to describe a storm, a battle, a palace;
to console a friend on the loss of a law-suit, or on the death of
a parent; to ask some favour; and so on.   Coustel also gives a
number of recommendations to the master for correcting these
prose compositions or 'themes,' "on the understanding that the
good custom is adopted of setting children to compose in Latin
as late as possible."   Of these rules the following may be noted:
(a) First correct the 'howlers'; (b) then those words and usages
which are not of the purest Latin; (c) then correct or improve
the style, giving reasons and going into detail wherever possible;
(d) in (b) and (c) do not merely point out the faults, but substitute
better words or phrases to take their place; (e) give fair copies
from time to time; (f) avoid being too severe; the diffuse and
flowery style which a boy often adopts will be toned down as he
grows more mature and reads more widely, and as his judgment
and literary taste develop.

In regard to Latin verses the Port-Royalists took a *via media*
between the Jesuits, who held them in the highest honour, and
those who, like the Oratorian father Lamy and the Abbé Fleury
were already beginning to condemn them as far worse than
useless; their attitude was that which Comenius had already
adopted.   It was recognised in the Little Schools that but few
children had any aptitude for verse-making and that in the case
of the majority it would be a pernicious waste of time.   "Out of
70 or 80 pupils," says Arnauld, "there may perhaps be two or
three who gain any advantage from verses[1]."   In another place
Guyot adds: "I think it sufficient if the children in the third
class have been shown how to scan Latin verses, to take them to
pieces and to put them together again.   In this matter we must
follow the genius of our pupils[2]."   Verse making then was not
obligatory at Port-Royal, and it was confined to those boys who
had a bent for it.   It seems sometimes to have been practised in

---

[1] *Œuvres*, Vol. XLI, p. 91.
[2] Trans. of *Epp. ad Atticum*, Preface.

the highest class under the conduct of the master, suggestions being invited from any pupil present. Arnauld describes the process: " Anyone has permission to say how he would turn the subject of each verse. Thus from one corner comes one phrase; from another comes an improvement on it. Having obtained permission to speak (which is asked and given merely by a sign to avoid confusion) the pupils judge, criticise, and give reasons for their preferences. Those who have the least enthusiasm exert themselves and all at any rate endeavour to distinguish themselves. The result is an exercise well-adapted to please the pupils and to develop those who have any talent[1]." We may compare with this the account given by Du Fossé of the 'Battle of Latin Verses' which used to take place in the Little Schools when he was a pupil there; reference has already been made to this practice.

Before leaving the subject of Latin at Port-Royal let us once more notice that the emphasis was wholly upon the literary side of the language. The Jesuits were content with the dry bones of linguistic and the University was hide-bound in scholasticism and rapidly declining in importance and influence; but when Port-Royal prophesied the dry bones came together and were covered with flesh and became quick with the breath of life. The object which the Port-Royalist schoolmasters steadfastly set before themselves was the development of responsible individuals, who could think for themselves and were not in bondage to Aristotle nor even to the Church; and they aimed at accomplishing this through the medium chiefly of Latin literature. In so far as they did this, they typified the Renaissance at its best—not the Renaissance of Ciceronianism but that of Vittorino Da Feltre. On the other side there was the strict Jansenist theology which resulted in a hot-house type of education and a distrust of the 'world.' The two views are not easily reconcilable and we find the conflict underlying many of the Port-Royal educational methods. It would seem that, whereas Saint-Cyran had adopted a somewhat narrow and exclusively theological view of education and would regard the classics as useful if well used, but extremely dangerous

[1] *Œuvres*, Vol. XLI, p. 91.

if badly used, this view was modified when an attempt was made to carry it out systematically in the schools. The change is due perhaps chiefly to Le Maître, Dr Arnauld and Nicole, in spite of the last-named's altered attitude in his later works. In so far then as the schools are concerned during their most flourishing epoch (1650—1656), we may be justified in saying that there was given in them a humanistic education of the most liberal type, in which the training of character and judgment was rightly held in highest esteem and in which a sound and wide knowledge of the vernacular and the classics was the staple of instruction.

We come now to the study of Greek in the Little Schools. The recovery of this language had been one of the most noteworthy features of the Renaissance; although the study of it was revived later in France than in Italy, Rabelais as early as the first part of the sixteenth century, had referred to "grecque, sans laquelle c'est honte qu'une personne se die sçavante[1]." From the *Ratio Studiorum* we gather that Latin and Greek had been placed on an equal footing in the Jesuit schools. The teaching of the Greek language was introduced into the University of France at the end of the sixteenth century; and thus, if Port-Royal were to keep abreast of the Jesuits and the University, she would of necessity have to make provision for Greek in the curriculum. In view of all this, surprisingly little is said about the study of this language in the educational treatises of the solitaries which remain to us. M. Carré tells us that the regulations drawn up for the schools in 1646 by Walon De Beaupuis do not mention Greek[2]. This is incorrect, for it is there stated that after 'goûter' the boys studied this language and said repetition in it. Guyot, however, says little about Greek; Coustel in a catalogue of the principal foreign languages has a passing reference to its value as being the 'language of the sciences'; Arnauld in his syllabus introduces it without further comment as a subject to be begun in the fourth class—i.e. the third from the bottom—and prescribes as authors in higher classes S. Luke's gospel in the original, Lucian, Aesop, Homer, Herodotus,

[1] *Pantagruel*, Bk II, ch. viii, p. 124. [2] p. xxx.

Thucydides, Xenophon, Euripides, Sophocles, Demosthenes, and Isocrates. But our chief proof of the estimation in which Greek was held in the Port-Royal schools is furnished by their schoolbooks; we still possess Lancelot's *Nouvelle Méthode pour apprendre facilement la Langue grecque* (1655), and his *Jardin des Racines grecques* (1657), both of which were composed for the benefit of his pupils. It was to Port-Royal again that Racine owed that knowledge of Greek tragedy which led him to compose *Phèdre*, *Andromaque*, *La Thébaïde*, and *Iphigénie en Aulide*. In fact it was owing to the honour in which Greek was held among the solitaries and especially to the appearance of Lancelot's *Jardin* that the Jesuit father Labbé taunted the solitaries with being 'la secte des Hellénistes de Port-Royal[1].' Lancelot complains that children as a rule are not made to begin Greek early enough. They should start as soon as they have made some little headway in Latin and thus make great progress "while they are more capable of exercising the memory than the judgment[2]." There is indeed something to be said for the method in which the mechanical rules of Grammar and Syntax, as well as a wide vocabulary, are committed to memory at a time when the mind is best able to do this. At the same time Lancelot opposes the contemporary method of teaching Greek through the medium of Latin, and would approach it directly from the vernacular; he points out that in its structure French is far more akin to Greek than to Latin, and the same would be true of our own language; hence the chief difficulty presented by Greek will be the acquirement of a vocabulary. Lancelot goes on to demand that Greek should be the chief study of the pupils during three or four years of their school-life. This seems to have been nothing more than the recommendation of an enthusiast, for we have no evidence that Greek ever held so important a place at Port-Royal. It is obvious that Greek was taught, especially in the upper forms; but attention was chiefly devoted to reading Latin authors and cultivating a good French style.

---

[1] He published a book in 1661 entitled: *Les Étymologies de la Langue Françoise contre la nouvelle secte des Hellénistes de Port-Royal.*

[2] *Méthode grecque*, Preface, p. xxix.

Greek at Port-Royal has a special interest to us because it gave birth to the two most important of all their school-books— Lancelot's *Méthode grecque* and his *Jardin des Racines grecques*. The former of these was based upon the works of Clénard, Ramus, Budé, Henri Estienne, Sanctius, and Vossius, to whom Lancelot did not forget to acknowledge his debt; but its claim to originality lay in the fact that it was written in French and not in Latin. It also contained several simplifications designed to aid the student; for instance the declensions were reduced in number from ten, as had previously been customary, to two: 'parisyllables' which are declined throughout with an equal number of syllables, and 'imparisyllables' which increase in the oblique cases; the conjugations were also reduced to two: verbs ending in -ω and those ending in -μι. The *Méthode* achieved an immediate success; in 40 years it went through nine editions and was translated into several foreign languages. It became well known in England; Gibbon was familiar with it; De Quincey, speaking of the year 1800 when he entered Manchester Grammar School, says that the "Port-Royal Greek Grammar translated by Dr Nugent was in use there and was about the best key extant in English to the innumerable perplexities of Greek diction."

The *Jardin des Racines grecques* appeared two years after the *Méthode grecque*. Whereas the *Méthode* had sought to facilitate the learning of Greek Grammar, the *Jardin* aimed at reducing the difficulties involved in acquiring a Greek vocabulary; it purported to be a collection of primitive or root words, from which other words were derived, set forth in French verse. In this manner both roots and derivatives could the more easily be retained in the memory and thus the learner's path would be made smooth; Lancelot's aim, indeed, in dealing with pupils, is, to quote his own phrase, 'soulager la mémoire.' M. Compayré tells us that in writing the *Jardin*, Lancelot was indebted to a work by Scapula which had appeared in 1600 under the title *Primigeniae voces linguae graecae*, and to which as a matter of fact Lancelot refers in his Preface. The name *Jardin des Racines grecques* would imply that the austere Port-Royalist was not above making a pun, and the pleasantry is

emphasised by a poetical prologue contributed to the work by
De Saci:

> Toi qui cheris la docte Grece
> Où jadis fleurit la sagesse;
> D'où les Auteurs les plus divins
> Ont emprunté leurs termes saints,
> Pour estre de nos grands Mysteres
> Les Augustes dépositaires:
> Entre en ce IARDIN, non de fleurs
> Qui n'ont que de vaines couleurs,
> Mais de RACINES nourissantes
> Qui rendent les ames sçavantes.
>
> Ces mots d'ou sont nez tant d'Ecrits
> Des plus admirables Esprits,
> Forment de leur tige feconde
> La plus belle Langue du monde.
> Prens donc ces Vers comme un Flambeau
> Qui t'éclairant d'un jour nouveau,
> Te mene aux hautes connoissances
> De ces Grecs les Roys des Sciences,
> Et t'ouvre les Thresors divers
> Des Maîtres de tout l'Univers.

The title of the work was probably suggested by Comenius'
Janua, Vestibulum, and *Atrium*, the first of which, as we have seen,
was well known to Lancelot and had been used by him in class.

We cannot accord to the *Jardin* such commendation as
is due to the *Méthode grecque*. It abounds in mistakes; the
so-called 'roots' are in practically every case not roots at all,
but derived words, while the etymologies are often ludicrous.
Common and rare or obsolete words, prose terms and poetic
expressions, are mingled confusedly; for since the arrangement
is alphabetic, there is nothing to indicate which words are of
most frequent occurrence and of the best usage for the learner;
in some cases too the exigencies of the rhyme have resulted in a
faulty or derived meaning being attached to a word, instead of
its primitive sense. The following paragraph (§ CXXVII), chosen
at random, is typical of the whole book:

1. Μῆδος, *conseil* et *soin* veut dire   εος, τό.
* Μηδικός, *medecin* s'en tire,
2. Μηκάομαι, *s'en va beslant,*

3. Μῆκος, *longueur* * μακρός, *long, grand.*   3 εος, τό. * οῦ, ὁ.

4. Μήκων, *pavot* fait dormir l'homme.

5. Μηλέα, *pommier*; μῆλον, *pomme.*

6. Μήν, *mois.*   7. Μήνη, *lune* reluit.

*   Νεομηνία, s'en produit.

8. Μῆνις, *la colère envieillie*   εος, ἡ.

9. Μηνύειν, *apprend, certifie*[1].

Again, at the time when Lancelot wrote, philology as a science was as yet unborn; Sanscrit was a sealed book to contemporary grammarians and etymologies almost as absurd as the famous 'lucus a non lucendo' were set forth with the utmost gravity. The *Jardin des Racines grecques* abounds in these far-fetched and unscientific derivations; the following are typical; πυραμίς from πῦρ, because pyramids "go to a point like a flame"; ἐλεδώνη (= polypus) from ἑεδώνη—i.e. ἑαυτὸν ἔδει—because it eats its own feet; premier from primus, which in turn is derived from πρόμαχος 'by syncope'; baron from βάρος "qui se prend aussi pour autorité et puissance." Many causes then contribute to making the *Jardin* unsuitable as a school-book; and yet its value as a mnemonic resulted in its holding a place of pre-eminence in French schools for close upon 200 years. M. Compayré, writing in 1877, after pointing out the grave short-comings of the work, cannot help adding a kindly word for this friend of his youth; he calls it "ce bon et vieux recueil de rimes naïves qu'on apprenait au dix-septième siècle et dont nous avons encore récité les décades dans notre enfance[2]." After a long service in French schools the *Jardin* was finally suppressed by a ministerial decree of December 4, 1863; and M. Dübner, who was an authority on French education and, like Sainte-Beuve himself, a great admirer of the work of Port-Royal, does not hesitate to borrow Rousseau's term and to say in 1866: "La lecture (si justement et si vivement recommandée par Port-Royal) et nos bons dictionnaires rendent complètement inutile ce livre 'ostrogoth[3].'" Nevertheless the book in a modernised form appears even yet to be used in France in spite of the decree of 1863. For example, the writer has before him a copy of it which bears no date but which was published about 1908

---

[1] p. 129.   [2] Vol. I, p. 262.   [3] Quoted by Sainte-Beuve, Vol. III, p. 621.

by Delagrave of Paris; it is entitled: *Le Jardin des Racines grecques, réunies par Cl. Lancelot, et mises en vers par Le Maistre De Sacy. Nouvelle édition augmentée de racines nouvelles, par J.-B. Gr. Pitay, revue par Helleu.* This edition, which is prefaced by an 'autorisation universitaire,' has been drastically revised.

Port-Royal did not utterly neglect the study of Geography and History; these subjects were regarded as of minor importance in the curriculum but as none the less meriting a place there; they were at the same time introduced mainly for the purpose of explaining the authors read in class. It must be borne in mind that until recent times the chief value of a good classical education must have consisted largely in its content. In a school where little or nothing besides the classics was taught, Latin and Greek authors must have formed the medium through which the pupil picked up most of his knowledge of men and things— such as it was. At Port-Royal the curriculum was not so narrow as this and subjects other than the classics were included in it; but it remains true to say that, with the outstanding exception of the vernacular, they were subsidiary and employed chiefly in the explanation of authors. It is noteworthy that neither History nor Geography is specifically dealt with as a school subject by Coustel; but we learn from Walon De Beaupuis' *Règlement* that in the schools after 1644 three periods a week each were given to History and Geography, these subjects being taken on alternate days. Nicole in his *Traité de l'Éducation d'un Prince* devotes several paragraphs to the study of History; he sums up its advantages as follows: it cultivates memory and judgment and since pictures, portraits, views and the like may be used, it stimulates the imagination and delights the child. He recommends that pupils should learn first a general outline of Universal History and that after this every day a detached historical incident (called 'l'histoire du jour') should be related in some detail and then reproduced by the pupils in their own words. This exercise was designed in order to cultivate the child's powers of expression. Arnauld gives us a variant of it: the child has to relate some historical event "which he has found in Valerius Maximus, or Plutarch or in any book he likes, the choice being left to him."

Arnauld also recommends the daily reading of some passage from the history of France. Nicole again advises the collection of historical parallels in order that the memory of one may help the memory of another by the association of ideas. He gives a rather curious list of instances : " For example, it is well that they should know examples of all the largest armies mentioned in their books, of great battles, of great massacres, of great cruelties, of great mortalities, of great prosperities, of great misfortunes, of great riches, of great conquerors, of great captains, of fortunate favourites, of unfortunate favourites, of the longest lives[1]." Again it was in the Port-Royal schools that De Tillemont first developed his genius as a historian and learnt not to trust in second-hand information but to go straight to original authorities. We may conclude then that History had a definite place in the curriculum and the existence of a stereotyped expression like ' l'histoire du jour ' confirms this. It is therefore a little disconcerting to find Nicole in the first part of his treatise on education telling us that "History is often more harmful than useful to princes[2]." Still, we have discovered inconsistencies in Nicole before, and it must be understood that History, like everything else which emanated from Port-Royal, must be carefully selected and if necessary expurgated. What Nicole means is simply that History, when rightly chosen and properly used, is a school subject of great value ; but it is dangerous if these safeguards are not taken. In a word, his attitude towards History is precisely that of Saint-Cyran towards the classics.

Of Geography there is less to be said. It is at the same time noticeable that Port-Royal preferred the Geography which is learned from personal acquaintance to that culled from a textbook. It is from this standpoint that Nicole recommends Geography as a study for small children, ' since it depends largely on the senses.' He advises the use of maps and pictures of notable places ; in order to give the latter meaning for the child interesting anecdotes should be told in connection with the principal cities, &c., shown. In order to correlate Geography with the other subjects of the curriculum, all places mentioned by authors should invariably be looked up on the map.

[1] *Essais de Morale*, Vol. II, p. 286.   [2] *op. cit.* Vol. II, p. 254.

Mathematics and Physical Science are not altogether omitted from the Port-Royal curriculum; in fact when the time given to these subjects in the Little Schools is compared with that devoted to them by the Jesuits, we can see that they were taught to a much greater extent than was usual at this period; although, judged by modern standards, they might appear almost neglected. We have evidence that Lancelot was installed as teacher of Greek and Mathematics when the Port-Royal school was opened in the rue S. Dominique d'Enfer in 1646; and he himself tells De Saci in a letter, written after the destruction of the schools and when he was acting as tutor to the Princes De Conti, that Arithmetic formed part of the curriculum followed by his pupils. Arnauld also composed for the use of the Port-Royal schools his famous *Éléments de Géométrie* which were judged by Pascal to be superior to a work of his own on the same subject. On the other hand, Coustel, in spite of the fulness with which he treats of the purely literary side of the curriculum, makes only a passing reference to Mathematics among those subjects 'dont il faut au moins avoir une légère teinture.' He says nothing about any kind of Natural Science. Nicole is equally silent as to Mathematics; he does certainly make mention of the possibility of teaching children Anatomy, but the chief inducement which he holds out for so doing seems to be that it will facilitate their learning the Latin names for the various parts of the body. He has not that passion for the concrete realities of this branch of Natural Science which had led Vesalius of Padua to abandon once for all the text-book of Galen and appeal to the actual results of anatomical dissection, or which inspired Rabelais when he wrote in Gargantua's letter to Pantagruel: "Par fréquentes anatomies acquiers toy parfaicte congnoissance de l'homme." Nor again does Nicole regard Anatomy as a valuable manual training, for which purpose "Anatomy, making sceletons and excarnating bowells" was recommended as a desirable occupation for school-children by William Petty in his letter to Hartlib. In the girls' schools no kind of Mathematics or Science was included in the regular curriculum; except that upon festivals the elder girls studied Arithmetic for an hour in the afternoon and then for

half-an-hour instructed their younger schoolfellows in this subject
—a somewhat unusual form of feast-day dissipation, but one
which throws a flood of light upon the dreary monotony of the
regular curriculum in the Port-Royal girls' schools. We can
conclude then that all forms of mathematical or scientific study
were, according to modern notions, much neglected at Port-
Royal; but they were not wholly neglected, as was so often the
case in contemporary schools. If any reason is required for this
other than the sound common-sense of the Port-Royalists and
their ardent desire "to develop the individual's native faculties
to the utmost possible extent," we can discover it if we
remember that some of the solitaries had been deeply impressed by the philosophy of Descartes and that they numbered
among them Pascal—the most brilliant mathematical genius,
perhaps, that the world has seen.

A word about the teaching of Modern Languages at Port-
Royal will complete our conspectus of the subjects taught in the
Little Schools. There are very few references indeed to these
languages as school subjects in the educational works of the
solitaries; in fact, we have no direct evidence that they ever
were definitely and regularly taught at Port-Royal. It was
probably felt by those who regarded travelling as a grave moral
danger, that a knowledge of Modern Languages was hardly
desirable for the young; and it is only in the case of 'enfants
de qualité' whom Coustel allows to travel under rigorous
supervision, that a knowledge of foreign languages is prescribed.
He gives no indication of these subjects having been taught at
Port-Royal. At the same time it must be remembered that
shortly before the final closing of the schools Lancelot published
his *Méthode italienne* and *Méthode espagnole*, which were drawn
up upon the same lines as his Greek and Latin grammars.
M. Compayré also tells us (though he gives no references)
that Racine understood Spanish and Italian when he left the
Little Schools. Nevertheless he was most probably not one
of their typical products in this respect; and there is in fact
nothing to make us believe that Modern Foreign Languages
ever formed part of the regular school course at Port-Royal.

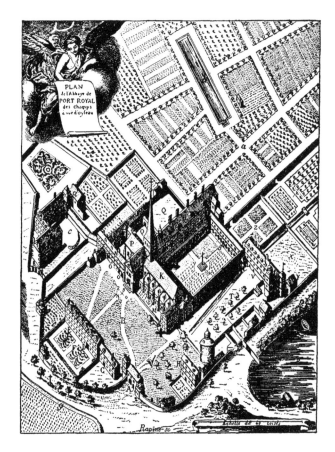

BIRD'S-EYE VIEW OF PORT-ROYAL DES CHAMPS.

(1) This view is taken from Les Granges, on the hills above Port-Royal
des Champs and to the North-West of the Abbey.

(2) The school was held in the building marked + +, at the North-West
end of the Chapel, and the North aisle of the Chapel itself was
reserved for the exclusive use of the solitaries and their pupils.

(3) The solitaries and their pupils slept in the building marked D E, to the
left of the main entrance to the Abbey.

CHAPTER VI

SOME DETAILS OF SCHOOL ADMINISTRATION

HAVING now completed our investigation of the teaching methods applied to the various subjects of the curriculum at Port-Royal, we must proceed to describe in outline the time-tables of the Little Schools. There are extant three Port-Royal time-tables: two for the boys' schools after the 1650 dispersion; and one for the girls' schools in Jacqueline Pascal's *Règlement pour les enfans de Port-Royal*. We have also Lancelot's *régime* for the Princes De Conti, which is of less interest for our purpose; our concern at present is with the first two only, since we are here dealing solely with the Little Schools managed by the solitaries. Of these two time-tables, one is in a memoir of M. Walon, a merchant of Beauvais, and brother of Walon De Beaupuis; he had been a pupil at Port-Royal. The other is a *Règlement* drawn up by De Beaupuis himself. They are both given in the *Supplément au Nécrologe*. The former, which is also reproduced in Fontaine's *Mémoires*, purports to be general rules for each of the groups at Les Trous, Les Granges, and Le Chesnai, while De Beaupuis' *Règlement* is described as a regulation for the Le Chesnai group alone; but since the two time-tables correspond in all essentials, it is very easy to combine them; having done so, we shall be in possession of a typical day's work in the Port-Royal schools which would probably hold good for any time in their career between 1646 and 1660.

About 5 a.m. the elder boys rose and the younger at 6, winter and summer alike; on getting out of bed each child said his private prayers before beginning to dress; there was a servant to help those children who were too young to be able to dress themselves. Morning prayers were then said in common in the dormitory where the master slept with his boys ; after which the elder boys attended Prime. This done, each pupil went to his desk and studied in silence till 7, when the lesson just learnt was repeated to the master in charge. At 8 o'clock came breakfast and in winter the children were allowed to warm themselves round the fire ; during the meal the silence which had lasted since rising, save for the repetition of the prayers and of the morning lesson, was broken and the boys were free to converse with one another on any subject they liked. At about 8.30 the second lesson began and lasted apparently till nearly 11 ; it consisted of a 'version'—that is to say, the reading of a French translation from Greek or Latin. For the elder boys three in-folio pages of Plutarch were prescribed ; for the younger Livy, Justinus, Sulpicius Severus, &c. ; the elder boys also did Latin composition. The compositions, when completed, were read aloud to the master for correction. The use of *vivâ voce* methods in teaching Latin seems characteristic of Port-Royal ; it is emphasised by Guyot in a passage already quoted.

At 11 o'clock the whole school assembled in one of the rooms, where they repeated the Confiteor, made an examination of conscience, and said a prayer. One of the elder children who had been confirmed also recited a text from the Book of Proverbs or from the New Testament in Latin. This done, they all went to wash their hands and then to the refectory for dinner. The children of each class sat at the same table, presided over by their form-master ; the meal began with soup and then the master helped each pupil to whatever was provided, special care being taken to see that every child had enough to eat and drink and made a good meal. At the same time any signs of daintiness in children were diligently repressed ; Saint-Cyran had already recommended that they should be accustomed to eat 'all sorts of vegetables, cod, and herring[1],' and Coustel desires that, although food should always be good and nourishing, children should not be allowed to become too fastidious in regard to it. In the same way moderation in eating and drinking is essential ; we must follow our Lord's example in this respect.

[1] Fontaine, *Mémoires*, p. 192.

Too great variety in food is regarded as injurious to children's health; and although it is right to feel pleasure in taking meals, yet they should always be regarded as means to an end; we should eat to live. While daintiness was deprecated at Port-Royal, stress was also laid on manners, and Coustel's regulations on this subject are evidently a faithful reproduction of Port-Royal practice. We can gather that conversation between pupils was hardly possible at dinner, for during the meal a history book was read aloud—Josephus or Godeau's *Church History*, or a work on French or Roman history; on Sundays and feast-days a devotional book was substituted—the *Christian Instruction* or the *Confessions* of S. Augustine.

After dinner there was an hour and a half's recreation; in fine weather the children played in a large enclosure marked off from the spacious park round the school; in winter or bad weather they amused themselves with billiards or draughts or a card-game in a large room warmed with a good fire. Throughout the recreation the children remained under a master's super-vision; for, as has been pointed out, this was an essential tenet of the Port-Royal educational doctrine. We are told that the master's presence "did not trouble them at all, because they were given complete freedom to play at any games they liked to choose." At 1 o'clock work began again, being prefaced by a short prayer. For an hour the whole school remained together in one room where they learnt Geography and History on alternate days; at 2 they returned to their various class-rooms; there the younger children copied sentences of Scripture, and the seniors learnt Virgil by heart and afterwards repeated it to the master in charge. In the middle of the afternoon they partook of 'goûter'—a light meal still patronised by French children, though not usually taken by adults. During the repast, the pupils were free to talk to one another, as at breakfast. When 'goûter' was over, they returned to work and the elder children studied Greek; when the lessons were learnt, they were heard by the form-master. At 6 o'clock came supper, during which a book was read, as at dinner. From 6.30 to 8 there was another recreation-time; the juniors played games, while the seniors conversed with the masters on some points of History or other useful subjects. Du Fossé describes for us the evening recreations of the school groups at Magny near Port-Royal des Champs in 1649. The master in charge was Le Fèvre—one of the most obscure, yet most lovable, figures among the teaching solitaries at Port-Royal; he was wont to take his boys out into the country after supper on fine summer evenings and to point out the constellations and planets, and to tell them the medicinal properties of vegetable and mineral products—"ce que nous considérions avec beaucoup de plaisir." On returning from the evening recreation a good half-hour was spent in preparing lessons for the next day. At 8.30 evening prayer was said, the children, the solitaries, and the servants all being present; then, after examination of conscience, each boy retired to his dormitory in silence, undressed quickly, and was in bed by 9. After seeing that his charges were all in bed, the master who was responsible for the dormitory himself retired; thus, as Fontaine says, "he was the last to go to bed and the first to get up."

On Sundays and festivals the time-table was somewhat modified. The children rose at the usual hour and then attended Prime. After this they read privately 'improving' books, such as Saint-Cyran's catechism, until 8 o'clock, when the Superior catechised them and gave them religious instruction. This lasted until Mass which they heard not at the monastery but at the parish church. Week-day attendance at Mass was not exacted from all the pupils at Port-Royal, but instead two senior boys were selected each day to represent their school-fellows; "since on this occasion," we are told, "they fulfil the office of angels, they are exhorted to behave with great reverence, and to present themselves at this bloodless sacrifice of Jesus Christ, in remembrance of that which He offered to His Father for our sins on Mount Calvary[1]." Any misbehaviour in church was visited with severe penalties; as has already been pointed out, this was one of the few offences for which the use of the rod was reserved. When the children returned on Sunday from Mass, they continued their devotional reading until dinner time. After the meal there were two and a half hours of recreation and this in fine weather consisted of playing in the garden or of

---

[1] *Suppl. au Nécr.* (1735), p. 55.

country walks towards Marly, Saint-Cyr, or Versailles[1]. At 2 o'clock the pupils went to their respective class-rooms and there continued their devotional reading until 4, when they all went to Vespers[2] at the parish church. The rest of the day passed as on week-days; and in fact the only things which distinguished festal from ferial days in the Little Schools seem to have been attendance at Parishional Mass and Vespers and the substitution of devotional or religious reading for the ordinary school-work.

From the above tables it will be gathered that on week-days about eight and a half hours per diem were devoted to school-work, and on week-days and festivals alike only about three hours were given to recreation; also it is noticeable that the physical exercise taken by the pupils was not usually of a violent kind; active games seem to have been chiefly patronised by the younger boys, while their seniors were usually content with more demure walks in the woods surrounding Port-Royal des Champs; at the same time they were given entire liberty within the school bounds, and anything like the 'crocodile' walks of the present-day French lycée must have been happily unknown in the Little Schools. The modern English schoolmaster may perhaps be struck with an apparent monotony and lack of adequate physical exercise in the Port-Royal schools; yet we are told in the *Supplément au Nécrologe* that "as all the exercises of the day were, in this manner, regulated and diversified, the children had no time to become wearied; and the greatest punishment that could be given to those who sometimes showed a disagreeable humour was to threaten to send them home[3]." As a matter of fact the *régime* of the Little Schools compares very favourably with that of the modern French lycée, in which some eleven hours are officially devoted to work and only two to recreation. Truly, the typical French boy seems to possess a peculiar toughness of physique, for which he is not usually given credit in this country; he appears to flourish under conditions which would

[1] The palace of Versailles was not yet built; it was begun in 1668.
[2] The Roman Catholic parish church evening service of 'Benediction,' usual at the present day, is of comparatively modern growth.
[3] pp. 57—8.

be intolerable to an English schoolboy, and yet to escape with remarkably little illness.

In spite of the fact then that the recreation time at Port-Royal seems to our modern English eyes to be woefully short, yet physical education was not overlooked in the Little Schools. Coustel in his *Règles* makes several references to the subject; recognising that one must take "reasonable care of the body in order that it may serve the soul in its functions," he lays down various recommendations for this, and points out *inter alia* the necessity for physical exercise; "dancing helps to give gracefulness; horse exercise strengthens the body; hunting in moderation disposes it to bear the fatigues of war of which hunting is a miniature; it is also advantageous to be able to swim well; without it, Caesar would have been lost before Alexandria[1]." But though Coustel specifies these forms of physical exercise, there is no evidence that they were employed in the Port-Royal schools; the exigencies of school administration obviously precluded most of them. However we find that when Lancelot was appointed tutor to the young Princes De Conti, after the dispersion of the Little Schools, he admitted dancing, riding, and hunting as recreations for his charges.

In another passage Coustel gives us a list of the recreations which were probably in vogue at Port-Royal des Champs; he specifies running, walking, 'jeu de paume,' and ball games It is to these that reference is doubtless made in the regulation of Walon De Beaupuis when he says: "We make them exercise their bodies during recreation times, either at running or at games of skill." Even in the girls' schools presided over by the nuns "quelques petits jeux innocents" were permitted. Allusion has already been made to the account given by Du Fossé of the fort which he and his companions built and of the games which centred round it. We may gather then that the country walks, the running, the games of skill, and the spontaneous 'divertissements' for which the recreation hours at Port-Royal gave opportunity, all contributed to keeping the pupils in good health and in cheerful spirits; so that there is probably no exaggeration in the statement of Walon De Beaupuis that the greatest

[1] Vol. I, p. 314.

punishment which could be given to a recalcitrant pupil was to threaten to send him home.

Before leaving the subject of physical education at Port-Royal it will be interesting to contrast the attitude of the Little Schools with that of the University in this respect. The statutes of Henri IV which reformed the University in 1600, show that physical exercises were held in very little esteem. Fencing, for instance, was absolutely forbidden, and 'maîtres d'armes,' flute players and dancers were rigorously excluded from all places under the jurisdiction of the Academy, and were "relegated to the other side of the bridges." Here again is a statute (No. 18) which conjures up a marked contrast with the Regulation of Walon De Beaupuis: "There shall be no recreation before dinner; neither shall there be any recreation after dinner."

On the other hand, the Jesuits had set a very different example and it is not improbable that Port-Royal had been to some extent inspired by them in the stress laid upon recreation and exercise; at any rate this stress would not be the natural outcome of the ascetic Jansenist theology, practised by many of the solitaries themselves, which despised the things of this world and tended to sacrifice the claims of the body to those of the soul. The Society of Jesus had from the first emphasised the importance of health and the care of the body; Ignatius Loyola himself, writing in 1548, had said: "Impress upon your mind this thought that the soul and the body have been created by the hand of God; we must render account to Him for these two parts of our being and we are not constrained to enfeeble one of them for the love of the Creator[1]." Thus the Jesuits would not allow their pupils to work for more than two hours on end and held all kinds of invigorating exercise in honour; swimming, horse-riding, and fencing were all practised. We can conclude then that, in this particular, Jesuit and Jansenist schools agreed and were alike in advance of much contemporary practice, although their position had already been anticipated in France by Montaigne and more especially by Rabelais. Care for the body had been a doctrine drawn by the Renaissance educators from Greek thought and was gradually beginning to displace

[1] Quoted by Compayré, Vol. I, p. 179.

the contempt in which mediaeval theology had held the physical framework of the soul—the 'flesh.' Physical training bulked largely in the curriculum of the Court schools of Italy (such as that of Vittorino Da Feltre) and of the later German Ritter-akademien; but it seems that by the seventeenth century it had also become an important element in the schools of the teaching congregations. It could never have been for long neglected at a time when war was far commoner than it is to-day and when the soldier's profession was regarded as the most honourable of all careers for a man of gentle birth.

When the weather was wet and outdoor physical exercises impossible, the children at Port-Royal were allowed to play billiards or other indoor games. Coustel very wisely points out that normally games such as chess, dice, and cards are very unsuitable for school-children who perforce have to lead a some-what sedentary life; still he would prefer in winter or bad weather that the children should play draughts, backgammon, or billiards, rather than that they should sit in a state of torpor round the fire. There was one particular game with cards which was in special vogue at Port-Royal, and which well illustrates their desire to make study pleasant and their anticipation in some respects of kindergarten methods[1]. On these cards were written the time and place of all the principal events of the history of the first six centuries after Christ; they included the principal Church Councils, Popes, Emperors, Saints and authors, together with a list of important events[2]. By this means the pupils at Port-Royal became possessed of a store of historical knowledge which was apparently rare among children of the time and which excited much admiration. Perhaps it was this game which first awoke in De Tillemont the genius for History which afterwards made him famous and won for him the praise of Gibbon.

The pupils at Port-Royal were not without their little holidays

---

[1] Compare the "Chartes, non pour iouer, mais pour y apprendre mille petites gentilesses et inuentions nouvelles," by the help of which Gargantua learnt Arithmetic —Bk I, ch. 23.

The game is described in great detail in *Vies des Amis de Port-Royal* (1751), pp. 79—82.

and festivals; a good instance is recorded by Du Fossé. Every year, he tells us, on the eve of the Epiphany, Walon De Beaupuis, the headmaster, gave a kind of 'party' to the children at his own expense. According to a custom which seems to have been universal in western Europe from the Middle Ages until quite recently[1], a cake containing a bean was served at supper time; after supper the pupil whose slice contained the bean was crowned King of the Bean with all appropriate ceremony. He was set on a throne and from the other boys present were chosen his officer, chancellor, and constable. No sooner was this accomplished, so Du Fossé tells us, than powerful plots, intrigues, and cabals were directed against the new sovereign, until he was finally driven from his throne unless he could find a large and strong enough body of loyal supporters to defend him.

Not only were proper feeding and adequate physical exercise or other recreation carefully ensured for the pupil at the Little Schools, but also his hours of sleep were definitely provided for. Coustel tells us that here, as elsewhere, moderation is desirable for children; he says that eight hours of sleep is not too much for them, and his estimate is confirmed by the time-tables drawn up for boys' schools and girls' schools alike. We may be sure that the children were not allowed to stay in bed after they had once been called, but that they were made to rise at once, just as the young Princes De Conti were compelled to do by Lancelot, "de peur qu'ils ne badinent dans leur lit."

Similarly the subject of clothing was not overlooked. Coustel in his *Règlement* has some wise advice as to dress which may be quoted here; his injunctions are as follows: (*a*) in dress one should submit to fashion so far as is seemly, but never in affectation; (*b*) if your clothes are shabby, let them at least be clean; (*c*) if your rank allows you to wear fine clothes, beware lest they serve only to show up your own vices or defects; (*d*) never be vain; clothes are a heritage of shame from our first parents and afford no excuse for pride. To avoid possible stumblingblocks which the wearing of clothes might cause, a

---

[1] A full account of this custom is to be found in Chambers' *Book of Days*, Vol. I, pp. 61 ff.

uniform dress was prescribed for the pupils of Port-Royal. This
was not unusual in the schools of the time and it still survives in
the modern French lycée or collège, the 'internes' or 'pensionnaires' of which often wear a semi-military uniform.

Before leaving this part of our subject it will be well to note
a subject of interest to the parents of the Port-Royal pupils—
the school fees. It seems that Saint-Cyran's original intention
was that fees should be proportioned to the means of the pupil's
parents ; and that in some deserving cases, free places should be
allowed. There is no evidence whatever that the Little Schools
were ever run for financial profits. But provisions and lodging
cost money, and accordingly the inclusive fee for pupils of rich
families was fixed at 400 livres—a sum which during the wars of
the Fronde and the scarcity of provisions, was raised to 500
livres. We may conclude that in those cases where fees were
paid in the Port-Royal schools the charges were decidedly high ;
this probably explains the presence of so many children of the
'upper' classes in the Little Schools. Adamson[1] estimates eight
livres in 1678 as being equal to about £3 of our money to-day.
If this be so, the fees at Port-Royal must have been as high as
from £150 to nearly £200 a year—the cost of education to-day
at Harrow or Eton ; though there was not in the case of the
Little Schools some three months of holidays every year, as is
the custom in our modern public schools. It must at the same
time be remembered that Saint-Cyran's intentions as to the
provision of free places for children of poor parents were faithfully carried out and we have several instances of pupils who were
educated free of charge; among these most probably was Racine.

Many of the pupils of Port-Royal did credit by their after-
career to their education received in the Little Schools. "The
education which was given to children in these schools," says
Besoigne, "can be estimated by the pupils who have come from
them[2]"; and he goes on to give a list of the more distinguished
alumni of Port-Royal. From several other sources we can
collect the names of pupils; we have indeed upwards of 30
names specified. But many of them remain mere names and

---

[1] *Pioneers of Mod. Educ.* p. 215.   [2] Vol. I, p. 199.

no very useful purpose would be served by quoting a list of them here.   The most famous Port-Royal pupil was of course Racine, who was for three years a member of the Little Schools ; he has already been dealt with in this book, but it must be remembered that he is hardly a typical product of the Port-Royal education.   It is true that he owes his knowledge of Greek to Lancelot and his appreciation of fine literature to Le Maître and Hamon; but in order fully to realise his genius, he had to become untrue to the spirit of his upbringing and this involved the well-known quarrel with Nicole.   It is noticeable that though Racine is described in the *Supplément au Nécrologe* as 'poète,' the only works attributed to him are the tragedies of *Esther* and *Athalie* ; *Cantiques Spirituels* ; and the *Histoire abrégée de Port-Royal*.   Far more representative of the best product of the Little Schools are Du Fossé and De Tillemont, to whom reference has already been made ; they both entered Port-Royal at the age of 10 and remained there until the community of the solitaries was broken up.   Both alike acquired considerable contemporary fame.   Du Fossé is the author of the *Lives of Saints*, some most interesting *Mémoires de Port-Royal* to which much of our knowledge of the schools is due, and an annotated continuation of De Saci's French Bible.   De Tillemont won even greater fame as a Church historian.

Two other illustrious Port-Royal pupils may be found in Jérôme and Thierri Bignon, sons of an Avocat Général who had entrusted their education to the care of Saint-Cyran and had thus given occasion for the definite establishment of the Little Schools in 1646.   The education which they received there "rendered them both excellent men"—so the *Nécrologe* tells us[1].   Jérôme became in succession Avocat Général, Conseiller d'honneur au Parlement, Conseiller d'État[2], Chef du Conseil, and Chief-master of the King's Library.   Thierri held the position of Premier Président du Grand Conseil when he

---

[1] p. 55.

[2] The Conseil d'État under Louis XIV was a small body of not more than four or five men.   According to the *Cambridge Modern History* (Vol. v, p. 3) it was the 'pivot of the state,' so that Jérôme Bignon attained to one of the highest civil offices of his time.

died in 1697. There is also Simon Arnauld, Marquis De Pomponne, the third son of D'Andilly, who belongs to Port-Royal both by birth and education; he lived to become successor to Lionne as Minister for Foreign Affairs to Louis XIV, and was largely responsible for the French alliance with Sweden.

Many other instances could be quoted of Port-Royal pupils who afterwards became famous in State or Church; it seems well established therefore that considering the very small total number of pupils who were educated in the Little Schools, a large proportion of them attained distinction in after life. The importance to us of the education given by Port-Royal depends not so much on those among its pupils who won contemporary fame, but are now nearly all forgotten, as on its whole attitude towards education and teaching, and on its influence upon subsequent educational thought. But at the same time it should be noticed that, judged by their pupils—and this is how their contemporaries would have estimated the value of the education which they gave—the Port-Royal solitaries could render a very good account of their work. They could not show a list such as that of the Jesuits: Condé, Bossuet, Descartes, Montesquieu, Corneille, Molière, Voltaire. But, at a time when the Port-Royal schools reached their maximum of some 50 children all told, the Jesuits had in the province of Paris alone nearly 14,000 pupils, and in addition many times this number in other parts of France. Moreover the Society of Jesus was paramount in French education for nearly 200 years, while the Port-Royal schools led a troubled existence for barely 14 years. All things then considered, we must give the solitaries the credit which is their due for the unusually large proportion of distinguished statesmen and ecclesiastics who were in their youth educated by them.

On the other hand, there were pupils at Port-Royal who can hardly be reckoned as typical products of its education. It has already been pointed out that "with a facility more Christian than judicious" there were received into retreat at Port-Royal certain courtiers and great ladies whose antecedents were not likely to shed lustre upon the community which they entered.

This naturally brought the Little Schools into communication with the corrupt court of Louis XIV and as a result the solitaries were given charge of some pupils who apparently profited little by the education they received at Port-Royal. There was for instance the Duke of Monmouth, who was an illegitimate son of Charles II, and afterwards espoused the Protestant cause and laid claim to the English crown; he entered the group at Le Chesnai at the age of nine and passed two years there (1658—60). There were also the two sons of the Princesse De Guémenée—De Montauban and De Rohan—of whom the former was feeble-minded and the latter was executed as a rebel. Still, it appears that these children were never definitely members of the Port-Royal schools; they stayed there from time to time, often in charge of their own special tutor, but their sojourns were interspersed with periods in which they were exposed to the infection of the 'world'; and we cannot therefore assert that the solitaries ever regarded such pupils as in any true sense typical members of the Little Schools.

The question now arises: how many pupils were there at Port-Royal? This point has already been touched upon, but it must be considered in rather greater detail. The educational work of the solitaries started about 1637 at Port-Royal de Paris with the two sons of Bignon, the Avocat Général, two nephews of Saint-Cyran, De Villeneuve, son of D'Andilly, a young Saint-Ange, Vitart (a cousin of Racine), and De La Ferté-Milon— eight pupils in all; by 1643 when Du Fossé and his two brothers entered the schools the total had risen to 11 or 12. When the schools were definitely organised and established in the rue S. Dominique d'Enfer in 1646, the numbers rapidly increased; there were four classes, each consisting of about six pupils taught together in a separate room; this raises the total to 24. The size of the school buildings and the first war of Paris in 1648 probably prevented any great increase of this number during the stay in the capital. The period after the first dispersion of the schools (1650) and their establishment in groups at or near Port-Royal des Champs was the most flourishing epoch of their existence.   The group at Le Chesnai—the largest of all—never contained more than 20 pupils[1]; that at Les Granges numbered at first about 15; that at Les Trous, which was the least important of the three, about 10.   The little group at Magny had comprised five pupils, but as they returned to Les Granges after six months, this number is probably included in the 15 already allowed for this group.   In fact if we add the 20 for Le Chesnai, 15 for Les Granges, and 10 for Les Trous, together with five for other groups—such as that at Sevrans—which were either very small or else existed only a short time and were soon merged in one of the bigger groups, we obtain a total of 50; and it seems probable that the numbers of the Port-Royal pupils never exceeded this figure.   It must be remembered also that there was a continual exchange of pupils and masters[2] alike between various groups; as Sainte-Beuve says: "Absolutely nothing was fixed in regard to the distribution and combining of the classes; masters and pupils alike must have passed several times from one house to another[3]."   This being so, there is a continual danger of reckoning the same persons twice over, unless special care is taken; and this forms another reason for not putting the total number of Port-Royal pupils at any one time above 50.

During the civil wars of 1649—53 the schools were much disorganised, as is proved by the retreat of the solitaries and some of their pupils to the Duc De Luynes' castle at Vaumurier; but when peace was restored, the schools were reorganised and the buildings at Les Granges were enlarged.   However, it seems that this was done chiefly in order to relieve the other groups

---

[1] In the *Vies des Amis de Port-Royal* (p. 86) it is said that a nephew of De Beaupuis gave the names of 17 boys at Le Chesnai " ajoutant qu'il ne se souvient pas bien des autres." It goes on to say that a note-book of De Beaupuis had been discovered in which the names of nearly 30 pupils were mentioned; but this would probably include all the pupils who passed through this group during the whole time of its existence; at any rate it contains the name of the Duke of Monmouth who, we know, spent only two years at Port-Royal.   Moreover, in the *Vie de Nicole* (pp. 26—29) the names of the pupils at Le Chesnai are given, and they total 18 in all.

[2] e.g. Nicole taught both at Les Granges and Les Trous at different times—see *Vies des Amis de Port-Royal*, p. 89.

[3] Vol. III, p. 475.

and to provide better quarters for those children who had been sent to their homes during the civil war. At any rate we find that by 1660 the number of pupils at Le Chesnai had sunk to seven; and this would seem to show that the largest group had been transferred from the private house of M. De Bernières at Le Chesnai to school buildings specially erected about 1653 at Les Granges, close to the convent of Port-Royal des Champs. It was at this time probably that Walon De Beaupuis left Port-Royal de Paris in order to take charge of the school at Le Chesnai. This is quite in keeping with the statement that the schools flourished between 1653 and 1656; but it does not prove that the number of pupils ever rose above 50 during this period. Another fact, which tends to prove that the total number of pupils did not appreciably increase, is that we have no record of an increase in the number of masters; one of the chief characteristics of Port-Royal education is the small group of about five children, or even less, presided over by a tutor. During the period 1650—6 we know that Lancelot and Nicole were teaching at Les Granges, De Beaupuis, Guyot, Le Bon, and De Bascle at Le Chesnai, and Borel at Les Trous; Coustel, and Le Fèvre, who died soon after leaving Paris, were also on the regular staff, while assistance was occasionally given by Le Maître, De Saci, and Dr Arnauld. Everything then points to 50 as being about the maximum number of the Port-Royal pupils during the establishment of the schools in the country; and to about half that number as the maximum during their establishment at Paris.

There now remains the more difficult question as to the total number of pupils which passed through the Port-Royal schools during the 14 years or so of their existence. Compayré estimates it as "un millier à peine pendant tout le temps que l'enseignement dura[1]." This is evidently an extreme over-estimate; even if the whole personnel of the school had been changed every year during the four years in Paris and the ten troubled years at Port-Royal des Champs, the total of 'barely a thousand' could not be reached. As a matter of fact, a considerable proportion of the Port-Royal pupils spent their whole

[1] Vol. I, p. 240.

schooldays in the Little Schools; as has been pointed out, these
gave both an elementary and a secondary education, in spite of
their name, and this fact in itself must have tended to make
children stay long at the schools. Du Fossé and De Tillemont
gained their whole education there; so apparently also did the
two Bignons, De Villeneuve, Des Champs and several others.
We have no means of estimating exactly the total number of
pupils in the Little Schools during their 14 years' existence; but
on the basis of some very rough calculations the writer is inclined to think that this total cannot at most be put higher than
250; it is indeed quite possible that it was well below this
figure.

CHAPTER VII

THE PORT-ROYAL GIRLS' SCHOOLS

IT has been and is still a very general custom for religious communities of women in the Roman Church to receive girls as boarders and to devote themselves to their education. Port-Royal was no exception to this custom, but the history of the girls' schools is less known to us in its details because of their lesser importance and their less troubled existence. It must be pointed out here that there was no connection whatever between the boys' schools and the girls' schools at Port-Royal. They were, it is true, both under the control of the same monastery; but whereas the girls or 'pensionnaires' were educated by the nuns within the precincts of the convent itself, the boys were lodged in 'dépendances' and were under the care of the solitaries. The same spiritual director or confessor visited nuns and solitaries alike and thus had a general interest in the educational work of both girls' and boys' schools. But as far as teaching staff and school administration are concerned, there was no kind of connection between the two establishments; each is absolutely independent of the other. It is necessary to insist on this point, for certain educational historians in treating of Port-Royal appear not sufficiently to have investigated whether the word 'écoles' in their authorities refers to the boys' or the girls' schools; and this may possibly have contributed to the discrepancies which exist as to the date of the final dispersion of the solitaries and the Little Schools[1]. Let it then be clearly understood that except for their general dependence on the convent of Port-Royal, the two educational establishments were in no wise connected.

[1] See Appendix A..

The education of girls at Port-Royal was in vogue long before Saint-Cyran set his solitaries to teach boys. Even as early as the first part of the thirteenth century the nuns of Port-Royal were devoting part of their time to teaching, and this work was carried on until the general laxity of discipline in religious houses set in during the sixteenth century. But when the young Abbess Angélique set about reforming Port-Royal in 1608 she apparently revived the educational work of the community. In 1626, when the community was transferred from the unhealthy site at Port-Royal des Champs to Port-Royal de Paris, the girls' schools were moved at the same time; and we find that five years later Sister Anne Eugénie De L'Incarnation, one of Angélique's sisters, was appointed 'maîtresse des pensionnaires.' In 1648 the community, having greatly increased in numbers, was divided into two parts, one of which remained in Paris while the other returned to Port-Royal des Champs; we have evidence that the teaching of girls was carried on in both sections of the convent, so that there were two separate schools. From this time onwards the girls' schools of Port-Royal flourished exceedingly and they appear to have been very little affected by the dispersion in 1656 of the Port-Royal solitaries and the boys whom they were educating. However, the complete suppression of the boys' schools and dispersion of the solitaries in March 1660 did not satisfy the Jesuits; "they had nothing more at heart," Racine tells us, "than to get the king to ruin the community of Port-Royal[1]." Accordingly, on April 13, 1661, a royal order was issued to this effect; and on April 23 the boarders were driven out and the nuns were forbidden to receive in future any more girls to be educated. Besoigne gives a list of the girls who were pupils at Port-Royal at this time and who were thus ejected. There were 21 at Port-Royal de Paris and 17 at Port-Royal des Champs; they included the daughters of the Duc De Luynes, as well as the children of a notary and a merchant; thus we may conclude that social distinctions counted for no more among the nuns of Port-Royal than they did among the solitaries.

It happened then that, a year after the boys of Port-Royal

[1] *Hist. abr. de P.-R.* p. 223.

were sent back to their parents, their sisters underwent a similar fate. But whereas the boys' schools were never restored in their old form and with their original masters, the royal interdict was revoked in regard to the girls' schools at the 'Peace of the Church' in 1669, and the nuns were allowed to receive boarders again. The first to arrive were the two little granddaughters of D'Andilly, one of whom—Charlotte—was only four years old at the time. Their father, M. De Pomponne, the Minister of Louis XIV, had himself been educated by the solitaries. The aged Abbess Agnès (Jeanne Arnauld) was overjoyed at this *auspicium melioris aevi*; it seemed as though all the persecutions, which Port-Royal had for the last 20 years or more endured, were now at an end. "The whole community," she writes, "is overjoyed to see these little doves who have brought an olive branch and opened the door which had been closed to small and great[1] alike." But the new lease of life lasted only 10 years, for on the death in 1679 of the Duchess De Longueville, the cousin of Louis XIV and protectress of the convent, and the outbreak of further persecutions of Port-Royal in the same year, the girls' schools were finally closed by royal order. We have in Besoigne a list of 42 girls who were on this occasion sent back to their parents. We can trace a successor of the educational work of the Port-Royal nuns in the girls' school founded by Nicole at Troyes in 1678. It was in charge of teaching sisters or 'black sisters'; but they were forbidden to teach in 1742 and were finally dispersed in 1749. Reference has also been made in a former chapter to the Jansenist 'Sœurs de Sainte-Marthe,' whose educational activities lasted down to our own days.

Such in outline is the history of the Port-Royal girls' schools; but of the details of their administration we know on the whole less than of the details concerned with the boys' schools. M. Cadet, however, is greatly mistaken in saying: "We have not, so to say, any information about the education of the girls

---

[1] She refers to the fact that since May 1661 the convent had been forbidden to receive novices and postulants, i.e. to recruit the number of the nuns. This interdict was also removed in 1669.

at Port-Royal....Where are the programmes of studies? What
methods did the mistresses employ? What books did they put
into the hands of their pupils? What traces have they left of
their teaching and of their system of education[1]?" All these
questions are answered at some length in Jacqueline Pascal's
Règlement pour les enfans de Port-Royal and in chapter XVI of
the Abbess Agnès Arnauld's *Constitutions du Monastère de
Port-Royal.* Thanks to them, as M. Compayré observes, we
know 'avec précision' what the education of girls at Port-Royal
was like. It is on this first-hand documentary evidence therefore
that our account of the Port-Royal girls' schools will almost
entirely be based.

It has already been pointed out that in the Port-Royal boys'
schools intellectual education was sacrificed to moral education.
In the girls' schools this process was carried still further and the
purely intellectual side of their education is almost completely
lacking. This is illustrated by the following clause in the
Constitutions: "Girls may be received in the monastery for
instruction in the fear of God during several years, but not for
one year only, because that is not sufficient to form them in
good morals according to the rules of Christianity[2]." Owing to
this lack of intellectual training, the girls' schools at Port-Royal
can never have the interest and importance of the Little Schools
conducted by the solitaries; in the former the type of education
given remained on the conventual level and was apparently not
distinguished in any important feature from the usual contemporary education given to girls in religious communities.
The girls' schools of Port-Royal introduced no new teaching
methods, though they may have employed some of those already
worked out by the solitaries (e.g. Pascal's reading method); and
although they also are inspired by the Jansenist theology of
Saint-Cyran, this is not mitigated by Cartesianism and warm-
hearted good sense to anything like the degree shown by the
solitaries in the boys' schools.

This is illustrated by the fact that preparation for the
'religious' vocation was the actual, if not the avowed, aim of
the girls' schools. The parents of pupils were required to

[1] p. 46.   [2] p. 99.

renounce their authority over their children and "to offer them
to God," unconcerned whether ultimately they became nuns or
returned to the 'world.' As far as the rules of the girls' schools
went, there was no compulsion used to drive children towards
the religious vocation; but the mistresses are instructed in
Jacqueline Pascal's *Règlement* to point out, when occasion offers,
the joy, contentment, and peace which arise from the life of
a nun. "If the children themselves," she continues, "broach
the subject of religion, one should make good use of the opportunity to tell them something of the happiness of a good nun
who lives truly according to her vocation, and of her constant
consolation in thinking of the great means which God gives her
of loving Him and of securing her own eternal happiness by
obedience and humility; since this is the only road to heaven
for all Christians, but especially for nuns. Children must be
made to understand that the religious life is by no means a
burden, but one of God's greatest gifts and a comfort for those
who desire to live faithful to their baptismal vows; that God
does not give this grace to everyone, nor even to all those who
desire it, and that since it is of so great excellence, we should
ask it of God humbly and make ourselves ready to receive it by
good actions[1]." It is significant also that the 'pensionnaires' at
Port-Royal wore a white dress, similar to that of the postulants;
though a dispensation from this was granted for a short time
to any who on entering the school objected to wearing this
costume. Marriage also was evidently deprecated by the nuns,
and the girls at Port-Royal must have had as distorted views
of this sacrament as had the *précieuse* Armande in Molière's
Femmes Savantes. In the *Lettres chrestiennes et spirituelles* of
Saint-Cyran, which is included in the list of books read by the
children in the convent schools, occurs the following passage:
"God has prevented you with His grace in giving you an
aversion for the world and in deterring you from taking upon
you so heavy a yoke as marriage; I know so much about it
from the various experiences of so many people that if there
were 100,000 souls that I loved like yours, I should always wish,
in imitation of S. Paul, never to see them involved in it, and

[1] pp. 494—5.

would do my utmost to prevent them from entering it[1]." In the same strain Agnès Arnauld, who was at the time Abbess of the Convent of Tard, wrote in 1634 to her nephew Le Maître to induce him to give up his intention of marrying: "You will say that I am blaspheming this holy sacrament on which your heart is set; but do not trouble yourself about my conscience which knows well how to distinguish the sacred from the profane, the precious from the base, and which pardons you in the spirit of S. Paul. Be content with that if you please, but do not ask me for approval and praise[2]."

It is evident then that in the girls' schools the state of marriage and of motherhood was considered far inferior to the 'religious life,' and that the real aim of their education was to recruit the convent. This is confirmed by other evidence; the *Constitutions* provide that girls may be kept to the age of 16 years "even though they do not wish to be nuns"; but in spite of the letter of the law we find Angélique giving notice to a Mme De Chazé that her daughter, who had been some years in the school and was aged about 15, "did not wish to be a nun, and that it was necessary to take her away[3]." We must therefore accuse Racine of somewhat misrepresenting facts when he states that the Port-Royal mistresses "were not content to instruct their pupils in piety, but they also took very great care to form their intellect and their reason, and laboured to render them equally fit to become one day either perfect nuns or excellent mothers and wives[4]." As far as the evidence from Jacqueline Pascal's *Règlement* and the Abbess Agnès' *Constitutions* goes, it seems conclusive that the education of intellect and reason was largely neglected and that preparation for domestic life was completely overshadowed by preparation for the religious life.

It may be remembered that Saint-Cyran's original idea in founding the boys' schools had been to supply the Church with candidates for Holy Orders. But the good sense of the solitaries

[1] Vol. I, p. 241.
[2] MS. in Bibliothèque Nationale quoted by Sainte-Beuve, Vol. I, p. 375.
[3] *Vies intéressantes*, Vol. III, p. 28.
[4] *Hist. abr. de P.-R.* p. 69.

had led them to avoid insistence on this point; their first aim was to produce the complete man whose reason had so been trained that he could of his own initiative preserve his baptismal innocency and repel the attacks of the demon ; and one of the means by which this process was attained was intellectual education, pure and simple—a wide education, fruitful in ideas, and based upon a carefully-regulated study of the classics. There is nothing to parallel this in the girls' schools at Port-Royal; their rules and constitutions speak continually of religious instruction and devotional exercises, but the purely intellectual side of their education is meagre in the extreme. Such as it is, however, it must now be considered.

The *Constitutions* lay it down that: " The girls shall be in a department separate from the nuns, with a mistress to instruct them in virtue ; to her assistants will be given the duty of instructing them in reading, writing, needlework, and other useful things, and not those which minister only to vanity[1]." The only additions which can be made to the three school subjects above-mentioned are the singing of plainsong, for which the Port-Royal services were noted, and an hour's Arithmetic as a special treat on festivals.

We know that Pascal's method of teaching reading was adopted by his sister for use in the girls' schools, and we also have evidence that the art of reading aloud was cultivated there. But the books read were exclusively of a religious nature ; there was nothing which corresponded to the 'version' or classical translation of the boys' schools. Jacqueline Pascal gives in her *Règlement* a list of the books used in the girls' schools ; they are as follows: Fontaine's *Translation of the Imitatio Christi*, Father Louis of Grenada's *Guide des Pécheurs*, *La Philothée*, the *Ladder* of S. John Climacus, the *Tradition of the Church*, Saint-Cyran's *Letters* and *Familiar Theology, Christian Maxims from the Book of the Hours, Letters of a Carthusian Father, Meditations* of S. Theresa on the *Pater Noster* and certain passages from her *Way of Perfection*, selected letters of S. Jerome, *Christian Charity*, and the lives of the Fathers and other saints. No

[1] p. 94.

other books than these and similar works were permitted in the
schools, and even these were not left in the pupils' hands; the
only books which they might keep to themselves were the *Book
of the Hours*, the *Familiar Theology*, the *Sayings of Christ*, an
Imitation and a psalter.   Reading therefore was rigorously
confined to works of a religious character; but it seems evident
that within these limits a wide selection was allowed.   An
unusually large number of them were read and questions were
invited on points not understood; this must have ensured at
least a good knowledge of the French language to those girls
who passed through the schools; we learn therefore from the
Jesuit father Rapin, who would naturally not be well-disposed
towards Port-Royal, that "everything there was polished—even
the little boarders whom they took the trouble to instruct in
purity of language as much as in virtue[1]."   To a small extent
also the reason and intellect may have been developed by
reading; but it is easy to over-estimate this feature of the
education given in the girls' schools.   Its avowed aim was
always a moral one; "our object," says Jacqueline Pascal,
"should be to accustom them never to listen to reading out of
pleasure or curiosity, but with a desire to apply it to themselves;
for this reason our method of making them understand it should
contribute far more to making them good Christians and to
bringing them to break themselves of their faults, than to
rendering them learned[2]."

We are told that the girls of Port-Royal also possessed a
psalter 'in Latin and French.'   Does this imply that any
knowledge of Latin was imparted to them?   We read of a
certain Mlle De Monglat, aged 14 at the time of the dispersion
of the 'pensionnaires' in 1661, who had a certain acquaintance
with the Latin language[3], and it is obvious from Jacqueline
Pascal's time-table of a day in the girls' schools that the prayers

[1] Rapin, *Mémoires*, Vol. II, p. 276.
[2] p. 521.
[3] *Supplément au Nécrologe* (1763), p. 2.   She could read at the age of three, and also
had a knowledge of Poetry, Geography, History (sacred and profane) and Latin by
the age of five or six.   This seems, however, due not to the schools but to the instruction given her by her aunt the Marquise D'Aumont, who lived in retirement
at Port-Royal from 1648 till her death in 1658.

were said in Latin. But there is no evidence that any systematic teaching of Latin Grammar or even vocabulary ever formed part of the curriculum; and we may therefore conclude that Latin, so far as it was learnt at all, was acquired almost parrot fashion. The girls knew the general sense of what they were saying because they had a parallel French translation to guide them; but beyond this they probably repeated the Latin words merely by rote, or at most with a very scanty knowledge of the meaning of isolated words or the force of grammatical constructions. This is often the case with devout but not highly educated Roman Catholics at the present day, and it explains the vogue of such manuals as the French *Paroissiens* or the English *Garden of the Soul*, in which the Latin and the vernacular are given side by side. So long as the intention is clear and the general meaning definitely understood, it is unbecoming to judge harshly of such practices; and the devout sincerity of the Roman Catholic peasant when he joins in the Gloria or the Credo (for in small parish churches in France these are often sung by choir and congregation alike) is in no wise inferior to that of his Anglican brother whose liturgy is in 'a tongue understanded of the people.'

About three-quarters of an hour every day seems to have been devoted in the girls' schools to the practice of writing. The children wrote in silence and were not allowed to show one another their productions nor " to write according to their fancy." They merely wrote out a set copy, or " when they were very good and had been granted permission," transcribed something —probably from one of the religious works above-mentioned. They were not allowed to write letters to one another without first obtaining permission from the mistress in charge and using her as post-office and (we may shrewdly guess) censor as well. M. Carré also conjectures that the girls learnt not only to write but also to compose in French. There is no direct evidence for this, but it seems probable; the pupils would not be employed in learning mere orthography up to the age of 16 or later, and thus we may infer that the elder girls were allowed to write French compositions of some kind; this conjecture is also borne out to some extent by the reference which Jacqueline

Pascal makes to the practice of writing letters by one pupil to another.

Of the needlework and other 'ouvrages utiles,' mentioned in the Abbess Agnès' *Constitutions*, we have some few details in Jacqueline Pascal's *Règlement*. The chief occupation of this kind seems to have been the knitting of worsted gloves[1]; the children were encouraged to devote any odd spare time to the task and for this purpose to carry some work of the kind with them wherever they went. No kind of art needlework was allowed—not even for vestments or church decorations; indeed, as has already been seen, such things were eyed askance by the almost puritanical Jansenism of Port-Royal.

The teaching of singing and Arithmetic, the only other subjects in the curriculum of the girls' schools, has been touched upon elsewhere, and in fact we have very little information as to either. A few minutes every day were given to singing and an hour upon festivals; after which, half-an-hour or so was spent by the elders in instructing the younger pupils. Arithmetic was confined to festivals and a similar method of learning followed by pupil-teaching was employed in regard to it also. We can conclude then that in such rare and short periods no great progress could ever have been made in either singing or the art of calculation. The former was apparently confined to reading simple plainsong melodies at sight from the ordinary four-line stave—a matter of very little difficulty to any child with a musical ear; while the latter must have been of the most elementary nature, and was doubtless regarded as strictly an 'ouvrage utile' for those who would one day most probably be nuns and whose duty it might be to keep the accounts of the convent, and to calculate the Epact, Golden Number, Dominical Letter and the dates of the various movable feasts.

The time-table of a day in the girls' schools of Port-Royal has been outlined for us by Jacqueline Pascal in the first part of her *Règlement pour les enfans de Port-Royal*; as it gives at first hand a far more vivid picture of the actual conditions of life there than any elaborate description could do, it will not be out

[1] 'gants d'estame.'

of place to transcribe its essentials here; it is interesting
to compare it with the time-table of the boys' schools from
1650 onwards, for by so doing the salient points of difference
between the two establishments are made obvious and the
superiority of the *régime* of the boys' schools becomes at once
apparent.

The eldest girls rose at 4, their juniors at 4.30 or 5, while
the hour of rising for the smallest of all was regulated by 'their
needs and their strength.' They dressed quickly and in absolute
silence save for the morning prayers; if by any chance one girl
had need to speak to another, she was obliged to ask the nun in
charge to act as intermediary and carry the message for her.
This 'great silence' lasted till 6 o'clock, the hour of Prime; at
the first stroke of the bell all fell on their knees in the dormitory
and repeated the office in a low tone, slowly and distinctly.
This done, a short silence ensued, during which the children
meditated on their faults of the preceding day and sought grace
to avoid them during the coming one. The girls now proceeded
to make their beds, after which they washed their hands and
rinsed out their mouths with wine and water before going down
to breakfast. During the meal one of the pupils read aloud the
history of the saint to whom the particular day was dedicated.
After breakfast—that is to say about 7.30 at latest—work began
and continued in the most profound silence. Even the little
girls, some of whom were as young as four, were taught not to
utter a word, although "after they had tried faithfully to work
and to keep silent," they were allowed to play. This each did
separately, for fear lest they should make a noise if they played
together. Jacqueline Pascal even tells us that this did not trouble
them at all; "quand elles y sont accoutumées, elles ne laissent
pas de se divertir fort gaiement[1]." How one pities the poor
little souls! The morning lesson consisted of the reading of
some religious manual, the subject being chosen as far as possible
in accordance with the Church season; during this hour also a
few of the eldest girls swept out the dormitories or cleaned the
cells. At 8 o'clock all alike assembled to hear a reading of
the Scriptures by one of the mistresses; the passage chosen

[1] p. 430.

was at the same time expounded and a short homily based on it. At 8.30 most of the girls assisted at the office of Tierce which was said in the convent chapel; as in the boys' schools, attendance at the church services was not rigorously insisted upon and, in theory at any rate, care was taken lest too many devotional exercises should arouse contrariance in some of the pupils. Permission to go to church therefore was regarded as a favour accorded to the elder girls and to those others who by their good conduct had qualified themselves for participation in the worship of Holy Church. After Tierce—that is to say about 9 o'clock—all those who were not very young or badly behaved assisted at Mass; they knelt two and two in the middle of the choir with their hands joined beneath their scapularies, in an attitude of reverent devotion. As in the boys' schools, any misbehaviour in church was punished 'avec force.' The infants and those children whose conduct had been bad were left behind in charge of a mistress; but since these little unfortunates were obliged to remain kneeling in perfect silence in the schoolroom during the whole time of the service, we can easily understand why attendance at church, where one could listen to the singing of the nuns and watch the movements of the celebrant, came to be regarded as a privilege and as a reward for good behaviour. When the girls returned from Mass they all had a writing lesson which lasted three-quarters of an hour, and this was followed by a very short singing lesson. At 11 o'clock came confession and examination of consciences; we learn from another part of the *Règlement* that the children were encouraged sometimes to confess their little faults publicly and aloud "in order to accustom themselves to penitence and humiliation." It is not necessary to enlarge upon the dangers involved in such a system; it seems a direct encouragement of morbid imaginings which perhaps is specially undesirable in young girls who are sometimes inclined to be already over-sensitive in this direction. When confession was over some of the elder girls repeated Sext and after this, at about 11.30, the whole school went to dinner. This took place in the convent refectory where the rest of the community as well as those who were engaged in teaching dined together. The girls were seated at table, not according to their classes as was the case in the boys' schools, but "as was judged best, the best girls being placed between those who were not so good, in order to prevent them from conversing." Silence therefore was observed during the meal and the children were instructed to keep their eyes cast down without looking to the right or the left. Daintiness was forbidden and the pupils were even made to begin the meal with the dish they liked least "par esprit de pénitence." None the less the mistresses were instructed to see that they made a good meal, so that this rule was evidently not carried to extremes. After dinner came an hour's recreation, in which the elder girls were not allowed to play with the younger ones, but amused themselves apart "plus doucement et plus sagement." We learn elsewhere that they usually took the opportunity to do some of their knitting. The silence and severity which had endured throughout the day so far was now somewhat relaxed and one is at first relieved to hear that the little girls were allowed if they liked to play at 'innocent games,' knuckle-bones and shuttle-cock being specified. But in the same breath Jacqueline Pascal goes on to say: "ce n'est pas que cela se fasse parmi nous présentement"; so that even this respite was less real than would at first appear. The children were all under constant supervision; not a word was allowed to escape them which was not overheard by the mistresses in charge. Yet some definite attempt does seem to have been made to ensure that this interval should be a real hour of recreation; Jacqueline Pascal specially lays it down that the mistresses should never speak to the children of their work or their faults during their playtime; if they do anything wrong during recreation, the mistress in charge should wait till it is over before reprimanding and punishing the offender.

At 1 o'clock the pupils returned to the schoolroom where they said the 'Veni Sancte Spiritus' and any child who 'had the devotion' openly confessed her faults, though no one was forced to do this. This confession lasted a quarter of an hour and was followed by a lesson on the Epistle and Gospel for the day, on a passage from some devotional work, on a part of the catechism, or on some 'mystery' of the Church. Jacqueline

Pascal gives an interesting list of subjects upon which she had given lessons of this kind during the four years previous to 1657. The syllabus in the first year comprises: symbolism, the sign of the cross, holy water, the Ten Commandments; in the second year: explanation of the office of the Mass; in the third year: explanation of the morning and evening prayers, of the practice of self-examination and of the other duties of a good Christian; also lessons on the Christian virtues, based on the writings of S. John Climacus; while in the fourth year the course of study included the subject of penitence and the doctrine of Grace as understood by the Jansenists. For these lessons a book called *The Tradition of the Church* and also Saint-Cyran's *Catechism* were used. The afternoon lessons lasted an hour and a half—from 1 o'clock till 2.30; they were followed by a repetition of Nones. Then the children said their catechism, taking turn and turn about to ask the questions and give the answers. This done, those children who could read did so in silence; while one of the elder girls of approved character, who had definitely decided to become a nun, retired with the very young children into a room apart and there taught them reading. About half-past three all pupils under the age of 14 partook of 'goûter.' At 4 o'clock the elder girls attended Vespers in the chapel "si elles méritent qu'on leur fasse cette grâce"; meanwhile anything which the other children had not understood in their lessons was carefully explained to them. After Vespers one of the elder girls read aloud from some religious work while the rest listened in silence. Then came supper which was taken in common with the whole community in the convent refectory and was conducted in the same manner as dinner; after this there was another hour's recreation. At 7.30 Compline was said; in the summer time the girls were allowed to repeat this in the garden and to recite the psalms while walking in procession. When this was finished they returned to the chapel and sang the anthem of the Blessed Virgin, except during the three hottest months of the year (June—August); thence they went straight to their rooms, undressed quickly and in silence, and were all in bed by 8.15. Each child had a separate bed. When they had retired one of the sisters visited each bed to see that its occupant was well tucked-up and warm enough; in each dormitory also a nun slept with the children and a light was kept burning all night long.

Such then was the ordinary day's routine in the girls' schools. It was slightly changed on festivals, the chief alterations being as follows: after Prime the whole school assisted at early Mass and again after Tierce at High Mass. There was no writing or singing lesson in the morning as on ordinary days, but its place was taken by the learning by heart of passages from the *Familiar Theology*, the *Treatise on Confirmation*, or of French hymns from the *Book of the Hours*, Latin hymns from the Breviary, or the Psalter. Before Nones came the Arithmetic lesson and after Nones half-an-hour's singing lesson, to both of which reference has already been made. The whole school attended Vespers and the Adoration of the Holy Sacrament which followed it; and the rest of the day was spent in much the same manner as on week-days.

In reading the above time-tables one is at once impressed by two of its features—the inordinate amount of devotional exercises and religious instruction, and the long and numerous silences imposed on the children. The emphasis laid on the former has already been explained by the fact that education in the girls' schools was exclusively moral and almost anti-intellectual, and that its real object was to prepare for the 'religious' life. It must be noted that in addition to the prayers and services specified above, every meal and lesson or other occupation was prefaced and concluded by appropriate devotions, and that at every hour throughout the day one of the girls took her turn to recite suitable prayers, kneeling by herself in a corner of the room where the other children were learning their lessons or having their meals. This regular repetition of the set prayers was regarded as avowedly more important than even the school-work itself, religious in character as it was. "The children are exhorted," says Jacqueline Pascal, "on no account to be too much attached to their work, but to leave it immediately the clock strikes, whether it be to go to the service or to say private prayers; they must be always ready to perform their duties towards God and to devote themselves to nothing save this[1]." Again, the pupils were encouraged to practice mortifications and penances; an instance of this has already been given in regard to meals, but the children were instructed in general terms that "the less one is pleased by any occupation, the more it pleases God." These regulations might well have been expected to arouse a contrariant spirit in the pupils, but we find that the opposite was often the case and that girls were sometimes over-eager to devise methods of mortification and had to be restrained. For instance, they of themselves (so we read) often asked permission to be deprived of their afternoon 'goûter'; but Jacqueline Pascal adds: "We do not easily grant exemption for children younger than 14, even when they beseech us for it, for fear lest they should ask this permission in order to be like the elder girls or out of hypocrisy[2]." Some of the children even seem on their own initiative to have tried to emulate one another in this matter. "It nearly cost two of them dear," says Besoigne, "who admitted the little Marie-Claire, sister of the Abbess (Angélique), into their pious but dangerous plot. They took it into their heads, in order to mortify themselves in imitation of the nuns, to gather weeds in the garden, pound them up and swallow the juice[3]."

In addition to the religious austerities furnished by continual prayer, private and public, and by mortification of the flesh, one is impressed, as has already been remarked, by the long silences which were imposed upon the girls of the Port-Royal schools. During the whole day, with the exception of one hour's playtime after dinner and another hour after supper, conversation was practically forbidden and the silence was broken only by the recitation of the prayers and canonical hours, or by the saying of lessons. Besides this there were certain times of rigorous and complete silence. In the morning from the time of rising to the hour of Prime, and in the evening from the ringing of the Angelus until retiring to bed, were the two 'great silences'; the utmost care was taken that during these periods the children should not have occasion to ask anything even of the mistress

---

[1] p. 431.   [2] p. 454.   [3] Vol. I, p. 42.

in charge. A similar silence was kept during the time when the choir offices or the Mass was being said in the convent chapel— even among those girls who did not attend the services. There were thus two hours every day during which a certain amount of freedom was granted to pupils for conversation among themselves; the rest of the day was spent in silence, more or less complete.

The girls' schools of Port-Royal contained pupils whose ages ranged from four, or younger, to 17 or 18, and it is a little difficult to imagine the effect which this *régime* of devotion and silence must have produced upon some of them. It seems to have been vaguely understood by the mistresses that it was not every child whose nervous system could endure a curriculum so rigid and monotonous; Jacqueline Pascal tells us in the 'avertissement' to her *Règlement* that the regulations were not invariably applied in all their rigour and that relaxation was allowed in special cases. She also seems to have understood that too little variety in mental food may produce mental indigestion, and we thus find her even advising that religious instruction should not be overdone. "We avoid," she says, "speaking too much (about religion and morals) for fear of overburdening their minds and I have found by experience that religious instruction is much more beneficial to them when they are not at all weary of it. For this reason I think it is well sometimes to allow several days to elapse without giving them any, and to let them become hungry as it were for this form of nourishment; the result is that they take in better what is said to them[1]." We may conclude that the *Règlement* for the girls' schools, like some of the rules for the boys' schools, was not applied in all its rigour; but even when we have allowed a liberal discount for the skill of the mistresses in diagnosing the needs of particular cases, we are still left with a *régime* which, considering the tender age of many of the children, must have proved at times intolerable to some of them. The boys' schools of Port-Royal were not exempt from the depressing influence of Jansenism; but in them free conversation was allowed at meals, 'great silences' were unknown, religious exercises were carefully not

[1] p. 432.

insisted upon, the curriculum was wide and interesting, and the end in view was to develop a reasonable and responsible individual. In all these particulars the Little Schools immeasurably surpassed the girls' schools, which never proposed to prepare for ordinary life in the world.

In the schools directed by the solitaries affection for the pupils formed the basis upon which all educational methods were built. It has been said that Saint-Cyran and the Port-Royal masters loved children not for their own sake but for the sake of God, whom they desired to serve by carrying on the work of education. An attempt has already been made to show that, whatever may have been their theory on this subject, their practice was based upon a direct, human, and natural love for children which appears nowhere more clearly than in the case of Saint-Cyran himself. But when we turn to the girls' schools we find it explicitly stated that the pupils were loved not for their own sake, but for the sake of God. Sisters are instructed not to wish to be loved by the pupils, except for the good of the children themselves; "they will not show any tenderness they may feel for them, and they will make a sacrifice of it to God, to obtain from His goodness that these children may benefit by the good education that will be given them[1]." Passages of this and a similar nature could be abundantly paralleled from Jacqueline Pascal's *Règlement*; she lays it down that the mistresses should be utterly devoted to their charges "because they are the children of God and we feel ourselves obliged to spare nothing to make them worthy of this holy estate[2]." They must never be treated with familiarity or confidence and must often be reminded that they are not cared for because ordinary spontaneous human affection is felt for them, but "qu'on les aime pour Dieu." Although provision is made for unfailing kindness and care on the part of mistresses towards their charges, yet there seems to have been a deliberate attempt to suppress that friendly and natural relationship between teacher and taught which is the peculiar glory of many of the secondary schools of this country. If a mistress felt affection towards her

[1] *Constitutions de P.-R.* p. 104.   [2] p. 478.

pupils for their own sake, she was encouraged to "offer them to God" and to merge her love for them in her love for God. The distinction is perhaps a little subtle, but it is none the less real. The result of it in theory was to reduce to exactly the same plane those mistresses who were naturally fond of children and those who were not; for both alike were supposed to undertake their work not primarily for the sake of the children, but for the sake of God.

The natural outcome of such a position was that the work of teaching was sometimes regarded in the light of an unpleasant penance imposed upon teachers. One finds this spirit especially in the writings of the Abbess Agnès, but to a less extent in Jacqueline Pascal's *Règlement*. Even Sister Anne Eugénie De L'Incarnation, who appears to have been one of the most successful and popular mistresses of the 'pensionnaires' at Port-Royal, had "a great natural dislike for teaching children." Lack of teaching ability and want of sympathy with children seem to have been regarded rather as qualifications for a mistress than the reverse; for the resulting humiliation and trouble afforded a penance which would be of great worth in achieving salvation. "Do not put forward as an excuse," writes Agnès to a sister, "that you do not discharge this duty well, and that you make many mistakes; for it is for this very reason that it may perhaps be found fitting to leave you there still, that you may better understand your incapacity....God permits the children not to behave as they ought that their insubordination may make you suffer and humble yourself[1]."

We are here far removed from the ideas of Saint-Cyran; he looked at the work of education from the point of view of the pupil's eternal welfare and not from that of the moral advancement of the teacher. For him, the highest natural gifts, a special grace, and professional training, were all alike important for the man who aspired to take in hand the great work of educating the young. But in the education of the girls at Port-Royal greater value was set upon the spirit which animated the teacher than upon the actual result accomplished. Thus Jacqueline Pascal speaks of the "pleasure and satisfaction there is in being

---

[1] *Letters*, Vol. ii, p. 465.

entirely devoted to God and in serving Him in truth and simplicity, keeping nothing whatever in reserve; nothing is unpleasant when we do it entirely in a spirit of love....Some will gain heaven while others will deserve nothing but punishment by the same action, according to the movement of their heart and the purity or impurity of their intention[1]." The Kantian ethic of this passage is entirely in accordance with Jansenism and with the theories of Saint-Cyran himself; but, as so often happened, he and still more the teaching solitaries rose superior in their practice to their own doctrine. The nuns on the other hand seem to have concentrated their attention on the spiritual welfare of the teacher rather than that of the pupil, and it is this which taints the whole of their educational system and renders it far inferior to that of the Little Schools.

At the same time this somewhat unnatural attitude of detachment from their pupils did not exclude constant attention and real kindness towards them on the part of the mistresses. Jacqueline Pascal tells us that the girls must be under constant, but benevolent, supervision; as with the boys in the Little Schools, " elles sont toujours accompagnées partout." The smallest children—' petites colombes'—must have the most care. In several passages of the *Règlement* there seems to breathe a truly maternal solicitude for the comfort and well-being of the children, which was perhaps not altogether due to an artificial affection born of a love for God. The very little girls must be watched "lest they fall and hurt themselves." Although daintiness is forbidden, the mistress in charge must see that children make a good meal. Again, as was said above, the pupils were visited in bed to ensure that they were warm enough. Special care was lavished on any pupil who fell ill; the case was put in charge of the convent doctor who was 'bon chrétien et bon médecin[2],' and a sister was told off to nurse the invalid. If the medicines are nasty the sufferer must not make a fuss, but implore divine aid in taking them and the sister in charge must always exhort invalids "offrir leur mal à Dieu."

---

[1] p. 490.

[2] E.g. Hamon (see p. 27) and Pallu, of whom Fontaine said, "It was almost agreeable to fall ill in order to have the pleasure of enjoying his conversation."

Should it be suspected that a child is malingering—"j'en ai vu quelques-unes de cette sorte," says Jacqueline Pascal—they should be put to bed and dieted for a day or so on eggs and broth. "Si le mal était effectif, ce régime leur est fort bon ; et s'il ne l'est pas, il est sans doute que dès le lendemain elles diront qu'elles n'ont point de mal[1]." In spite then of the distorted view of education which seems to have been general in the Port-Royal schools, we get occasional glimpses of a more spontaneous motherly solicitude for children's needs, a shrewd insight into their weaknesses, and a sanity of method which contrasts strangely with that somewhat morbid other-worldliness which characterises too much of the work of these schools. As Miss Hodgson well remarks: "Jacqueline Pascal if a Port-Royaliste, was also a Frenchwoman[2]."

The result is that in the Port-Royal girls' schools we find a curious combination of severity and kindness. The author of the 'avertissement' which prefaces the Règlement quotes with approval the words of one of the Popes: "Sit rigor, sed non exasperans; sit amor, sed non emolliens"; but this can hardly be said to have been put into practice in the convent schools. Severity there certainly was, but its monotony must surely at times have proved extremely exasperating; love there was also, though it was not of the type which has a weakening effect upon character. The spring of both alike was repression and mortification of the natural passions, however innocent these in themselves might be.

There remain several topics yet to be touched upon in reference to the education of girls at Port-Royal. As in the boys' schools, stress was laid upon good manners. The girls were instructed in the formulae of politeness and taught when and how to bow gracefully. They were encouraged to be clean and neat, without on the other hand giving too great attention to the adornment of the body, "which must one day serve as food for worms." They were not allowed to gossip about their schoolfellows' superiorities or inferiorities, and, like the boys in the Little Schools, were instructed "se prévenir d'honneur l'une

[1] p. 528.   [2] *Studies in Fr. Educ.* p. 85.

l'autre par une sainte civilité." We may take it then that the *tutoiement* was likewise forbidden, for the girls were not allowed upon any pretext whatever to kiss or caress one another; not even were the elder girls permitted to show these signs of affection towards the infants of three and four who were received into the convent. This is but another instance of the attempt to suppress the ordinary and natural affections in the hope of enlarging thereby the individual's devotion towards the Creator.

The question of punishments is one of interest. There seems to have been an earnest desire not to overdo these, and it was recognised by Jacqueline Pascal that continual badgering serves only to accustom children to being chidden, so that punishment —"ce qu'il faut toujours éviter autant qu'on le peut"—loses its force. Nevertheless, when punishment is clearly indicated, it must be administered faithfully, though never in a spirit of anger. In order to avoid the temptation of making untrue excuses, children are first to be punished in silence and then to be asked why they have been punished. This method is obviously open to grievous abuse, though it was reserved for cases in which the mistress was perfectly sure that a fault which deserved the punishment had been committed. Among those offences which were visited with the most rigorous penalties was misbehaviour during the church services or the silences in the schoolroom which coincided with them. Such faults were not reprimanded by the mistress in charge until after the prayers or service was ended, so that children might be the more impressed with the solemnity of the occasion; but "as soon as the office is said they must be punished according to the magnitude of the fault and with greater severity than when prayers are not being offered to God[1]." Bad faults were to be corrected with unvarying regularity in order to emphasise the impression made by the punishment on the offender.

We have already seen that Saint-Cyran classed together misbehaviour in church and lying as worthy of the cane ; in the girls' schools the former offence seems to have been regarded as even more heinous than the latter. It is true, of course, that lying

[1] pp. 482—3.

was a serious misdemeanour in the girls' schools, but we hardly find there the "très grande horreur du mensonge" which Du Fossé tells us characterised the education of the solitaries. "Lying," says Jacqueline Pascal, "is extremely common with small children; we must therefore do all we can to prevent them getting into this bad habit; for this reason I think we should warn them with great kindness in order to get them to confess their faults, telling them that all that they have done is clearly seen, and when they confess of their own accord they should be pardoned or their punishment mitigated[1]." This may perhaps be a wise treatment for girls who are sometimes said to be more prone to the telling of untruths than boys; but one cannot help preferring the solitaries' use of the cane and their very great horror of falsehood to the attitude of the Port-Royal mistresses who regarded lying merely as a "bad habit" which could be expiated by confession.

The punishments in vogue in the girls' schools compare on the whole somewhat unfavourably with those employed by the solitaries. Jacqueline Pascal devotes a chapter to them and the following may be quoted as typical: asking the pardon of the mistress or schoolfellow offended; kissing the feet of the person injured; exclusion from the church services ("il faut surtout prendre garde que la privation d'aller à l'église ne leur soit pas indifférente"); the wearing of placards with the transgression writ large upon them (a similar penance it will be remembered was imposed upon the young David Copperfield and it may be doubted whether this punishment fitted the crime any more successfully at Port-Royal than it did in his case); confessing the fault aloud in the refectory and in the presence of the nuns of the community. These penances merely serve to emphasise the ascetic and conventual nature of the education given to girls at Port-Royal.

The regulations laid down by the *Règlement* and the *Constitutions* for the conduct of the mistresses are merely a somewhat weak reproduction of those already drawn up for schoolmasters by the educational writers among the solitaries. We find the same emphasis on the importance and arduousness

[1] p. 488.

of the teacher's task and the same insistence upon the fact that
strength for carrying it out can only be obtained by absolute
reliance upon God and constant prayer to Him for the children
and the work of educating them. We even find in Jacqueline
Pascal echoes of Saint-Cyran's own expressions, e.g. "il faut
moins parler à elles qu'à Dieu pour elles"; "je répète ici ce que
je ne puis trop dire, et que je ne fais pas assez, qui est de plus
prier que de parler." It is noticeable again that solidarity
among the assistant mistresses and the head mistress is laid
down as an essential, so that there may be no possible inconsistency in the attitude of the teachers towards the taught.

Before leaving the subject of the Port-Royal girls' schools,
some reference must be made to the age and numbers of the
children taught in them. Pupils seem to have been recruited
in a somewhat half-hearted way, and in fact, when the nuns
were deprived of them in 1661, they appear to have been on the
whole more relieved than distressed; "it was," says Besoigne,
"easy to console themselves on their own account because of
the relief which this release procured for them[1]." Still, as a
discipline, the *Constitutions* of the convent ordained that
12 girls under 10 years of age should be received, and that when
they passed this age they might be allowed to stay till their
16th or even their 18th year; a large proportion of them doubtless became postulants. As they passed the age of 10, new
juniors were taken in their place to fill up the requisite number
of 12. Especially welcome were little girls who had lost their
mother, and orphans such as these were often received as early
as their third and fourth year[2]; by their care of these motherless babies, as the Abbess Agnès very beautifully says, the nuns
"will make their virginity fruitful before God, whose spouses
they are, as He is the Father of souls and spirits[3]." These very
small children were not always subjected to all the rigours of
the ordinary *régime* of the girls' schools. Their lessons were

---

[1] Vol. I, p. 177.
[2] The Mlle De Monglat aforementioned was received at the early age of two.
Suppl. au Nécr. (1763), p. 2.
[3] *Constitutions de P.-R.* p. 102.

split up into very short periods interspersed with playtimes, but even here the spirit of severity appears; if they played during a lesson time the mistress in charge said nothing until the end of a period, when, instead of letting the little girls out to play, work began again; " cela les surprend et fait qu'elles se tiennent une autre fois sur leurs gardes."

Taking into account the normal number of 12 children below 10 years of age, the motherless babies (who were probably not counted in this total), and the elder girls who were allowed to stay on till the age of 16 or 18, we should probably arrive at a total number of about 20 pupils in the girls' schools. This is in fact borne out by Besoigne's information that in 1661 21 pupils were ejected from Port-Royal de Paris and 17 from Port-Royal des Champs; again he tells us that when the two houses were finally closed in 1679 they contained together 42 pupils. So that although the Port-Royal girls' schools lasted longer than the boys' schools, they probably never reached the maximum number of the pupils in the Little Schools, and they certainly fell far below them in general importance.

How then are we to explain the admiration with which Racine speaks of the 'excellent education' of the girls' schools? Besoigne uses the same expression. Clemencet says that the 'pensionnaires' were trained 'perfectly well.' Du Fossé, who was himself educated in the Little Schools and his sisters in the girls' schools, joins in the contemporary chorus of praise of these latter. Boileau in 1693 pays homage to the education given in the Port-Royal girls' schools when he says:

> L'Épouse que tu prends, sans tache en sa conduite
> Aux vertus, m'a-t-on dit, dans Port-Royal instruite
> Aux lois de son devoir règle tous ses désirs[1].

The explanation is that the education of girls at Port-Royal was essentially conventual, but it was good of its kind. In comparison with the methods of the Little Schools and of modern girls' schools it suffers greatly, but judged simply and solely from the conventual standpoint it merited the praise which contemporaries gave it. When Sainte-Beuve says: " Certes

---

[1] *Œuvres* (1765), p. 77 (Sat. x).

l'éducation qu'on donnait au dedans de Port-Royal aux jeunes filles avait en son genre autant d'excellence que l'éducation donnée au dehors aux jeunes garçons[1]"—a phrase to which M. Compayré takes exception—the emphasis is obviously on the words "en son genre"; and with this emphasis the statement is absolutely true. The brighter days of Mme De Maintenon and Saint-Cyr had not yet dawned and the idea that women were entitled to an intellectual education was as yet almost unknown in France. They were to receive an education which would fit them either to enter conventual life or to fulfil the ideal which Chrysale sets up in the *Femmes Savantes* :

> Il n'est pas bien honnête et pour beaucoup de causes,
> Qu'une femme étudie et sache tant de choses,
> Former aux bonnes mœurs l'esprit de ses enfants,
> Faire aller son ménage, avoir l'œil sur ses gens,
> Et régler la dépense avec économie
> Doit être son étude et sa philosophie[2].

It was the first of these two aims that the Port-Royal girls' schools set before themselves and there seems every reason to believe that they achieved no small measure of success. They never seriously attempted to prepare their pupils for ordinary domestic life. In this respect useful work was already being done in the east of France by the Ursuline teaching community founded by Anne De Xainctonge in 1606. The plan of education adopted by them was modelled on that of the Jesuits ; but they were un-cloistered and their primary object was to provide free of cost a thorough preparation for domestic life for the daughters of poor parents[3]. The Society of Anne De Xainctonge was then in some respects in advance of the Port-Royal girls' schools, although it is a little difficult to compare the two institutions owing to their differences of aim and organisation. Madame De Maintenon in the latter part of the seventeenth century made a similar endeavour to provide a training for home-life for girls drawn from the higher classes of society. But at

---

[1] Vol. IV, p. 115.   [2] Act II, Sc. vii.

[3] For further details as to this most interesting Teaching Congregation see Morey, *La Vénérable Anne De Xainctonge*, Besançon, 1901. The Society is still in existence and has houses at Oxford and Malvern.

Port-Royal the education given to girls was first and foremost a preparation for the 'religious' life. Any criticism then of the Port-Royal girls' schools tends to involve a criticism of the whole conventual system and this is fortunately outside our province. None the less it remains true that from the strictly educational point of view (and that is the standpoint which the writer endeavours to adopt), the boys' schools have a real and permanent value, while the girls' schools have no more nor less importance than any other good French convent school of the period.

CHAPTER VIII

THE EDUCATIONAL PREDECESSORS AND SUCCESSORS
OF PORT-ROYAL

In order to realise the true significance of the educational work of the Port-Royalists, it must be compared, not with present day methods, but with those in vogue when the Little Schools first came into existence. Hence, before proceeding to deal with the impression which Port-Royal has left upon subsequent education, a short account must first be attempted of the state of contemporary schools and of the standard to which education had already attained; and some estimate must be formed of the extent to which the Port-Royalists were indebted for their educational ideas to their predecessors.

In the history of French education three revivals of learning have been traced. The first dates from the time of Charlemagne and is associated with Alcuin and his palace school. The second connects itself with the name of Peter Abelard and occurs at the end of the eleventh century; it saw the rise of Paris to be an educational centre of European repute and heralded the establishment of the University there. The third took place in the fifteenth and sixteenth centuries and was a phase of that widespread movement known as the Renaissance. Since we are concerned with the state of French education in the seventeenth century the first two of these revivals of learning have only an indirect interest for us; but it will be necessary to estimate what the Renaissance had already done for French education in order to appreciate rightly the services of the Port-Royalists.

The chief educational establishment of the period which lies between the second and third of the three revivals of learning above alluded to, is the University. That of Paris is said to have been founded in the year 1200 and between the beginning of the thirteenth and the end of the fifteenth century no less than fifteen other universities came into existence in France. It must be remembered, however, that these institutions were hardly universities in the modern sense. The regular academic course in arts was begun by boys of 12 or 13 who had been prepared either at home or in one of the grammar schools under ecclesiastical jurisdiction. The mediaeval French university thus gave what was definitely a secondary education ; the degree of licentiate was taken by boys of 15 or 16 and the master's degree half a year later. It was not until the close of the arts course that the student entered the faculty of theology, law, or physic, and there began what would correspond to the modern university career.

The curriculum of the arts faculty was spread over three years ; during the first two Aristotelian Logic was the staple subject of instruction and it was studied by the aid of the commentaries of Porphyry and Boethius. In the last year the *Physics* and *Nicomachean Ethics* were read and a smattering of Mathematics and Astronomy acquired. Logic, then, was the chief subject in the secondary education given by the Universities. But it was not merely a theoretical science; in its applied form as Dialectic it was put into practice by frequent disputations. Vives, who studied at Paris University early in the sixteenth century, tells us : "A boy is set to dispute the first day he goes to school, and bidden to wrangle before he can speak. It is the same in Grammar, in Poetry, in History, in Dialectics, in Rhetoric, in short in every branch of study. Nor is it enough to dispute once or twice a day. They dispute till dinner, after dinner, till supper, after supper....They dispute at home, abroad, at the dinner table, in the bath, at church, in the town, in the country, in public, in private, in all places and at all times[1]."

The influence of the Renaissance made itself felt in France quite a century after it had first manifested itself in Italy. Hence in the first half of the fifteenth century Vittorino Da Feltre was carrying on the work of his school at ' La Giocosa,' at

[1] *De causis corr. art.*, *Œuvres*, Vol. VI, p. 50.

a time when barren scholasticism with its formal disputation still held the field in secondary education in France. But when the power of the new learning began to make itself felt on the northern side of the Alps, there were not wanting those who ventured to criticise the Dialectic of the schoolmen. One of the earliest to do so was Rabelais, and he did not hesitate to turn to ridicule contemporary school methods. In the description of Gargantua's education by 'ung grand docteur sophiste, nommé maistre Thubal Holoferne,' we are told that, after a lengthy preliminary training, the pupil read the *De modis significandi* with a host of commentaries, and, after eighteen years and eleven months of study, knew the book so thoroughly that he could say it backwards, "et prouuoit sus ses doigtz a sa mere, que de modis significandi non erat scientia." The chief reproach hurled at the Dialectic of the Universities by their contemporaries of the early Renaissance in France, is that it was mere eristic, like that of the Athenian sophists who were attacked by Plato. To quote the words which Rabelais puts into the mouth of Thaumaste, the learned Englishman who wished to dispute by signs: "Au reguard de disputer par contention, ie ne le veulx faire; aussi est ce chose trop vile, et le laisse a ces maraulx sophistes lesquelz en leurs disputations ne cherchent verité, mais contradiction et debat[1]." The account given in the chapter which follows this quotation, of the disputation between Thaumaste and Panurge is, according to Tilley[2], "a fair caricature of the whole system. The process is hardly more absurd, the result not a whit more barren than many of the disputations which took place in the Paris schools."

Rabelais was followed by Montaigne in his attack upon scholasticism and the formalism of contemporary school methods. Both alike also condemned the use of the cane and the 'collège' system which characterised the Universities of the period. In 1464 the revenues of a scholarship founded by Louis XI at the 'collège' of Navarre (one of the constituent 'collèges' of the University of Paris) had been set aside for the purchase of a constant supply of rods for the correction of erring students; thus we may gather that corporal punishment was in vogue

---

[1] *Pantagruel*, Bk II, ch. xviii, p. 155.   [2] p. 108.

even in the arts faculty of the Universities. Montaigne, who had gained his experience in the College of Guyenne, at the University of Bordeaux, protests vigorously against the brutality of contemporary school methods—"quelle maniere pour esveiller l'appetit envers leur leçon à ces tendres ames et craintifves, de les y guider d'une tronque effroyable, les mains armees de fouets!" Moreover, this severity of discipline does not seem to have succeeded in maintaining a high standard of morals among those boys who were being educated in the 'collèges' of French universities. "Il n'est rien si gentil que les petits enfants en France," says Montaigne again, "mais, ordinairement, ils trompent l'esperance qu'on en a conceue; i'ay ouy tenir à gents d'entendement que ces collèges, où on les envoye, les abrutissent ainsin[1]." The remedy, prescribed alike by Rabelais and Montaigne, is that children should be educated at home by tutors; but this is obviously not a final and satisfactory solution.

We may gather then that, at the time when the Renaissance dawned over France, secondary education presented many striking defects; chief among them were the formalism of the curriculum, the harshness of the discipline, and the corrupting influences of the boarding school. As has been seen, Rabelais and Montaigne united their protests against this state of affairs and outlined schemes of education which would by pleasant processes develop reason and encourage independent thought, while at the same time safeguarding morals. It is pertinent to ask how far, if at all, their criticisms and suggestions influenced contemporary school practice. It has already been pointed out that the English educational writers of the sixteenth and seventeenth centuries produced very little effect on the school methods of this country, and it remains to be seen if the same fate befell Rabelais and Montaigne in France.

It seems true to say that, although these authors were read with avidity and exercised a considerable influence especially upon the thought of the seventeenth century in France, yet so far as their educational doctrine is concerned each alike was a 'vox voceferantis in deserto.' The reason is not far to seek.

[1] Bk I, ch. xxv.

In the case of Rabelais, men read his book merely for pleasure; they never took *Gargantua* and *Pantagruel* seriously or looked for a deeper truth underlying the broad humour and quaint conceits which enable one still to enjoy 'a jolly chapter of Rabelais.' In his preface the author of *Gargantua* had said: "les matieres icy traictees ne sont tant folastres comme le tiltre au dessus pretendoyt"; but we seldom read prefaces to-day, and perhaps the men of the sixteenth and seventeenth centuries were no more conscientious in this matter than we are. The chapters in *Gargantua* and *Pantagruel* together, which deal with education, are only half-a-dozen or so in number and would be easily overlooked by the ordinary reader. There is another reason why Rabelais had but little influence on the schools of his country; during the seventeenth century secondary education passed to a large extent from the University into the hands of the Teaching Congregations of the Church. In the eyes of these latter Rabelais was a person of no great repute; he had made unrestrained fun of the corruptions and perversions of religion which he found in vogue, and his leanings towards the views of the Reformers must have compromised him considerably. Add to this the fact that his work abounds in coarseness of the broad, straightforward type, and it is easy to see why Rabelais' works were put upon the *Index* and why his educational theories had borne practically no fruit by the fourth decade of the seventeenth century and were perhaps unknown to the Port-Royalists when they began their teaching work.

The general influence of Montaigne was probably greater even than that of Rabelais: to quote M. Émile Faguet: "Every seventeenth century man of letters read his works incessantly and was deeply imbued with their spirit. In all these writers are to be found deep traces, echoes, imitations, and even plagiarisms of Montaigne[1]." But though it is probable that Montaigne made a greater impression upon the education of the time than did Rabelais, yet even in his case the result was small. The reasons are not unlike those already mentioned. Montaigne was read for pleasure rather than for profit; again, his remarks on the subject of education are scattered up and

---

[1] *Camb. Mod. Hist.* Vol. v, p. 64.

down his *Essais*; and even so M. Compayré is obliged to confess: "Il est donc quelque peu malaisé de saisir, à travers les pensées indécises et fugitives du livre des *Essais*, un véritable système d'éducation[1]." Moreover, Montaigne, like Rabelais, incurred the disapproval of the Church and was placed on the *Index*. This was due not to his favouring the Reformers nor to any immodesty in his work, but rather to his religious indifference and his inclinations towards scepticism and agnosticism. A *réchauffé* of the educational doctrines of Montaigne was prepared by his 'plagiarist' (to use Brunetière's word), Charron; and Tabourot in his *Bigarreures* (1648) draws his inspiration from the same source. But we may doubt whether they did much to popularise Montaigne's educational theories and therefore whether his writings had any appreciable influence upon the schools of the time. By educated men of the world he was read and enjoyed; but by the churchmen, under whose control were the schools, he was regarded with suspicion and it was felt that his principles must at all costs be refuted. Their attitude may perhaps be summed up in the words of Pascal: "Montaigne is incomparable for confounding the pride of those who, without faith, boast of true righteousness; for disabusing those who cling to their opinions, and who think they find in the sciences unshaken truths, independently of the existence and perfections of God....He is absolutely pernicious for those who have a leaning towards impiety and vice. Therefore reading him should be regulated with much care, discretion, and regard for the position and morals of those to whom it is recommended[2]." As to those Port-Royalists who concerned themselves especially with the educational work of the community, we have it upon Sainte-Beuve's[3] authority that they show no traces whatever of having been influenced in the slightest degree by Montaigne.

As far as secondary education is concerned, then, the influence of Rabelais and Montaigne had been very small. But their aim had not been purely educational, although one might gather that this was so from a perusal of some of the modern

[1] Vol. I, p. 91. [2] Fontaine, *Mémoires*, Vol. III, p. 80.
[3] Vol. II, p. 421.

histories of education. They were "teachers of genius but teachers by accident"; the real break from the formal education of the Middle Ages was due not to them but rather to Ramus. He was not only a practical teacher and an ardent educational reformer, but he also had the courage to endure an almost continuous persecution and finally to lay down his life for the faith that was in him. It is he, far more than Rabelais or Montaigne, who is responsible for the substitution in French schools of the modern education according to reason for the mediaeval education according to authority. Thus he may well be regarded as being in a real sense the forerunner of the Port-Royalists, and as such he merits our attention.

Ramus did not shrink from carrying war into the enemy's country; the title of the thesis which he presented before the University for the degree of master-in-arts was: *Quaecumque ab Aristotele dicta essent commentitia esse*; and to call in question the inspired word of Aristotle was heresy of the very worst description. This was not merely the temerity of a hot-headed young man—Ramus was only 21 at the time; for he ceased not throughout his life to wage war upon the scholastic formalism which appealed always to authority and discouraged the development of an independent faculty of reason. In the same spirit Ramus condemned the blind imitation of Cicero; it is true that the inane attempt to equal Cicero's style which had become the loftiest ambition of Italian scholars, and which to-day is known as Ciceronianism, never found much favour in France; but to presume to criticise the text of Cicero and the underlying ideas was in the eyes of the University little short of a sacrilege. Ramus was president of the 'collège' of Presles, one of the constituent 'collèges' of the University of Paris; and thus, unlike Rabelais and Montaigne, he was able to put his educational reforms into immediate practice. In spite of the enmity which his innovations aroused, he was appointed, through royal favour, professor of eloquence and philosophy at the Collège de France; in 1562 he presented a plan of reform of the University to the King, and although it was long before some of his suggestions were put into practice, others (including some which affected the faculty of arts) were incorporated in the great reform carried out by Henri IV in 1600. But since the faculty of arts gave a secondary and not a university education, Ramus had at any rate made an attempt to banish scholasticism from the secondary school long before Port-Royal appeared and completed the work.

In many other ways Ramus introduced innovations which proved successful and which were carried on by the Port-Royalists. He did his utmost to popularise the use of the French language for literary purposes and thus he helped forward a movement which culminated in the style of Pascal and the establishment of that wonderful instrument of expressiveness and lucidity—modern French prose. For this reason he wrote his *Dialectic*, which foreshadows the Port-Royal *Logic*, in French; as well as his school-books—the Latin, Greek, and French 'gramères.' These works are the first of their kind in the French language and since they had a wide vogue, their influence in displacing Latin as the medium of teaching and learning must have been considerable. Another reform in which Ramus points the way to Port-Royal is his desire to syllogise about realities rather than about abstractions. Referring to the schoolmen, he says: "They have never regarded their rules but under the shadow of scholastic disputations; they have never brought Logic into the dust and sunshine of everyday use; they have never called it into the conflict of human examples." The same thought appears in the Second Discourse of the Port-Royal *Logic*: "Since the ordinary examples do not show how the art of Logic can be applied to anything useful, they are accustomed to confine Logic to itself, without extending it further[1]." Ramus and the solitaries alike are never so blinded by the merely theoretical as to lose sight of the practical. 'Peu de préceptes, beaucoup d'usage,' is the motto of the grammars of Ramus; and it is quoted with approval by Lancelot in the once famous *Nouvelles Méthodes* which emanated from Port-Royal. In yet another particular Ramus anticipated Arnauld and Pascal, if not the practice of the Little Schools; he regarded the study of Mathematics as worthy of an attention which it never received in the Universities

---

[1] Baynes' trans. p. 16.

of his day; his text-books on Arithmetic and Geometry for long remained classics, while at his death he left a substantial sum for the endowment of a chair of pure and applied Mathematics in the University of Paris.

Ramus then is for us a figure of no small importance; he marks the first successful attempt to break away from mediaeval tradition in French secondary education; and since in several particulars he anticipated the reforms of the Port-Royalists, and he was at the same time well-known at least to some of them, we may conclude that he contributed in some measure to the formation of the educational doctrine which was put into practice in the Little Schools.

In spite of the work of Ramus and the great reform of Henri IV, the University steadily declined during the seventeenth century. In many respects it remained blind to the better way which had been revealed to it and preferred to perpetuate mediaeval methods. Appeal to authority still maintained much of its ancient power; freedom of thought and imagination was discouraged; the use of the vernacular was forbidden; and disputations and formal grammatical exercises still formed the staple of the secondary education given to boys in the faculty of arts. More paralysing than all these was a lack of funds; the faculty of theology alone continued to flourish, but the rest could not afford even to pay their professors regularly.

It was at this juncture that there rose into prominence the Teaching Congregation of the Jesuits, who took the leading part in French secondary education throughout the seventeenth century and who are responsible for the tragic end of the Port-Royal schools. In some ways their methods were still mediaeval and had made no advance upon those of the University; education with them rested not upon reason, as Ramus would have had it, but upon authority; the classics were taught by them more as linguistic than as literature. But their success was due to many causes. Their school methods were far less harsh than those of the Middle Ages and they made a very real attempt to render school-work and school-life pleasant and interesting. Again they possessed a system of organisation, set forth in their *Ratio Studiorum* and *Ratio discendi et docendi*, which embodied some of the best practice of the time and incorporated—so it is said— much of the experience of Sturm in his school at Strasburg. The Jesuits were also indebted to the example of the schools of the Brethren of the Common Life or Hieronymians, whose society had been founded as early as 1384 and was among the first of the teaching institutions north of the Alps to adopt the new learning. In some ways these form an interesting parallel to the Port-Royal schools; the teaching brethren lived in common but were bound by no vows; they opposed scholasticism, favoured the vernacular, gave prominence to the intelligent study of the classics and Hebrew, as well as of the Bible, and—like many of the later Port-Royalists—were inclined towards mysticism. Among their pupils they numbered Erasmus and Thomas à Kempis, and their schools, starting from Deventer, soon spread over the Netherlands, Germany and Northern France. These institutions declined throughout the sixteenth century and were finally superseded by the schools of the Jesuits; but they are worthy of remark because of their points of similarity with Port-Royal and also because it was largely upon their constitution that the organisation of the Jesuit 'collèges' was modelled.

Most important perhaps of all the advantages which the Jesuit schools enjoyed was the fact that instruction in them was not only efficient, but in many cases gratuitous; this gave the Jesuits an enormous advantage over the poverty-stricken University and it is for this reason as much as any other that the former were, during most of the seventeenth century, in the ascendancy. It should be noticed that the reform of the University in 1600 had been carried out by the King—i.e. it was a secular reform; but with the rise of the Jesuits, secondary education passes once more into the hands of the Church. It preserved its ecclesiastical character throughout the seventeenth century, for the work of the Jesuits was shared by the Oratorians and Port-Royalists. It is not until well into the eighteenth century that secular education revived once more under the care of Rollin, and even he is to a great degree inspired by Jansenism.

To a certain extent the educational movement of the Jesuits was a reactionary one, chiefly in that it definitely reverted to the deductive methods of the Middle Ages, and that it tended to crush out individuality and spontaneity in the pupil. It is unlikely then that Port-Royal, with its respect for human reason and its desire to develop every faculty to the fullest, owes much to the Jesuits. As a matter of fact, the two Congregations were bitter enemies and the Jansenist books of the early eighteenth century, at any rate, are full of recriminations against the Society of Jesus. In the earlier Port-Royal educational treatises the Jesuits are hardly ever mentioned, except when reference is made to the moral dangers to boys educated in their 'collèges.'

Our short survey of French secondary education from the Renaissance to the seventeenth century has revealed only one source from which Port-Royal drew inspiration—Peter Ramus. There was, however, another educationalist who was well known to the teachers of the Little Schools and about whom something must be said. This is the Moravian bishop, John Amos Comenius.

As is the case with most of the educationalists of the Protestant reformation, the work of Comenius chiefly influenced the elementary school; but it also left its mark upon secondary education. Comenius was a convinced advocate of education according to reason, of the accommodation of school methods to the pupils' mental capacity, of the use of *Realien* wherever possible in instruction. In all these particulars Port-Royal was at one with him; but since the more important works in which he set forth his educational theories were not published until after the Little Schools had been fully organised and were in complete working order, it is doubtful—as was pointed out in a former chapter—whether Port-Royal is indebted to Comenius to any extent for its general educational doctrine. In one respect, however, the solitaries did draw their inspiration from the school-books of Comenius which were well known to them; the Moravian reformer had insisted upon the use of the vernacular, especially in connection with the teaching of Modern Languages, and in this respect, though with certain modifications as has already been explained in greater detail, the Port-Royalists may be considered as followers of Comenius.

Among the most illustrious of the schools that were contemporary with Port-Royal were those of the Oratorians. The Oratory of Jesus had been founded in 1611 by Cardinal De Bérulle as a seminary for the education of priests only. But, owing to the insistent wishes of Louis XIII, the society devoted its attention more and more to the education of children, chiefly of high rank, and it soon became famous throughout France; ultimately, after the expulsion of the Jesuits in 1762, the Oratorians took over many of their 'collèges' and did much to fill the gap made in French education. Not only was the Oratory a contemporary of Port-Royal but there are many remarkable resemblances between the two teaching institutions. In both alike the masters took no formal vows, and thus afford a contrast to the practice of the Jesuits; their attitude again, unlike that of the Society of Jesus, was distinctly national and Gallican, rather than ultramontane. Both show the influence of Descartes and are opponents of the scholasticism of the Jesuit 'collèges' and the University of Paris. The educational systems of the Oratory and Port-Royal are also in many respects strikingly alike; discipline in both is mild and general teaching methods are based on love rather than fear. They agree again in regarding the aim of education as threefold: the cultivation of the intellect is necessary in order to develop the judgment and this in turn regulates the will and produces moral conduct. Religious zeal, disinterestedness, and devotion to the welfare of the pupil characterise equally the Oratorians and Port-Royalists. More than this, their curricula have much in common: the vernacular is studied for its own sake; Latin is taught as literature rather than as mere language; an important place is given to Greek; and History and Geography are also included in the time-table. In all these respects then there is a noticeable correspondence between the education given in the Little Schools and in those of the Oratory.

The points in which they differ are comparatively unimportant. At Port-Royal French was the medium of instruction throughout; with the Oratorians this was the case only in the teaching of History but with other subjects Latin replaced the vernacular in all classes above the fourth. Again, if we may believe Sainte-Beuve, the instruction given in the Little Schools was on the whole more solid than that of the Oratory; Port-Royal produced scholars like De Tillemont and saints like Du Fossé, but the typical products of the Oratorian schools were 'honnêtes gens,' respectable and competent persons, but not of striking character either intellectually or morally. One may perhaps be permitted to regard Sainte-Beuve's remarks on this head as somewhat exaggerated; on the whole the products of the Oratorian schools will bear comparison with those of the Little Schools, for among their pupils they could count Malebranche; though it should be remembered that the Oratory outlived the expulsion of the Society of Jesus in 1762, while the Port-Royal schools endured for scarcely 14 years. Be this as it may, the education given by the Oratorians in some particulars shows an advance upon that of the Little Schools; for instance, the study of the Sciences and Mathematics was carried to a remarkable length by the Oratory, and included algebra, geometry, plane and spherical trigonometry, analytical geometry and the calculus.

None the less, the resemblance between Port-Royal and the Oratory almost entirely overshadows these points of difference. It cannot possibly be a mere coincidence; but because the two educational institutions were contemporary it is very difficult, if not impossible, to decide exactly how far each borrowed from the other, or to what extent they were indebted to a common source of inspiration. It should be noticed that, although the Oratory was founded in 1611, it was at first merely a theological seminary and its school-work did not begin till later. Still the spread of its educational work was extraordinarily rapid and by 1637, when that of Port-Royal first began, there were more than fifty Oratorian colleges already established; while in 1638 at the bidding of Louis XIII, the Society took over the Collège de Juilly as an academy for the education of children of noble birth.

The Oratory then was in the field well before Port-Royal appeared and we might argue from this that the solitaries owe most of their doctrines to the Oratorians. But these latter did not set to work with a ready-made and inflexible educational code like the Jesuit *Ratio Studiorum*. It was not until 1645 that there appeared their *Ratio Studiorum a magistris et professoribus congregationis Oratorii Domini Jesu observanda*, which dealt with the teaching methods to be adopted in their schools; moreover even this scheme admitted of progress and of improvements based upon the results of experience. But by 1645 the Little Schools were practically launched; Saint-Cyran's educational views had already been worked out and communicated to Lancelot and De Beaupuis. Again, we owe much of our knowledge of the curricula and methods of the Oratorian schools to the works of two of the most eminent of their masters —the *Entretiens sur les Sciences* by Father Lamy[1], and the various *Méthodes* written by Father Thomassin. But of these the former was published in 1683 and the latter between 1681 and 1693—that is to say, long after the Port-Royal schools had ceased to exist. Thus it seems probable that the solitaries owed less than would at first appear to the theories of the Oratorians. It is true that there was friendship between the two societies in the face of their common enemy—the Society of Jesus; and this helped to give rise to the accusation that the Oratory was infected with Jansenism. We may even conjecture that school matters may have sometimes formed a topic of conversation between the solitaries and certain of the Oratorians; but there is a noticeable absence of references to the Oratorian schools in any of the Port-Royal educational authors, and this is the more remarkable in that the solitaries habitually refer to those to whom they are indebted for ideas and suggestions. On the whole then, while acknowledging the extreme probability of an interchange of views and methods between the Oratorian masters and the teaching solitaries, the present writer inclines to a belief that the coincidences between the doctrines and practices of the two societies are also largely due to their being inspired from a common source—namely, Descartes.

---

[1] Lamy was an enthusiastic Cartesian, and on this account was expelled from his chair of Philosophy at Angers. He refers in terms of the highest praise to the Port-Royal *Logic*—of which he compiled an abridgment—and also to the *Nouvelles Méthodes* of Lancelot. See especially *Entretiens sur les Sciences* (1683), p. 55.

The state of French secondary education, therefore, in the
first part of the seventeenth century, at the time when the Port-
Royal schools first came into being, may be summed up as
follows : the University was decadent and retrogressive so far as
secondary education was concerned ; the Jesuits led the way in
this department of education and were brilliantly successful, but
their fundamental principles were still mediaeval ; the Oratorians
had shown in some particulars an advance upon their rivals but
were overshadowed by their success.   The work of Ramus had
as yet left little lasting impression upon the schools of the times,
and that of Comenius was only just beginning to be felt.
Scholasticism was still rampant and mediaeval methods were
still in vogue.   As for the education of girls, it was to a large
extent neglected, and such as did exist was due entirely to the
benevolence of the Church.   It was provided chiefly by convents,
to many of which a small girls' school was attached.   Several
sisterhoods existed, however, which devoted themselves wholly
to the work of teaching.   There were, for instance, the Sisters of
the Christian Doctrine, a branch of the Teaching Congregation
of the 'Doctrinaires' who were founded in 1592 and for at least
two centuries carried on an important educational work, chiefly
in the south of France.   There were also the 'Filles de la
Congrégation de Notre-Dame' who gave gratuitous instruction
in the vernacular, arithmetic, and needlework.   More interesting
were the Ursuline community, founded by Anne De Xainctonge
early in the seventeenth century, whose aim it was to do for girls
what the Jesuits were doing for boys.   It may be objected that all
these are instances of elementary education, whereas our concern
is chiefly with the secondary education of the first part of the
seventeenth century in France.   The answer is that for girls
this type of education was the only one which existed ; and, as
was pointed out in the chapter which dealt with the Port-
Royal girls' schools, virtually no advance upon contemporary
practice was made in them and therefore they are of far less
importance in the history of education than the Little Schools
for boys.

There are two other sources, besides Ramus and to a lesser

extent Comenius, from which Port-Royal drew inspiration, although neither is directly connected with the work of the school. The first of these is S. Augustine. Saint-Cyran, the founder of the Little Schools and the first formulator of the Port-Royal educational theory, had worked out a theology, in company with Jansen, which was based entirely upon the writings of S. Augustine; and, as has already been explained, it is from this theology that the fundamental tenets of the educational doctrines of the Port-Royalists are deduced. At the same time there was another influence at work—that of Descartes.

Descartes followed—probably unconsciously—in the footsteps of Ramus in two respects: in his emphatic assertion of the freedom of the judgment and the supremacy of the reason; and also, as a result of this, in his use of the vernacular for a learned work. But he went further than Ramus in that he applied reason to the central problem of metaphysics and set forth what he considered to be the firm and universal truth underlying all existence. In doing this he did not oppose religion, for his ratiocination lay in a sphere untouched by the doctrines of the Church. As has been well said : " His *Meditations* gave the world what the world had never seen before— proofs of God, freedom and immortality put into language strictly reasoned, but not too hard for average minds to follow. These three things proved, however, Descartes made his bow and departed, leaving the field clear for theology[1]." Unlike Montaigne, therefore, Descartes ran little risk of offending the Port-Royalists by depredations upon the enclosed preserve of orthodoxy. Hence, while the solitaries laid an emphasis upon the gift of grace and the necessity of faith in spiritual matters— subjects upon which the arguments of Descartes had nothing to say—both alike evinced a passionate desire for logical clearness and the spirit of free enquiry in all branches of human knowledge. How far Port-Royal owed this attitude to Descartes is a matter which will be investigated shortly.

The Jansenist theology, which inspired Saint-Cyran, is directly responsible for the educational theories which underlay

---

[1] Viscount S. Cyres in *Camb. Mod. Hist.* Vol. v, p. 72.

the teaching in the Port-Royal schools which he founded. This, being distinctly a theology, did not preclude the additional influence of Descartes; but the mere evidence of dates proves that it is very unlikely that Cartesianism could have entered the Little Schools *viâ* Saint-Cyran. The *Discourse on Method*— the first of Descartes' works—was published at Leyden in 1637, and in May of the following year Saint-Cyran was imprisoned ; he was not set at liberty until February 1643 and died eight months after his release. It seems probable then that Saint-Cyran had never read Descartes—perhaps had never heard of him ; moreover, even if Saint-Cyran had read the *Discourse on Method*, it is probable that he would have regarded it with suspicion, as savouring somewhat of the heresies of the reformers. Sainte-Beuve, indeed, referring to Descartes, speaks of " son génie novateur, mais religieux, qui certes eût donné de l'ombrage à Jansénius ou à Saint-Cyran[1]." We are surely justified in concluding that there is no tincture whatever of Cartesianism in the source from which the fundamental doctrines of Port-Royal education were drawn ; if in any respect the views of Descartes and Saint-Cyran coincide we must regard this as accidental or—most unlikely—due to their both being influenced by some earlier thinker.

The pure spirit of Jansenism then, as typified by Saint-Cyran, had little sympathy with Descartes; and it is from this spirit that the Little Schools drew much of their power. But Saint-Cyran died before the schools were well established and, although they were carried on to the very end according to the tradition which he left behind, they were at the same time influenced by Cartesian theories, introduced by members of the Port-Royal community who, like the famous Dr Arnauld, had departed in some measure from the original Jansenism of Saint-Cyran. In 1652, during the last phase of the wars of the Fronde, the Port-Royalists, in whose hands was the teaching work of the Little Schools, were obliged owing to the disturbances in Paris and the neighbourhood to take refuge at the château of the Duc De Luynes at Vaumurier. During their confinement there frequent discussions on the Cartesian philosophy took

[1] Vol. II, p. 396.

place, for the Duc De Luynes himself had prepared the first French translation of the *Meditations*, which was published in 1647. But the adhesion of Port-Royal to the new doctrines was only partial, for many of its members were true to the spirit of Jansen and Saint-Cyran, and they regarded Descartes with suspicion as a possible enemy to the Faith. De Saci, for instance, upon whom fell not only Saint-Cyran's mantle as director of Port-Royal, but also a double portion of his spirit, is an uncompromising opponent of Cartesianism. While deploring the position of authority which Aristotle had usurped even in religion itself, he regards Descartes as merely another 'tyrant' who is ready to take his place. "He said to me one day," says Fontaine, De Saci's companion and biographer, "that he wondered at the action of God with regard to these new opinions; that M. Descartes was with respect to Aristotle like a robber who came to kill another robber and carry off his booty[1]." Similarly Nicole who was one of the principal masters in the Little Schools says: "Whatever be the eulogies which are bestowed upon M. Descartes' philosophy, it must none the less be recognised that the real result which it achieves is to make it quite clear that those who have spent their lives in philosophising about nature have never had dealings with the world of realities, but merely with dreams and phantoms....If I could live my life again I would take care not to be numbered among the 'décartistes[2].'"

The two Port-Royalists who looked most favourably upon Cartesianism were Lancelot and Dr Arnauld; but of these, the latter had only an indirect influence upon the teaching in the Little Schools and was, as has been already said, not a wholehearted follower of Saint-Cyran. For the influence of Descartes then upon the Port-Royal schools we have to rely chiefly upon Lancelot, who was not only a master in them during the whole time of their existence, but was also the author of some of their most important school-books. To him is due the important innovation of teaching foreign languages directly through the vernacular; but this may well have been inspired by the actual

[1] Fontaine, *Mémoires*, Vol. III, p. 75.
[2] Nicole, *Letters*, Vol. XLII, pp. 290 and 300.

example already set by Ramus, as much as to the somewhat indirect implications of the Cartesian philosophy.

It is in two books—the best-known and perhaps the most important of all those which emanated from Port-Royal—that the influence of Descartes is strongest and most easily traced. These are the *Grammaire générale et raisonnée* and the famous Port-Royal *Logic*. It must be remembered that these are not strictly school-books in the same sense that the *Jardin* or the *Nouvelle Méthode latine* deserves that name; they were prepared rather for those whose secondary education was almost, if not quite, completed. They were neither of them published until after the Port-Royal schools were closed; so that when M. Cadet tells us that "the greatest merit of the Port-Royal *Logic* is to have introduced Cartesianism into teaching[1]," he must be referring not to the teaching in the Little Schools, but to that of the successors of Port-Royal. At the same time, although Dr Arnauld is responsible for the main body of both the *Grammaire générale* and the *Logic*, Lancelot and Nicole also contributed to them; so that the spirit which animates these works may well have left its impress upon the Little Schools, even though the books were published after the schools had ceased to exist. For this reason it will not be out of place at this stage to examine the *Grammaire générale* and the *Logic* and to endeavour to estimate briefly what they owe to Descartes.

The *Grammaire générale et raisonnée*, in spite of its importance and influence, is a small book of some 140 octavo pages of large print. In the *Life* of Dr Arnauld we are told that "it is the result of conversations which M. Lancelot, who was entrusted with the teaching of languages in the Port-Royal schools, had with this great man....M. Lancelot wrote out the answers which M. Arnauld gave to his questions; and thus was composed the first work that went deeply into the art of speaking, and developed the first foundations of the *Logic*[2]." The scope of the work is explained in its title; it seeks to set forth the principles which are common to all languages and the more important differences which exist between them, and at the same time to explain these phenomena. It is in this latter respect that the

---

[1] p. 30.   [2] *Vie de Messire Ant. Arnauld*, Vol. 1, p. 218.

Grammaire générale follows Descartes; just as this philosopher had set aside everything which could admit of doubt in order to discover an ultimate in knowledge and a criterion of truth, so Arnauld in the *Grammaire générale* goes back to the very beginnings of language in order to explain the varied phenomena which it now exhibits. This was a notable achievement in the middle of the seventeenth century, but—judged by modern standards—it was an almost entirely useless one. The beginnings of language as conceived by Arnauld are no less imaginary than the beginnings of political society, as described by Hobbes or Rousseau. The Port-Royal *Grammar* suffered because so little was known at the time of philology and ancient languages; there was a general belief that Hebrew was the source of all other tongues; but the philology of the period, although sometimes ingenious, was essentially uncritical, unhistorical and speculative. The importance of the *Grammaire générale* is that it applied the Cartesian reasoning to a sphere in which Descartes himself had not yet employed it—to the study of language. In every other respect the work of Arnauld and Lancelot has long since been superseded by that of scholars such as Grimm, Humboldt, Bopp, Max Müller, and Skeat.

The Port-Royal *Logic* has a far greater value than the *Grammar*, and for this reason has remained in use down to our own times; in fact the science of Logic in its essentials has made but little progress from the time when it was first put forth in Aristotle's *Organon* until the present. The Port-Royal treatise owes something to the *Dialectic* of Ramus but more to the writings of Descartes. It begins by following the latter in clearly asserting the supremacy of human reason over authority in all branches of secular knowledge. To quote from the Second Discourse which prefaces the *Logic*: "There is nothing contrary to reason in yielding to authority in those sciences which, treating of things above reason, ought to follow another light—and this can only be that of Divine authority. But there is no ground whatever in human sciences, which profess to be founded only on reason, for being enslaved by authority contrary to reason[1]." In this spirit the writers of the *Logic* adopt the four

[1] Baynes' trans. p. 23.

rules which Descartes had laid down for the conduct of the understanding and proceed to examine the various operations of the mind; the treatment of these under the four headings of the Term, the Proposition, the Syllogism, and Method, which are so usually adopted in modern treatises on Logic, dates from the *Logic* of Port-Royal. It is not an extremely profound work, but it is always interesting and full of common sense. At the same time it is practical; it does not confine its attention to chimaeras and the mortality of man, but it brings the science of Logic into the ordinary life of the reader. A random selection of a few of the examples used to illustrate rules, would be sufficient to prove this. The work of the Port-Royalists in the realm of Logic is admirably summed up by Spencer Baynes, the translator of their treatise: "They brought to its examination the same spirit of inquiry and power of analysis, which had been already employed with so much success in other branches of philosophy (e.g. by Descartes in Metaphysics), and the science emerged from their hands in a new and better form[1]." It is in fact the most thoroughly Cartesian of all the writings of the solitaries and yet it had an independence and an originality of its own. As Lantoine points out: "Tout le suc du *Discours de la Méthode* a été exprimé dans ce petit livre....C'était alors malgré la tentative de Ramus (i.e. his *Dialectic*) et même après Descartes une nouveauté[2]."

As has been remarked in a former chapter, the education given at Port-Royal tended to be more moral than intellectual. This is due to the persistence of the Saint-Cyran tradition throughout the history of the Little Schools. There was always a tendency for the theological contribution of Saint-Cyran to outweigh the intellectual contribution of Descartes; and for this reason the pedagogy of Port-Royal never quite loses its stern religious character. But it is in the influences of these two men, which at times conflicted in spite of Descartes' disclaimer of any interference with theological matters, that we may find the explanation of occasional contradictions between the strict educational doctrine of Port-Royal, as deduced from Jansenist theology, and the actual school practice of the teaching solitaries.

[1] Introd. p. xxix.   [2] p. 142.

None the less it remains a fact that much of the direct influence of Descartes, as illustrated in the *Grammaire générale* and the *Logic*, passed by the Little Schools. The chief Cartesian at Port-Royal was Dr Arnauld who was not to any very important extent concerned with the work of the schools. But he is one of the best known of all the Port-Royalists, and the *Logic* is certainly the work by which the community is to-day most generally remembered. The result is that the Port-Royalists are often indiscriminately cited as followers of Descartes and it is inferred from this that their educational doctrines are equally Cartesian. This, as has been shown above, is true only to a certain degree.

The main sources of Port-Royal educational doctrine therefore are threefold: the original spring is the theology of S. Augustine as interpreted by Saint-Cyran, but Peter Ramus and to a greater extent Descartes are responsible for a modification in practice of the crude Jansenist theories. There were, however, many subsidiary sources; for the Port-Royal educational writers made extensive use of their predecessors and were not like certain modern educationalists (e.g. Herbert Spencer[1]) who take upon themselves to write without first reading what has already been said on the subject. The solitaries' debt to Comenius has already been dealt with in some detail; their treatises contain frequent references to Quintilian, the greatest of the classical writers on education since Plato, as well as to the remarks of Cicero and Seneca on this subject; they adopted in its entirety the modified tutorial system which Erasmus had elaborated; Coustel, at any rate, was familiar with the writings of Vives. Lancelot again, when writing his *Nouvelles Méthodes*, made full use of the labours of his predecessors and modestly acknowledges his indebtedness to them. He consulted the writings of Sanctius of Salamanca, of the Dutch scholars Scioppius and Vossius, of Clénard, Budé, and Henri Estienne.

The Port-Royalists, then, were not only practical teachers as

---

[1] He confessed to M. Compayré that the only writer on education with whom he had even the slightest acquaintance was Pestalozzi. See Compayré's monograph on Herbart, p. 88.

well as educational theorists but they were also familiar with the literature of their subject, and this gives an added value to their treatises. At the same time they were not mere plagiarists, for they made an original contribution of the highest importance to the cause of education. In order to sum up the advance which they made upon their contemporaries in the work of teaching, we may say that they put into actual practice in the class-room principles which were only just becoming explicit in the writings of the most advanced thinkers of the time. The power of scholasticism and appeal to authority still held sway throughout French education—in the University, in the 'collèges' of the Jesuits, even to some extent in the schools of the Oratory. But the Port-Royalists broke once and for all with the spirit of mediaevalism ; they applied to teaching those truths which were being disseminated by Descartes on the Continent and by Bacon in England, and by so doing joined in the movement which had already been started by Comenius. How far they were inspired by Descartes and Comenius (they probably knew nothing of Bacon), is another matter and one which has already been considered ; but the fact remains that in their educational doctrines and practice the Port-Royalists were far in advance of any of their contemporary educators in France—not excepting even the Oratorians. They mark in French education the transition from the *régime* of the Middle Ages, which had remained undisturbed in its essential characteristic—that of the supremacy of authority over individual judgment—to the modern spirit of freedom in intellectual matters. It is by this spirit that all their school methods are animated and this explains the remarkable contrast which they exhibit when placed beside those of contemporary schools. In fact almost everything which Pestalozzi said, and which has inspired the reforms which have revived education during the last hundred years, is implicit in the treatises and practice of Port-Royal. Had it not been for the relentless persecution and untimely end of the Little Schools, and the principles inherent in their organisation which would have precluded their permanence, the history of education in Europe might perhaps have been spared the dreary monotony of the eighteenth century—broken only by occasional outbursts of earnest educational activity in France where the smouldering ashes of Port-Royal could not be prevented from bursting into flame.

Having now estimated the extent of the advance which the Port-Royalists made upon their predecessors, it remains for us to discover how far their influence affected subsequent teachers and writers upon education before finally summing up the importance of Port-Royal in the history of this subject.

One of the earliest followers of the solitaries in the sphere of teaching was Rollin, principal of the College of Beauvais and Rector of the University of Paris. He is best known nowadays as the author of an *Ancient History* and of the treatise *De la Manière d'enseigner et d'étudier les belles lettres par rapport à l'esprit et au cœur*—a work which is usually given the shorter title of *Traité des Études*, and which first appeared in 1726. But besides committing his educational doctrines to writing, Rollin by virtue of his position was able to introduce certain reforms into the University itself. He was a personal friend and admirer of Dr Arnauld and a passionate adherent of Jansenism ; and hence he naturally drew inspiration from the work of the teaching solitaries. Still it is only in certain details that Port-Royalism was introduced into the University by Rollin ; the vernacular was no longer excluded ; Latin lost some of its ancient domination ; the explanation of authors came more into vogue ; and on the whole the University henceforth ceases to be influenced by the Jesuit school methods and inclines more towards those of Port-Royal. But the central and dominating feature of education as interpreted by the University remained unaltered and the last remnant of scholasticism held out there with vigour. As Sainte-Beuve points out : "Ce ne fut qu'une partie de la réforme littéraire de Port-Royal qui s'introduisit, et non pas la méthode vraiment philosophique. À cet égard, l'ancienne Université garda ses errements jusqu'à la fin ; elle s'affaiblit, et ne se régénéra pas[1]."

Rollin himself in his own practice and in the *Traité des*

[1] Vol. IV, p. 103.

Études goes much further than the reforms which he succeeded in introducing into the University. In his own classes he put into use Arnauld's *Règlement des Études pour les lettres humaines* and he followed Port-Royal in making little use of set Latin proses and in regarding the vernacular as worthy of study for its own sake. More important still is his conception of the purpose of education, which he defines as 'former l'esprit et le cœur.' Here he unites the intellectual education of Descartes and the moral education of Jansenism which had already been combined in a manner on the whole successful by the masters of the Little Schools. But although this is the case, one rises from a perusal of Rollin's *Traité* with a feeling that there is no advance at all upon the methods of Port-Royal. In some respects Rollin copies the practice of the Little Schools; in others he prefers to be blind to the improvements which the solitaries had introduced. For instance he recommends colloquial Latin and ignores modern languages; he is an ardent partisan of Latin verses; he is willing to teach the pupil all the legends of ancient Greece and Rome, but lays much less stress on the history of his own country. Rollin, then, is after all only a half-hearted follower of Port-Royal, but he does merit our attention because he succeeded in introducing some of the sweetness and light of the Little Schools into the darkness of the University and because his influence upon subsequent educational reforms in France helped indirectly to perpetuate the influence of Port-Royal.

Of all the reforms initiated by the solitaries that which produced the most immediate effect was the introduction of the vernacular into the schools, not only as a medium of instruction but also as a subject worthy of study in itself. It has already been said in a former chapter that the common practice of the period had been to teach reading through the medium of Latin. This was the case even in the elementary schools under the jurisdiction of the Precentor of Notre-Dame; the code issued in 1654 by this official enacts that "before children are put to reading French they must first know how to read Latin well in all sorts of books"—though it goes without saying that the Latin words, even when correctly read, conveyed no meaning whatever to a child at this stage. It was this wide-spread contemporary practice that the Port-Royalists combated so energetically in the sphere more especially of secondary education. As was pointed out on page 46, their example was soon followed by the Jesuits. The University also was before long affected by this reform; even before the time of Rollin, Pourchot, who became Rector in 1692 and who numbered among his pupils Racine's son Louis, had procured the adoption of the text-books of Gaullyer, which were written in French. Pourchot had also introduced Cartesianism into the philosophy syllabus of the University.

In elementary education the French language was employed by S. Jean-Baptiste De La Salle, the founder of the 'Christian Schools.' His regulations are given in the *Conduct of the Schools*— a document which was compiled gradually between 1670 and 1695, but not published till 1720, and which corresponded roughly to the *Ratio Studiorum* of the Jesuits: "The first book in which the children of the Christian Schools shall learn to read shall be filled with all kinds of French syllables....The book in which they shall learn to read in Latin is the Psalter; only those shall learn it who know how to read perfectly in French." In this respect then the practice of the Christian Schools was closely parallel with that of the Port-Royal girls' schools.

S. Jean-Baptiste De La Salle applied Port-Royal's recommendations as to vernacular teaching to the elementary education of very poor children. At the other end of the social scale it was adopted with suitable modifications by the Abbé Fleury, who succeeded Lancelot as tutor to the Princes De Conti. In many respects he is a more thorough-going innovator than the Port-Royalists, for he no longer recognises the classics as the essential basis of a liberal education, but relegates them to the position of "studies of the third degree." But in many respects he obviously draws his original inspiration from the solitaries, with whose work and theories he was well acquainted, and nowhere more so than in his use of the vernacular for teaching purposes. Not only is it to be the medium of instruction, but power of self-expression in French is to be cultivated by the pupil; "let him compose in this language—first narratives, letters, and other easy pieces; then let him write a eulogy upon some great man or a moral essay, which must however be well thought out and free from nonsense or insincere sentiments; he should express seriously his real views[1]." Truly, as Compayré points out, when the Princes De Conti exchanged Lancelot for Fleury they could not have found very much difference in the methods of their new tutor.

The doctrines of the Port-Royalists bore fruit not only in the practice of their immediate successors but also in the educational writings of these latter. It is doubtless true that the work of Port-Royal was merely part of a great progressive movement which was bent on destroying the last remnants of scholasticism and substituting the unquestioned supremacy of reason for that of authority. Nevertheless, to quote the words of Sainte-Beuve: " Que ce soit le Père Jouvanci[2] dans son livre, *Ratio discendi et docendi*, l'abbé Fleury dans son *Traité du Choix et de la Méthode des Études*, le Père Lamy de l'Oratoire dans ses *Entretiens sur les Sciences*...; qu'enfin ce soit Rollin et son *Traité des Études*, je les admets chacun pour sa part et les vénère tous. Seulement Port-Royal a précédé: son influence sur tous ces traités plus ou moins postérieurs est évidente[3]."

The influence of Port-Royal was not confined to French writers on education, for it even affected Locke. There is a passage in his *Thoughts concerning Education* (§ 175) in which he treats of learning by heart and takes up exactly the same attitude upon the question as that of Coustel and Nicole. This might seem to be merely a coincidence; but in a note upon this passage Mr Quick observes: "There are some excellent remarks on learning by heart and against learning 'great parcels of the authors,' in a work certainly known to Locke, as he translated part of it into English, the Port-Royalist Nicole's

---

[1] *Traité du Choix*, p. 242.

[2] Jouvanci or Jouvency was a Jesuit father who published his *Ratio discendi et docendi* in 1711. See also p. 46.

[3] Vol. IV, p. 101.

Pensées. The chapter I refer to is *de l'Éducation d'un Prince*[1]." This quotation suggests that Mr Quick was not very familiar with Nicole's works; for Nicole was not the author of the *Pensées* and the treatise (it can scarcely be properly described as a 'chapter') *de l'Éducation d'un Prince* appears in the second volume of the *Essais de Morale.* Nevertheless it is interesting to know that Locke was familiar with at least one Jansenist educational writer, and perhaps the influence upon him of Port-Royal is not confined to this single matter of learning by heart.

If the Port-Royalists left their impression upon Locke, we might well expect that they would influence Rousseau. In his *Confessions* he has left abundant evidence that he was familiar with some at least of the works of the solitaries. During his studies at what has been called the 'University of Les Charmettes' he applied himself especially to those books "which combined devotion and knowledge"; and he specifies more particularly the works of the Oratory and Port-Royal, which he set himself to "read or rather devour." In another place he tells us that he read the Port-Royal *Logic*; and reference has already been made to his vain attempts to master Latin Grammar from the 'vers ostrogoths' of the *Nouvelle Méthode latine.* But in spite of these references we have no evidence that Rousseau had ever read any of the definitely educational treatises of Port-Royal, unless the *Logic* can be included under this heading. Coustel, Guyot's prefaces, Nicole's *Traité*, and the passages on Saint-Cyran's educational views, given by Fontaine and Lancelot, were probably quite unknown to him and his *Émile* was almost certainly composed quite apart from any direct Jansenist influence. His views on the use of emulation in education are in some ways strikingly like those traditionally ascribed to the Port-Royalists; but there is no positive evidence that he was indebted to them in this particular; and indeed the whole spirit of the *Émile* quite warrants the supposition that he worked out this theory independently. As a matter of fact the educational doctrines of Rousseau are in some points diametrically opposed to those of Port-Royal. He believes in original goodness; they,

[1] p. 234.

in original sin. He advocates a negative education according to Nature; they, a carefully regulated moral and intellectual training. In emphasising the part which the development of the judgment should play in education Port-Royal and Rousseau are in accord; but the author of the *Émile* was more probably influenced by the general spirit of the 'Enlightenment' and the works of Voltaire and Diderot than by the perusal of the Port-Royal *Logic*. While then recognising that Rousseau was familiar with several of the school treatises of the solitaries, we have no evidence at all that his *Émile* owes anything to their general educational theories.

The influence of Port-Royal is more apparent in a contemporary of Rousseau's—Dumarsais, the author of the article on education in the great *Encyclopédie*, which appeared between 1751 and 1772. Dumarsais was brought up by the Oratorians, who, as has been seen, had much in common with Port-Royal; but his chief source of inspiration is from the solitaries and also from Comenius to whom he refers in his article. Like the Port-Royalists he emphasises the value of translation into French and deprecates the too frequent employment of set Latin proses; he advocates careful explanation of authors and the modelling of prose composition upon their style and vocabulary. At the same time he lays too great stress on a feature which Port-Royal had been one of the first to bring into prominence. In his desire to remove unnecessary obstacles from the path of the learner, Dumarsais would banish all difficulties indiscriminately. Port-Royal successfully combined the education according to interest with the education according to effort; but in Dumarsais the latter is almost wholly wanting. In order to facilitate the early stages of learning Latin, he would Frenchify the order of the Latin text and amplify any phrase which is not absolutely clear, quite irrespective of the laws of Latin Grammar. For example, the first stanza of Horace's *Carmen Saeculare*:

> Phoebe sylvarumque potens Diana;
> Lucidum coeli decus, o colendi
> Semper, et culti; date quae precamur
>   Tempore sacro

is treated thus:

O Phoebe, atque Diána   potens   sylvárum
O Phoebus, et Diane   puissante des forêts;
                qui es Déesse

(ô vos)   decus   lúcidum coeli, ô (vos)
ô vous ornement brillant du ciel, ô vous

        colendi   semper, et
qui devez être honorez toujours, et

        culti   semper;   date
qui avez été honorez toujours;   donnez
                        accordez-nous

(ea negotia) quae   précamur
ces choses que   nous prions
            nous vous demandons

(in hoc) témpore sacro[1].
dans ce temps sacré.

The Port-Royalists would have protested against this juggling with the Latin language just as strongly as they protested against the unreasoning use of it to the exclusion of the vernacular, or against the learning of Grammar rules in the barbarous verses of Van Pauteren.

In 1762, the year in which Rousseau's *Émile* was published, the Jesuits, who for more than 150 years had held almost undisputed supremacy in French secondary education, were expelled from France. The reasons for their downfall were numerous and it is no part of our business here to discuss them in great detail. These causes were largely political; the Jesuits, by their powerful organisation and unscrupulous methods, which apparently did not even shrink from attempts upon the lives of the King of Portugal and Louis XV of France, had concerned themselves with every department of society and were making a bold bid for absolute supremacy in the state. They had in fact become a menace to the secular authorities in France. At the same time there was widespread dissatisfaction with the educational methods in vogue in their 'collèges,' and this was a matter of great national importance considering the large

[1] *Œuvres*, Vol. I, p. 47.

share of French education which was in the hands of the Society. No advance had been made upon the *Ratio Studiorum*; formal instruction in the classics still constituted the staple of the curriculum; the French language and French history were almost entirely neglected; corporal punishment was practised in the 'collèges' to a brutalising extent; the masters were often incompetent and inexperienced—"Des jeunes gens, à peine sortis du noviciat, remplissaient les chaires et enseignaient aux autres ce qu'ils eussent dû apprendre eux-mêmes." These then are some of the reasons, pedagogic as well as political, which explain the holding of an enquiry into the methods of the Society. It was conducted by the Parlement of Paris and the provincial Parlements, and the result was the final ejectment of the Jesuits from their 'collèges' and the confiscation of their property in order to recompense their creditors.

It was easier to abolish the system of education of the Jesuits than to supply one more desirable to take its place. The Parlement of Paris accordingly appealed to the provincial Parlements for suggestions as to some general plan of secular education; and the chief interest of these suggestions for us is that they often embody many of the doctrines of Port-Royal and of Rollin, himself a follower of the solitaries. For this reason the expulsion of the Jesuits in 1762 and the constructive educational policy of the French government which ensued, have well been described as the revenge of Port-Royal for the malignant persecution and tragic fate which their educational work had received a hundred years previously at the hands of the Society of Jesus.

Among the projects of reform set forth at this juncture is the *Essai d'éducation nationale* by La Chalotais which was laid before the Parlement of Rennes. Being a plan for national and secular education it differed in a very fundamental respect from the theories of Port-Royal; but it should be remembered that the solitaries, though ecclesiastics, were essentially Gallican and in so far contrasted strongly with the ultramontane tendencies of the Jesuits. In many of the details of his educational proposals, La Chalotais shows the influence of the Port-Royalists, for whom he had a great admiration and whose educational works (e.g. Nicole's *Éducation d'un Prince*) figure among those which he recommends in his *Essai*[1]. He protests against the tyranny of Latin in the schools and pleads for the rehabilitation of the vernacular; the two languages should be set on a footing of equality. La Chalotais regards translation from Latin into French as more important than Latin prose composition—a definitely Port-Royalist doctrine. Like Guyot, he would set children to write only about those matters with which they are perfectly familiar. He even prescribes a study of the *Grammaire générale et raisonnée* as preliminary to the learning of particular languages[2]; though here he seems to be untrue to his own principles which emphasise the importance of proceeding wherever possible from the particular to the general.

Better known and more important than the reforms proposed by La Chalotais are those of Rolland, who in 1768 presented to the Parlement of Paris his *Compte rendu, ou plan d'éducation et de correspondance des universités et des collèges*. The influence of Rollin and of Port-Royal is as obvious in his case as in that of La Chalotais; and although many of his reforms had to wait until the Napoleonic *régime* before they were put into practice, yet they did ultimately come into effect and have not yet ceased to operate. Rolland's *Compte rendu* is divided into two parts, the first of which deals with the internal and external organisation of the various educational institutions, and the second with teaching methods. In the former part there is practically nothing which Rolland could have borrowed from Port-Royal, but in the second part he is less original and as M. Compayré says: "Jusque dans les nouveautés qu'il y propose, c'est à l'esprit de Port-Royal que Rolland obéit[3]." He makes the usual appeal for a regular and systematic study of French; he recommends a larger use of 'versions' and the oral explanation of authors; he advocates the study of History, both ancient and modern. In the study of Philosophy, which is to form part of a higher education, Rolland appears to fall behind the Port-Royalists in that he recommends scholasticism; but the reason he gives for this is one of which the solitaries would

---

[1] E.g. on pp. 35, 53, 101, 128.   [2] *De l'Éducation publique* (1762), p. 80.
[3] Vol. II, p. 230.

have approved, even if they had regarded it as quite inapplicable to the case in point : " The precision of scholastic methods," says Rolland, "contributes in no small measure to the formation of the judgment and to learning how to reason." And it is because he recognises the importance of these two elements in a complete education that he speaks in the highest terms of the value of the Port-Royal *Logic*.

The Parlements of 1762 then, in their constructive efforts to replace the educational system of the Jesuits, "took up again, not without enthusiasm, the interrupted work of Jansenism." The year 1762 does indeed mark the triumph of Port-Royal ; the seed which the Jesuits had trampled into the ground had germinated and brought forth fruit. The solitaries had given all their energies to combat scholasticism ; and now after a hundred years their efforts were to be rewarded. For, in spite of the amiable weakness of Rolland above recorded, the formal education of the Middle Ages received its quietus in the expulsion of the Jesuits in 1762 ; and although no constructive educational policy could be satisfactorily accomplished during the years of unrest which led up to the Revolution and the ' Sturm und Drang Periode' of the last years of the eighteenth century, yet when the new educational system arose in France under the *ægis* of Napoleon, we find it utterly purged of linguistic formalism and scholastic methods, such as still persisted in some of the most famous and influential secondary schools of this country for at least another sixty years.

The educational proposals which were set forward in the course of the years preceding the Revolution and during the Revolution itself seem in many ways to be the very reverse of those advocated by Port-Royal. The aim of education according to the solitaries was the development of judgment and the power to reason in the individual and to ensure, as far as might be, his eternal salvation ; in the educational ideas of the latter part of the eighteenth century man is a πολιτικὸν ζῷον and nothing more ; his τέλος is to serve the State. Questions of morals and intellect, so far as they refer more especially to the individual, take a subordinate place. This view is especially characteristic of Talleyrand, and the 'rapports' presented to the Convention in 1792 and 1793. In yet another respect the educational ideas of the Revolutionary period are the very antithesis of those of Port-Royal. Teaching is no longer regarded as the work of the Church, but must be secularised; and again education is now considered to be the right of all members of the community—a view which would have little commended itself to Saint-Cyran and the rest of the Port-Royalists.

In spite of the many proposals set forward there was hardly a commensurate constructive activity; but, after the storms of the Revolution were past and the Napoleonic era had begun, there was set up a complete system of public education, characterised by excessive centralisation; and this marks the beginning of the modern French secondary school system. The most important features of this scheme are concerned with the external organisation of the various educational institutions and therefore have nothing in common with the doctrines or experience of the Port-Royalists. It is none the less noticeable that the curriculum of the lycées established under the 'décret' of 1808—in spite of the marked tendency of the Revolutionary educationalists to give chief prominence to Science and Mathematics—reverts to the old *régime*; Latin and French run parallel in the lower classes, Greek is introduced in the second school year, and a modicum of History and Geography is included. In short, if we leave out of account religious instruction, we have come back once more to the curriculum of Port-Royal with practically no modifications. The inspiration of the Little Schools and the solitaries was almost certainly not a direct one, but it was none the less real in that it was probably derived through the medium of Rollin. In spite, then, of the turmoil of the Revolution, the peaceful spirit of Port-Royal had not yet ceased to operate; it still lived in the person of Royer-Collard[1] the great French statesman of the early nineteenth century who was himself descended from a family closely connected with Port-Royal, and whom Sainte-Beuve calls " l'élève...de l'esprit de Port-Royal."[2]

[1] See Philippe, *Royer-Collard; sa vie, etc.* p. 11.

[2] Very appropriately the rue Saint Dominique d'Enfer has been renamed the 'rue Royer-Collard.' *op. cit.* p. 304.

The influence of Port-Royal can be traced through the nineteenth century in various reports, proposals, and laws relating more especially to secondary education in France. In the report presented by Villemain in 1843 the original attitude of Saint-Cyran and the solitaries once more appears; secondary education is to be confined to those who are preparing for the "learned professions, for great intellectual accomplishments, and for the principal occupations of society[1]"; and Villemain sums up his plan of secondary education by saying: "Fundamentally it is the system of Port-Royal[2]." In 1850 again there was published in Paris a tract entitled "Idées sur l'éducation par un professeur de philosophie[3]." It reproduces to quite a remarkable extent the theories of the solitaries upon education: e.g. a limited 'internat catholique'; the admission only of children of good morals and the exclusion of those likely to have a bad influence; distrust of the theatre; a very important place to be given to religious instruction; mildness of discipline; emphasis on moral as opposed to intellectual education. Many of these recommendations are such as might be made by any ecclesiastic; but their combination in this tract would be most unlikely had not the author been inspired by Port-Royal.

M. Compayré goes so far as to say that the Port-Royalists, and to a lesser degree the Oratorians, are the inspiration of all those who in modern France propose improvements in secondary education; "pour ne citer qu'un exemple," he continues, "il est impossible de ne pas remarquer que la circulaire ministérielle du 25 septembre 1872 est allée chercher dans les livres jansénistes l'inspiration de la plupart de ses critiques et la substance de ses projets de réforme[4]." As an example of the criticisms contained in this 'Bulletin administratif' and inspired by Port-Royal, we may take the complaint that too much stress is laid on Latin prose and verse composition, and that too little care is given to teaching pupils how to acquire the power of writing clearly and simply in their native language. The 1872 Bulletin adopts exactly the attitude of the Little Schools on the subject of Latin

[1] p. 5.   [2] p. 8.
[3] See " French Tracts relating to Education ; 1830—1852," in the British Museum.
[4] Vol. I, p. 241.

verses: "This type of exercise takes a great deal of the time of promising pupils; it is a barren waste of time for the rest. The advantage gained is not proportionate to the effort expended[1]." It was not until the programme of 1890 that Latin composition was at last given that place in the French secondary school curriculum which Port-Royal had advocated more than 200 years before; and the classics at last began to be taught for the sake, above all, of reading—a proposal to be found in Coustel's *Règles de l'éducation* and in Arnauld's *Règlement des Études*.

[1] p. 579.

CHAPTER IX

CONCLUSION

IN spite of the apparent failure of the Little Schools and notwithstanding the many vicissitudes of French education from the middle of the seventeenth century down to the present day, it is evident that the influence of Port-Royal has not ceased to be felt. As has been shown, it can be traced in the writings of French educationalists and in the laws and proposals of the French government during the last two centuries; but it can also be detected in another and no less important sphere—that of the school-books which emanated from Port-Royal. Some reference to their influence has already been made in Chapter V, and it is not necessary to repeat it here. Let it merely be remembered that Lancelot's *Méthodes* were for at least a century regarded as among the best works of their kind extant[1], and were translated into several foreign languages; that the *Logic* was translated into Latin and English soon after it first appeared and into Spanish and Italian in the course of the eighteenth century, and that it remains to this day one of the best short treatises on this subject. It is more than probable that in many of the old-fashioned grammar schools of this country the school-books of Port-Royal were in use until well into the nineteenth century, while in France—as has been seen—at least one of them has recently appeared in a revised edition, in spite of its suppression by a ministerial decree of 1863.

But in addition to the laws and school-books which have been influenced by or owe their origin to Port-Royal, the tradition of their methods still persists in the French secondary schools; the emphasis on the mother-tongue, the study of Latin

The *Méthode latine* was used by Péréfixe in the education of Louis XIV.

and French hand in hand, the recognition of the unique value of
Latin translation for giving command over the vernacular, the
employment of the classics as literature to be read and enjoyed
rather than as linguistic to be anatomised and labelled, the
inclusion of Modern Languages in the curriculum, and the belief
that History and Geography must form an essential part of a
liberal education—all these, though to-day common-places, were
unknown before Port-Royal and to a large extent owe their
origin to the initiative of the teaching solitaries.

To Port-Royal then France owes the conception of an education both wide and deep. The range of interests displayed by
the pupils in the Little Schools struck many contemporaries.
Dr Sainte-Beuve[1], a close friend of the solitaries tells us how he
had tested some of the pupils of less than 16 or 17 years old
and was astonished at their "vast and immense knowledge of
all kinds of things, of all the countries of the world and all
the periods of history, so that they were able to converse
pleasantly with every kind of person, to understand all kinds of
affairs and even to take part in them[2]." This is a type of pupil
that some of our modern schools have hardly yet succeeded in
producing. And it is noteworthy that the typical pupil of the
Little Schools was not of the flashy order that knows a little of
many things, but all things badly. The aim of Port-Royal was
always to develop solid intellectual power, to impart the capacity
for independent thought, and with all this to train the morals
by means of a code resting not on convention or prescription,
but on real personal conviction. There was ever among the
solitaries an unfaltering pursuit of Cartesian clearness in every
department of knowledge, and at the same time an intense moral
earnestness and deep piety; and these characteristics, intellectual
and ethical, are nowhere more apparent than in their educational
doctrines and practice.

Again, their theories are based on a thorough knowledge of
children; they had no elaborate psychology and were content
to adopt the faculty-theories of Aristotle; but at the same time

[1] Not to be confused with his illustrious nineteenth century namesake, the
historian of Port-Royal.
[2] See Carré, p. 28 note.

their tutorial system had given them unique opportunities for child-study and they had made full use of these. We have indeed in their writings the germs of modern genetic psychology as applied to teaching, the Pestalozzian doctrine of *Anschauung*, and even an adumbration of Froebel's employment of play in the education of young children.

Yet with all this the Port-Royal schools could never have been permanent, for they contained within themselves the germs of premature decay, and the persecutions of the Jesuits merely prevented these germs from developing. At the same time this fact affords no palliation for the conduct of the Society of Jesus in respect to the Little Schools. The tutorial system of the solitaries was essentially of very limited application; it was extremely expensive, inasmuch as its cost was comparable to that of education at one of our modern English front-rank public schools, and was therefore necessarily reserved for the favoured few. Anything like a universal education could never have been carried out along the lines laid down by Port-Royal. We have in the Tabourin schools an instance of how little some of the methods of the solitaries could be employed in an under-staffed elementary school.

Not only is Port-Royal's tutorial system impossible on a large scale, but its success in the Little Schools was largely due to the character of the teaching solitaries themselves. It was the unique good fortune of the Port-Royal schools to possess a staff which, all things considered, was one not only of extraordinary brilliance but also of absolute devotion to the work of education. It would be difficult to find in all history, before or since, a school which numbered among its masters at the same time a Nicole, a Lancelot, a Coustel, a De Beaupuis, and which could avail itself of the help or advice of a Dr Arnauld, a De Saci, a Le Maître and a Pascal. Moreover, the influence which the Port-Royal masters had over their pupils took the form of a close and personal intimacy, since each class consisted of not more than five or six boys. For this reason again the education given by the solitaries could never have been carried out on a large scale; nor could it ever have been made permanent, for not even Port-Royal itself could have maintained a supply of masters comparable with those with whom we are familiar. It is extremely improbable that a second generation of teachers could have carried on the work of De Beaupuis and his staff with undiminished glory. As M. Carré well observes: "Il fallait pour les écoles de Port-Royal des apôtres, et tous les temps n'en produisent pas[1]."

This being the case, it is really fortunate for the reputation of the Little Schools that their life was so short and that no opportunity was offered for the extension of their teaching work. Within the limits set to their activity and in circumstances which are little likely to occur again, their educational methods were possible and successful and it is to this fact that their glory is in some measure due. But if the experience of Port-Royal is of value only under these unique conditions, it has no bearing whatever on our modern educational problems, when schools are large and often understaffed with quite ordinary teachers. Fortunately this is not the case; both in their particular teaching methods and in their general educational theory the Port-Royalists may with advantage be studied to-day, and even when they point us to what must be under existing conditions an unrealisable ideal, we as schoolmasters should be among the foremost of mankind to recognise the value of ideals in shaping our ordinary and every-day life. Methods, which work well in small classes of four or five, may be suggestive, even if not rigidly applicable, in the case of large forms and under modern school conditions; views, which to-day seem old-fashioned and belong to an intellectual and religious outlook to which we are not accustomed, may none the less contain for us an inspiration which will take effect in our own teaching.

Setting aside then the question of particular teaching methods and curricula, wherein many schools of the present day might even yet copy the Little Schools with advantage, let us consider whether there are any particular points of the Port-Royalist educational doctrine which bear upon modern problems. There are at least two of these, and the latter is to a large extent

[1] p. xxxiii.

the outcome of the former: firstly the fact that the ultimate aim of the school should be to develop not intellect but character, and secondly the fact that reciprocal affection should be the basis of the teaching relationship.

The solitaries realised implicitly what modern psychology teaches us—that ideas affect the direction of the will and that character is a 'completely fashioned will.' Thus they saw that the way to train character was, as far as possible, to give their pupils only such ideas as were desirable with this end in view. But they knew far too much about boys to jump to the conclusion that character can best be trained by giving ideas of the direct moral instruction type—that is to say, formal lessons on specific virtues. In spite of their Jansenist austerity and strong religious bias, the solitaries would never have approved of the moral instruction syllabuses which have been put forward of late years and which have now largely taken the place of religious instruction in French schools. They would have recognised that a mass of improbable anecdotes about little boys of superhuman goodness, interspersed with tags of the Moody and Sankey order[1], are quite likely to have a positively bad influence upon a child, because he is thereby led to associate all moral teaching with this sickly stuff. The solitaries well knew what 'contrariant ideas' were, although they had never read Mr Keatinge's stimulating book on *Suggestion in Education*; Nicole lays it down that children should learn all the precepts of morality without knowing that there is such a thing or that one ever had the idea of instructing them in it.

The method adopted by the solitaries as a means for moral education was twofold: the indirect influence of the ordinary class subjects and the more general effects of environment both in and out of school. In teaching the usual subjects of the school curriculum, the solitaries never neglected an opportunity of introducing moral instruction as it were by accident, *à propos* of something which had arisen in the ordinary work of the form. This method had a preventive as well as a positive side, as is shown by the great emphasis always laid by Port-Royal on the

[1] E.g. the Moral Instruction syllabus issued a few years ago by the Leicester Education Committee.

careful expurgation of texts to be read in class. In both these cases we have yet something to learn from the solitaries; there is a tendency nowadays either, as was above remarked, to give formal and direct moral lessons as part of the school curriculum, or on the other hand to regard moral education as outside the province of the school and therefore to make no provision for it. Some of the best educational theorists and practitioners of the present time and of past ages concur as to the falsity of both of these views.

Again it may perhaps be questioned whether sufficient care is always exercised nowadays in the choice of books put into the hands of children by school authorities. There is, for instance, a tendency to prescribe most unsuitable passages from the Old Testament for study in class, merely because they form part of the Bible. In the choice of classical authors again the criterion seems often to be too exclusively language or history ; the present writer at the age of 16 was set to read some not very judicious selections from Martial and a complete and unexpurgated Teubner text of Suetonius. It is of course easy to overdo expurgation and probably Port-Royal erred on this side. But it seems equally unwise to put the unrevised works of certain Roman Empire authors into the hands of adolescents ; there is surely a *media quaedam via* along which safety lies.

The formative influences of environment were regarded by the Port-Royalists as of first importance in moral training. Judged from a modern standpoint they carried this side of the question to an enervating degree ; they curbed and controlled the environment of their pupils to such an extent as to produce a kind of hot-house education which would be neither possible nor, perhaps, desirable to-day. Under modern conditions when the pupils of the day schools of our big cities are inevitably exposed to influences of every sort, evil as well as good, over which the school can have no control, and when even the pupils of our boarding-schools spend several months of the year among conditions which the school has no power whatever to regulate, the cloistered seclusion of the Little Schools is impossible. But it should be remembered that Port-Royal used this hot-house type of education only as a means to an end ; the child must be isolated from the infection of evil until he is strong enough to resist it of himself; he must be protected until his own developed judgment is able to triumph over the depraved inclinations of the natural man and to choose the right path unfalteringly and consistently. The whole problem is as acute to-day as it was in the time of Port-Royal, and the extreme measures adopted by the solitaries may perhaps be justified by the fact that society under Louis XIV was more openly and militantly corrupt than it is at present. But we have still to solve the problem as to how far we should attempt to regulate the formative influences brought to bear on our pupils by their general environment. The matter is one which cannot now be so summarily settled as it was by the solitaries. The absence of an undisputed national religion, the wishes of the parents, the claims of the State, have all entered in to complicate the problem ; so that now it needs to be reconsidered in the case of almost every individual pupil. But, none the less, a critical though not unsympathetic study of the doctrine and experience of the Port-Royalists cannot fail to be of value in an attempt to settle how far the indiscriminate influences of the world at large should be allowed to have free play in the moulding of a character which is to be at once independent and self-reliant and at the same time beyond reproach as regards morality.

The question of school-environment involved at Port-Royal —as indeed it must always involve—the character and personality of the teacher. The solitaries never lost sight of the immense importance of teaching ; they never forgot that a boy will be in the future to a large extent what his teachers make of him. This is as true to-day as ever it was. The unique worth of the individual soul, the fact that a nation's hope lies in its children, the power of education as an instrument for social and moral progress—all these have not lost in force with the flight of time. And they all imply—what the solitaries recognised so clearly— that no profession is more really a vocation, involving a definite ‘call’ and a special ‘grace’ (as Saint-Cyran would have said), than that of the teacher. Schoolmastering tends too often to be the last hope of those who have either wasted their time at the University or have failed in the Indian Civil Service examination, or a convenient means of making a livelihood while reading for Holy Orders or the Bar; or, finally, the obvious solution for those whose days at the University are ended and who find it difficult to decide upon a career. It will not be until the pay and prospects of the teaching profession in this country are made commensurate with its dignity and importance, and until —as Coustel advocated—some form of professional training is made indispensable, that our schools will be staffed by the best products of the Universities—men who, at the same time, will be teachers by conviction and not by accident or misfortune. Would that the views of Port-Royal on these subjects were more widely held amongst us to-day!

One more aspect of Port-Royal educational doctrine and practice must be briefly touched upon in estimating their value for the present generation. The solitaries were unanimous in basing their teaching upon affection. The education which preceded and was contemporary with the Little Schools said: "Make your pupil fear you and then he will do what you tell him." Port-Royal on the contrary with one accord said: "Be 'keen on boys,' win their confidence, and when you have once gained their affection you can straightway lead them wherever you wish." Morever, the solitaries were among the first European educationalists to adopt this attitude which through the writings and influence of Pestalozzi has recently become popular amongst us, although the old-fashioned education according to fear is even yet rife in some quarters. Accordingly, they were also among the first to abolish the brutalising discipline which made Comenius call contemporary schools "terrors for boys, shambles of young intellects." They exercised all their ingenuity in making the process of learning as far as might be pleasant and easy; for they recognised that there is always enough in the school curriculum to exercise the will and to make education a discipline, without adding artificial obstacles by bad methods of teaching. The Port-Royalists would have been entirely in accord with those modern reformed methods of teaching, which seek where possible to make the process of learning an interesting and pleasant one for the pupil. They had too profound an affection for boys and too deep a sense of the infinite importance of education to be content that school-life should be associated with a dull grind which would leave none but painful recollections in the mind of the pupil when he had escaped from its thraldom.

The influence of Port-Royal in education must not then be judged by the evidence of the pathetic ruins which still stand in that deserted valley near Chevreuse. To the contemporary observer the destruction of the schools in 1660 must have seemed complete and irremediable. But, as with Christianity itself, this apparent failure was the beginning of a triumph far beyond the dreams of those who witnessed it. Port-Royal being dead yet speaketh. Its influence is still at work and its writings may still be a source of inspiration to those who are willing to receive it. The services which the solitaries performed in the study of the vernacular, in the reformed teaching of the classics, and in the extension of the curriculum have left a deep impression on the history of education; but, more than all this, their intense moral earnestness, their recognition of responsibility, their devout humility, their whole-hearted devotion to the cause of education, their unfeigned love of children—all these have left behind a sweet savour which can never pass away. And in these respects those of us who have still to carry on the great work of educating the young will do well to follow in the footsteps of the teaching solitaries of the Little Schools.

APPENDIX A

ON THE DATE OF THE DESTRUCTION OF THE PORT-ROYAL BOYS' SCHOOLS

A CAREFUL reading of a few of the histories of Port-Royal which have appeared from the early eighteenth century down to our own time will soon reveal the fact that there is among their authors a remarkable discrepancy as to the date of the final closing of the boys' schools and the dispersion of the solitaries. Accounts, which otherwise agree in minute detail, seem to favour the years 1660 and 1661 with considerable impartiality. Among modern authors Sainte-Beuve (*Port-Royal*, Vol. III, p. 477 and Vol. IV, pp. 109 ff.) gives the date as March 10, *1660*; Compayré (*Histoire des doctrines de l'Éducation en France*, Vol. I, p. 242) *1660*; Cadet (*L'Éducation à Port-Royal*, p. 19) *1661*; Monroe (*History of Education*, p. 430) *1661*; Miss Hodgson (*Studies in French Education*, p. 59) *1661*; Adamson (*Pioneers of Modern Education*, p. xx) *1661*; Carré (*Pédagogues de Port-Royal*), with a characteristic slipshodness which mars an otherwise useful book, gives March *1661* on p. xiv and Lent *1660* on p. 261; Beard also appears to fall into the same confusion in his first volume—contrast Vol. I, p. 304 and p. 326; but in Vol. II, p. 137 he clearly says March 10, *1660*. Mrs Romanes (*Story of Port-Royal*, p. 287) gives March *1660*.

Since then modern opinion is almost equally divided on this question, recourse must be had to the original authorities, in order to discover the facts of the matter. Here the evidence is overwhelmingly in favour of *1660*. In the small *Supplément au Nécrologe* (1761), p. 38, we read: "M. De Beaupuis en (des écoles) eut toujours la direction jusqu'à leur entière destruction en *1660*"; and on p. 12 (*à propos* of Coustel): "forcé de quitter cet emploi en *1660* que ces écoles furent détruites." Again in the small *Nécrologe* (1760) on p. 292 we read: "après la destruction de ces Écoles en *1660*"; and in the big *Supplément* (1735), p. 370: "les petites Écoles ne purent subsister long-tems. Dès 1656 une descente que le Lieutenant-Civil fit au Chesnai et aux Granges donna l'allarme. M. De Beaupuis seul resta ferme au Chesnai et fit encore pendant quatre ans tête à l'orage avec la moindre partie de son petit troupeau, que les allarmes causées par la visite avoient beaucoup diminué. Mais au *mois de Mars 1660* on fut forcé par les ordres de la Cour d'abandonner absolument le projet de l'éducation des Enfans." So also we find in Clémencet's *Histoire Générale de Port-Royal* (1756), Vol. IV, p. 25: "Nous avons vû de quelle manière on attaqua dès l'an 1656 ces écoles chrétiennes et comment on dispersa une grande partie des enfans, dont MM. de Port-Royal avoient soin et que l'on avoit mis aux Granges, soit à Vaumurier, soit à Magny, soit aux Trous, soit au Chesnay. Mais en *1660* tout fut absolument détruit. Le *10 de Mars de cette année* le Lieutenant civil fit encore, par un nouvel ordre, une visite à Port-Royal des champs, aux Troux[1], et au Chesnay, pour examiner si on n'y avait pas rassemblé de petites écoles, et pour les détruire." It may be added that *1660* is the date given in the *Life of Lancelot* which prefaces his *Vie de Saint-Cyran* (1738—no pagination to preface); and in the *Vies des Amis de Port-Royal* (1751), p. 117; also in the *Vies choisies des MM. de Port-Royal* (Poulain, Vol. IV, pp. 143, 186), and in a short history of Port-Royal prefaced to a *Manuel des Pèlerins de Port-Royal des Champs* (1767). Again the *Mémoires sur la vie de M. Walon De Beaupuis* (1751) gives *1660*, and Du Fossé's *Mémoires pour servir à l'histoire de Port-Royal* more definitely specifies Lent *1660*. It is true that in the 'Table Chronologique' on p. xxij of the small *Nécrologe*, the date *1662* is given for the destruction of the schools and the driving out of the solitaries, but its position in the table shows that it is an obvious misprint for 1660.

It would seem well-established, therefore, that the Port-Royal boys' schools were dispersed on *March 10, 1660*. This is the evidence of the *Nécrologes* which are really contemporary

---

[1] There is here a note to the effect that Angélique De S. Jean says that in *1660* there were no longer any children to be found at Les Troux except those of M. De Bagnols.

documents (see note p. 31) and it is followed by the best modern authorities such as Sainte-Beuve. How comes it then that the 1661 date has gained such wide acceptance, especially among modern educational historians in France, England, and America alike? Its origin is to be found in Tronchay's *Abrégé de l'Histoire de Port-Royal* (1710); the passage (p. xxij) is as follows: " Le lieutenant-civil retourna le 10 May 1661 à Port-Royal des champs et en chassa les enfans qui étoient encore dans des Villages circonvoisins aux Troux et au Chesnay. La perte de Port-Royal fut résolue dans le Conseil du Roy le mercredi-saint, 13 Avril de l'année suivante. On voit assez à la sollicitation de qui on prenoit ces violens desseins par la proximité des fêtes où l'on en faisoit la résolution. Le lieu-tenant-civil alla le vendredi de Pâques 23 Avril faire sortir toutes les Pensionnaires (i.e. girl-boarders) de Port-Royal de Paris. On chargea de la même expédition un Commissaire pour la maison de Port-Royal des Champs et il l'executa le lendemain 24 Avril." It goes on to say that on May 6 the lieutenant-civil turned out four boarders from Port-Royal des Champs; while on May 13 he unfrocked at Port-Royal de Paris the last seven novices and turned them out together with all the postulants.

The use of the phrase 'l'année *suivante*' in the second sentence of the above quotation suggests that '1661' at the beginning of the passage is a misprint for *1660*; for we have abundant and indisputable evidence from many sources in-cluding a large number of contemporary letters written by the Abbess Angélique, that the events above referred to as taking place during 'l'année *suivante*,' happened in *1661*. Moreover 'Mars' in a written manuscript of the early eighteenth century might easily have been mistaken by the printer for 'May'—the contemporary form of the modern French 'Mai'—owing to the custom of prolonging the bottom of the cursive 's' into a kind of tail. Again April 13 actually *was* Wednesday in Holy Week in the year 1661, though if the 13th fell on a Wednesday the 23rd would obviously fall on a Saturday and not 'vendredi de Pâques' as Tronchay says. However, his dates will in no way whatever suit the year 1662, in which Easter Day fell on April 9. His phrase 'l'année suivante' must therefore refer to 1661 and the date of the destruction of the schools, taking place in the year previous, must be 1660 and not 1661 as he says. Even Tronchay's evidence then when critically investigated points to *1660* as being the right date and 'May 10' may be either a misprint or a mistake for 'March 10.'

Tronchay has apparently been followed by Besoigne in his *Histoire de Port-Royal* (1752), Vol. I, p. 406; a somewhat lengthy quotation will be necessary here, in order to get the facts into the chronological order which he gives: "Le lieutenant Civil d'Aubrai fut envoyé par la Cour le 23 Avril 1661 pour ordonner de faire sortir dans 3 jours toutes les pensionnaires (i.e. girl-boarders) qu'on élevoit dans la maison et toutes les postulantes. Un Commissaire du Châtelet fut chargé dans le même tems d'une pareille expédition pour Port-Royal des Champs. La perte de cette Communauté avoit été résolue le Mercredi-Saint, 13 Avril....Dans le mois du Mai suivant, le même Lieutenant-Civil muni des Ordres de la Cour, alla au Chênai et aux Troux, pour dissiper les petites écoles qu'on y tenoit et qu'on y avoit transférées de Port-Royal lors de la première expédition qui s'étoit faite en 1656. Il fit celle-ci avec éclat....Le maison du Chesnai appartenoit à M. de Bernieres, Maître des Requêtes, dont il a déjà été parlé....Le petite Communauté qui étoit au Chesnai, consistoit en deux Précepteurs et sept enfans, deux fils de M. de Bernieres, un de leurs cousins, et quatre enfans de quelques-uns de ses amis : le reste étoit les domestiques de la maison et les gens de la Ferme. Ces Officiers entrérent, trouvérent les sept enfans occupés à leurs petits exercices, et furent même témoins de quelque répétition que leurs maîtres leur firent faire devant ces Messieurs. Après quoi ceux-ci firent commandement aux deux Précepteurs de sortir sur le champ et de s'en aller à Paris, et donnérent 24 heures aux domestiques pour avertir les parens et faire retirer les enfans. Un Commissaire du Châtelet demeura pour achever de faire exécuter l'ordonnance.

"De là ces Messieurs allérent à Port-Royal des Champs et vinrent d'abord aux Granges, où ils ne trouvérent rien du tout

...(except a M. Charles[1]; then they visited Port-Royal itself and found only D'Andilly and his son)....Le lendemain ces Messieurs partirent pour les Troux....Ils ne firent pas meilleure capture aux Troux. Il ne s'y trouva que les deux enfans de M. de Bagnols, qui étoient les maîtres de la maison, et qui y demeuroient avec le Précepteur que M. leur pere leur avoit donné avant que de mourir: Ainsi ils laissérent les choses dans l'état où ils les avoient trouvées. Revenons à Port-Royal de Paris....Le quatriéme Mai le Lieutenant-Civil revint à Port-Royal avec une Lettre de cachet par laquelle le Roi ordonnoit d'ôter l'habit à ces sept derniéres Novices et de les faire sortir avec toutes les Postulantes; faisant défense aux Religieuses de recevoir des filles, ni de leur faire prendre l'habit. Le lendemain pareil message à Port-Royal des Champs."

It is obvious from the above extract that Besoigne refers to a visit by the lieutenant-civil to Le Chesnai, Les Granges and Les Trous—i.e. the site of the three principal school groups— and the driving out of those masters and pupils who still remained after the partial dispersion of 1656; and that he definitely and deliberately gives May 1661 as the date of these events. This cannot be explained away on the hypothesis of a misprint as in the case of Tronchay.

The chronology as given by Besoigne is as follows:

Death of Mazarin	March, 1661
Royal order to destroy Port-Royal	April 13, 1661
Dispersion of Girls' Schools	April 23, 1661
Dispersion of Novices and Postulants	May 4 and 5, 1661
Dispersion of Boys' Schools	May 10[2], 1661

The chronology to be gathered from all the other sources quoted above, is as follows:

Dispersion of Boys' Schools	March 10, 1660
Death of Mazarin	March 9, 1661
Royal order to destroy Port-Royal	April 13, 1661
Dispersion of Girls' Schools	April 23, 1661
Dispersion of Novices and Postulants	May 4 and 5, 1661

[1] His real name was Charles Du Chemin, but he was always called 'M. Charles' at Port-Royal—see the *Vies choisies de MM. de Port-Royal* in Vol. IV of Poulain's *Nouvelle Hist. Abr. de Port-Royal* (1786), p. 50.

[2] The day of the month is not given by Besoigne, but is supplied from Tronchay.

As will be seen, the date of the dispersion of the boys' schools is the only one on which any doubt exists. How then can Besoigne's variation, which has been almost exclusively followed by present-day educational historians, be explained?

One hypothesis is that Besoigne followed Tronchay uncritically; it is true that they both give May 1661 as the date, but, as has been pointed out, the use of the phrase 'année suivante' by Tronchay suggests a misprint of 1661 for 1660 and of 'May' for 'Mars.' Also the account of the boys' school dispersion comes strangely out of its chronological order in Tronchay if May 10, 1661, really is what he intended to write.

Another hypothesis is that Besoigne does not mention the visit to the boys' schools on March 10, 1660, but that he gives instead an account of a second visit in 1661 by the lieutenant-civil to the places where the groups had been held, in order to make sure that his orders of the previous year had been thoroughly carried into effect. This might seem to be supported by the latter part of the quotation from Besoigne and the use of the word 'encore' in the first sentence of the passage from Tronchay. There are several objections to this and together they seem fatal. Firstly, the comparative desolation of the schools when the lieutenant-civil visited them, obviously dates from his previous visit in 1656. Secondly, there is not the slightest suggestion of a second visit in 1661 to Le Chesnai, etc. in any of those Port-Royal histories which record the dispersion of the groups by the lieutenant-civil on March 10, 1660. And, finally, many of the events given by Besoigne as happening in May 1661 are recorded in the other histories as taking place either in 1656 (e.g. the finding of M. Charles at Les Granges— see Sainte-Beuve, Vol. III, p. 169) or on March 10, 1660 (e.g. the detail about the two children of De Bagnols, who had died in 1657, at Les Trous).

There is yet one other hypothesis; it may be that Besoigne and Tronchay are wrong merely in the month (i.e. 'May' for 'Mars') but in giving the year they follow the new-style chronology, which had been adopted in France in 1564, while the other authorities adhere to the old Roman calendar. This

can be paralleled by an event from contemporary history.   The
Pope had issued a bull—'In eminenti'—against the *Augustinus*
of Jansen.   His followers (to quote Jervis' *History of the Church
of France*, Vol. I, p. 387) "pretended that it could not be genuine
because it professed to be issued at Rome on the 6th of March,
1641, whereas the copy despatched to Brussels by the Nuncio
at Cologne was dated 1642.   This arose simply from the
difference between the old and the new calendars as to the
time of commencing the year.   The ancient computation, according to which the year began on the Feast of the Annunciation,
March 25, was in use at Rome, and therefore the 6th of March
fell within the year 1641 ; but the Nuncio, writing from Cologne,
had followed the modern almanac which of course reckoned the
whole of that month in 1642." Similarly Besoigne and Tronchay
may have used the new calendar which made March 10 fall
within 1661, while other authorities put it in the year 1660
according to the old Roman reckoning.   But surely it is
extremely improbable that these two alone of all the Port-
Royal authorities should have used the calendar which already
had been in vogue in France for over 100 years; and, even
thus, their giving the month as May and not as March still
needs explanation.

All things, then, considered, the first of our three hypotheses
seems, to the writer at any rate, the most plausible.   Besoigne
was apparently led away by a misprint or a mistake in Tronchay,
and has aggravated the error by investing it with such a wealth
of detail that it possesses a verisimilitude.   There is another
matter that may have contributed to his making this mistake.
We have abundant evidence that the *girls'* schools were closed
on April 23, 1661 (e.g. Racine, *Histoire de Port-Royal*, pp. 71 and
74 ; *Relations*, pp. 1, 2 ; small *Nécrologe* (1760), p. xxij—Table
Chronologique—where '1761' is an obvious misprint for '1661';
also many of Angélique's contemporary letters—e.g. Vol. III,
p. 527, Letter MXXXI).   Even Besoigne himself (Vol. I, p. 412)
gives a list of 'pensionnaires' who were pupils at Port-Royal
and who were turned out in April 1661 ; and in his *Chronologie
des principaux événements de Port-Royal* he never mentions the
boys' schools, but under the date 1661 gives : "Novices et

pensionnaires chassées de Port-Royal par le Cour." In May of the same year the remnant of the novices and all the postulants were also driven out. It may be quite possible that Besoigne did not clearly enough distinguish between the girls' schools and the boys' schools. He gives in his preface a list of the authorities which he used in preparing his history, and in addition to Tronchay he mentions several sources in which the date March 10, 1660, is clearly cited. It may well be that, when using these, he carelessly took the word 'écoles' to denote the boys' schools when it properly concerned the girls' schools, and thus understood the date 1661 to refer to the destruction of the former and not of the latter. This, coupled with the obvious mistake in Tronchay and the knowledge that most of the persecutions of the nuns of Port-Royal, in whom Besoigne is primarily interested, took place in 1661 and not in 1660, probably led him to put the destruction of the boys' schools and dispersion of the solitaries in 1661 also; but enough has been said to prove that this date is beyond doubt wrong. Curiously enough, no writer hitherto seems to have noticed that any discrepancy on this subject exists among the authorities; and still more remarkable is the fact that Compayré is apparently the only modern educational historian of note who follows Sainte-Beuve and the majority of the original authorities and who therefore gives the correct date—1660.

APPENDIX B

BIBLIOGRAPHY

N.B. The dates given in the following lists refer not necessarily to first editions, but to those editions copies of which were consulted by the writer and which are quoted in the references. The date and place of publication are given in every case in which this information was specified on the title page of the book. The lists are not intended to be an exhaustive statement of the authorities which have been used.

I. ORIGINAL PORT-ROYAL AUTHORITIES

(A) For the History of the Little Schools

Nécrologe de l'Abbaye de Notre-Dame de Port-Royal des Champs. Amsterdam, 1723.

Supplément au Nécrologe de l'Abbaye de Notre-Dame de Port-Royal des Champs. Paris, 1735.

Nécrologe des plus célèbres Défenseurs et Confesseurs de la Vérité des dix-septième et dix-huitième Siècles. 1760. [This *Nécrologe* consists of seven volumes, of which the last three are entitled *Supplément*, and were published in 1761.]

Tronchay: Abrégé de l'Histoire de Port-Royal. Paris, 1710.

Besoigne: Histoire de Port-Royal. Cologne, 1752.

Clémencet: Histoire générale de Port-Royal. Amsterdam, 1756.

Guilbert: Mémoires historiques et chronologiques sur l'Abbaye de Port-Royal des Champs. Utrecht, 1755—9.

Racine: Histoire abrégée de Port-Royal. Vienne and Paris, 1767.

Poullain: Nouvelle Histoire abrégée de l'Abbaye de Port-Royal. 1786. [The first part of this work is not based on any original documents, but is merely a *réchauffé* of the histories of Besoigne, Clémencet and Racine. It cannot therefore be reckoned as an independent authority so far as the schools are concerned.]

Fontaine: Mémoires sur MM. de Port-Royal. Cologne, 1738.

Du Fossé: Mémoires pour servir à l'Histoire de Port-Royal. Utrecht, 1739.

Recueil de plusieurs pièces pour servir à l'Histoire de Port-Royal. Utrecht, 1740.

Mémoires et Relations sur ce qui est passé à Port-Royal des Champs. Amsterdam, 1716.

Manuel des Pèlerins de Port-Royal des Champs. "Au Désert," 1767.

Lancelot: Mémoires touchans la Vie de M. De Saint-Cyran. Cologne, 1738.

Lettres Chrestiennes et Spirituelles de Messire Jean Du Vergier De Hauranne, Abbé de Saint-Cyran. 1648. There is also a larger collection, published at Paris in 1744, which contains the letters which Saint-Cyran wrote to his little niece ; see p. 13.

Vies des Amis de Port-Royal. Utrecht, 1751.

Mémoires sur la Vie de M. Walon De Beaupuis. Utrecht, 1751.

Vie de M. Nicole. Liège, 1767.

Vie de Messire Antoine Arnauld. Cologne, 1695.

Vie de M. Le Nain De Tillemont. Cologne, 1711.

Relation de Plusieurs Circonstances de la Vie de M. Hamon. 1734.

Vies intéressantes des Religieuses de Port-Royal. Utrecht, 1750.

Vie de la Rev^de Mère Angélique. 1737.

Lettres de la Mère Angélique. Utrecht, 1742—44.

(B) For Port-Royal Educational Theory and Practice

Coustel: Les Règles de l'Éducation des Enfans. Paris, 1687.

Walon De Beaupuis: Règlement des Écoles de Port-Royal. This is given both in the *Supplément au Nécrologe* (1735), p. 58, and in Fontaine's *Mémoires* (1738), p. cxviii.

De Sainte-Marthe: An account of the educational ideas and practices of Saint-Cyran, written by M. De Sainte-Marthe, a Port-Royal solitary, and addressed to a certain M. Chamillard, is to be found in the *Supplément au Nécrologe* (1735), p. 49.

Dr Arnauld: Mémoire sur le Règlement des Études dans les Lettres humaines. Œuvres (Paris and Lausanne, 1780), Vol. XLI, pp. 85—98.

Le Maître: Règles de la Traduction française. This is included in Fontaine's *Mémoires* (1738).

Nicole: Traité de l'Éducation d'un Prince. Essais de Morale (Paris, 1714), Vol. II.

Lancelot: Letter to De Saci on the Education of the Princes De Conti. This is given in the *Supplément au Nécrologe* (1735), p. 161.

Lancelot: Prefaces to his school-books (see below).

Guyot: Prefaces to his school-books (see below).

Agnès Arnauld: Les Constitutions du Monastère de Port-Royal. Mons, 1665.

Jacqueline Pascal: Règlement pour les enfans de Port-Royal. This is bound up with Mère Agnès' *Constitutions*.

Jacqueline Pascal: Letter to her brother, Blaise Pascal, dated Oct. 26th, 1655.

Varet: Éducation Chrestienne des Enfans. Brussels, 1669.

(C) Port-Royal School-Books

Lancelot: Nouvelle Méthode pour apprendre facilement et en peu de temps la Langue latine. Paris, 1681.

Lancelot: Nouvelle Méthode pour apprendre facilement la Langue grecque. Paris, 1655.

Lancelot: Le Jardin des Racines grecques mises en vers françois. Paris, 1664.

Lancelot: Nouvelle Méthode pour apprendre facilement et en peu de temps la Langue espagnole. Paris, 1660.

Lancelot: Nouvelle Méthode pour apprendre facilement et en peu de temps la Langue italienne. Paris, 1660.

Lancelot: Quatre Traitéz de Poësies latine, françoise, italienne et espagnole. Paris, 1663.

Arnauld and Lancelot: Grammaire générale et raisonnée, contenant les fondements de l'Art de Parler. 1660.

Arnauld and Nicole: La Logique ou l'Art de Penser. 1662.

Arnauld: Nouveaux Éléments de Géométrie. 1667.

The following is a list of the more important "Versions" prepared by the solitaries:—

Guyot: Nouvelle Traduction des Captifs de Plaute. 1666.

Guyot: Lettres morales et politiques de Cicéron à son amy Attique. Paris, 1666.

Guyot: Nouvelle Traduction d'un nouveau Recueil des plus belles Lettres que Cicéron escrit à ses amis. Paris, 1666.

Guyot: Billets que Cicéron a escrit (*sic*) tant à ses amis communs qu'à Attique son amy particulier. Paris, 1668.

Guyot: Lettre politique de Cicéron à son frère Quintus, et le Songe de Scipion. Paris, 1670.

De Saci: Les Fables de Phèdre. 1647.

De Saci: Comédies de Térence. 1647.

De Saci: Traduction des quatrième et sixième Livres de l'Énéide de Virgile. 1666.

De Saci(?): Traduction des Lettres de Bongars. 1668.

Coustel: Traduction des Paradoxes de Cicéron. 1666.

De Brienne: Traduction des quatres premiers Livres de l'Énéide de Virgile. 1666.

Nouvelle Traduction des Bucoliques de Virgile. (? author.) 1666.

Nouvelle Traduction des Géorgiques de Virgile. (? author.) 1678.

Nicole and Lancelot: Epigrammatum Delectus, cum Dissertatione de vera Pulchritudine et adumbrata. "In usum Scholae Etonensis," 1686.

Les Fleurs morales et épigrammatiques tant des anciens que des nouveaux
Auteurs. 1669. This is a selection, with translations, from the *Epigrammatum Delectus*, which was first published in 1659.

N.B. In addition to the above school-books, a number of
theological and devotional works and translations were prepared
by the solitaries for use in the boys' and girls' schools.

II. NON-PORT-ROYAL AUTHORITIES

Erasmus: Christiani Matrimonii Institutio. Basel, 1526.
Rabelais: Œuvres. Charpentier reprint. Paris, 1856.
Montaigne: Essais. Dent reprint of Florio's Translation. London, 1897.
Vives: Opera Omnia. Valencia, 1782—90.
Comenius: Opera Omnia Didactica. Amsterdam, 1657.
Comenius: Janua Linguarum Reserata. Lissa, 1631.
Comenius: Orbis Pictus. Nuremberg, 1658.
Despauterii Grammatica. 1528.
Despauterius Novus. La Flèche, 1650.
Ratio atque Institutio Studiorum Societatis Jesu. Rome, 1606.
Ascham: Scholemaster. Cassell reprint. London, 1909.
Brinsley: Ludus Literarius or the Grammar Schoole. London, 1612.
Locke: Some Thoughts concerning Education. Quick's edition. Cam-
bridge, 1902.
Descartes: Meditations and Discourse on Method. Veitch's edition.
Edinburgh, 1902.
Pascal: Provinciales et Pensées. Flammarion reprints. Paris, N. D.
Rollin: De la manière d'enseigner et d'étudier les belles lettres, par
rapport à l'esprit et au cœur. (Commonly known as *Traité des
études*.) Amsterdam, 1745.
Fleury: Traité du Choix et de la Méthode des Études. Paris, 1686.
La Chalotais: Essai d'Éducation Nationale. Geneva, 1763.
Rolland: Compte rendu, ou Plan d'Éducation. Paris, 1783.
Dumarsais: Œuvres. Paris, 1797.
Rousseau: Confessions. Garnier reprint. Paris, 1875.

III. SOME OF THE MORE MODERN WORKS CONSULTED

Sainte-Beuve: Port-Royal. Paris, 1908.
Carré: Les Pédagogues de Port-Royal[1]. Paris, 1887.
Cadet: L'Éducation à Port-Royal[1]. Paris, 1887.

[1] These books consist of extracts reprinted from various Port-Royalist writers on
education, together with introductions and notes supplied by the editors.

Hallays : Le Pèlerinage de Port-Royal. Paris, 1909. This book originally appeared as a series of articles published during 1908 in the Feuilleton of the *Journal des Débats*.

Séché : Les Derniers Jansénistes. Paris, 1891.

Beard : Port-Royal. London, 1861.

American Journal of Education, 1878 ; Article on the Port-Royal Schools. This article is taken almost directly from Beard (see above).

Rea : The Enthusiasts of Port-Royal. London, 1912.

Romanes : The Story of Port-Royal. London, 1907.

Théry : Histoire de l'Éducation en France. Paris, 1861.

Compayré : Histoire des Doctrines de l'Éducation en France. Paris, 1904.

Monroe : Text-book in the History of Education. London, 1907.

von Raumer : Geschichte der Pädagogik. Stuttgart, 1857.

Hodgson : Studies in French Education. Cambridge, 1908.

Farrington : French Secondary Schools. London, 1910.

Lantoine : Histoire de l'enseignement secondaire en France au XVIIme et au début du XVIIIme siècle. Paris, 1874.

Bréchillet-Jourdain : Histoire de l'Université de Paris. Paris, 1862—66.

Desmaze : L'Université de Paris. Paris, 1876. This book consists of a collection of Documents, Acts, Registers, 'Pièces Justificatives,' &c., relating to the University of Paris.

Crétineau-Joly : Histoire de la Compagnie de Jésus. Paris, 1859.

Rochemonteix : Un Collège de Jésuites aux XVIIe et XVIIIe siècles. Le Mans, 1889.

Perraud : L'Oratoire de France au XVIIe et au XIXe siècle. Paris, 1865.

Waddington-Kastus : Ramus ; sa vie, ses écrits, et ses opinions. Paris, 1855.

Woodward : Erasmus concerning Education. Cambridge, 1904.

Woodward : Vittorino da Feltre and other Humanist Educators. Cambridge, 1904.

Keatinge : The Great Didactic of Comenius. London, 1896.

Morey : La Vénérable Anne De Xainctonge. Besançon, 1901.

Laurie : Educational Opinion from the Renaissance. Cambridge, 1905.

Adamson : Pioneers of Modern Education. Cambridge, 1905.

Norwood and Hope : The Higher Education of Boys in England. London, 1909.

Cambridge Modern History : Vol. v, "The Age of Louis XIV." Cambridge, 1908.

Jervis : History of the Church of France. London, 1872.

Brunetière : Études Critiques. Vol. IV, "Jansénistes et Cartésiens." Paris, 1880.

Tilley : The Literature of the French Renaissance. Cambridge, 1885.

Lodge : Richelieu. London, 1908.

Hassall : Mazarin. London, 1903.

Hassall : Louis XIV. New York, 1895.

APPENDIX C

CHRONOLOGICAL TABLE

Date	Port-Royal Events	Other Educational Events	Literary, Scientific and Religious Events	Political Events	
1598				Edict of Nantes.	1598
1599	Angélique first nominated Abbess of Port-Royal.	Jesuits' *Ratio Studiorum* issued in its final form.			
1600		Henri IV reforms the University of Paris.			
1605			Bacon's *Advancement of Learning*.		1605
1607	Angélique's conversion; she begins to reform Port-Royal.				
1608					
1610				Death of Henri IV.	1610
1611		Foundation of Oratorian Order.			
1612	S. Cyran and Jansen studying theology together at Louvain.	Ratke's Report to German Diet at Frankfort. Brinsley's *Ludus Literarius*. Ratke at Augsburg.			
1614					
1615					
1616			Shakespeare died.		
1618				Outbreak of Thirty Years' War.	1618
1620	S. Cyran introduced to Mère Angélique by D'Andilly.		Bacon's *Novum Organum*.		1620
1625	Nicole born.				

Year	Port-Royal	Education	General
1626	Community removes to Paris (Port-Royal de Paris).		
1628			Capture of La Rochelle.
1631		The *Janua Linguarum* of Comenius. Locke born. Ratke died.	
1632			
1635	S. Cyran introduced into Port-Royal as "director."		
1636	Beginning of educational work of Port-Royal.		Corneille's *Le Cid.* Descartes' *Discourse on Method.*
1637			Desmarets' *Les Visionnaires.* Richelieu founds the Academy.
1638	Lancelot enters Port-Royal. S. Cyran arrested; school driven to Port-Royal des Champs and thence to La Ferté Milon.	Establishment of Oratorian Collège de Juilly.	
1639	School returns to Port-Royal des Champs.		
1640		Busby at Westminster.	Posthumous publication of Jansen's *Augustinus.*
1642		De Condren's (Oratorian) *Méthode Latine.*	Death of Richelieu. Mazarin becomes First Minister.
1643	S. Cyran released (Feb. 6). S. Cyran died (Oct. 11).		Arnauld's *De la Fréquente Communion.* Corneille's *Polyeucte.*

Date	Port-Royal Events	Other Educational Events	Literary, Scientific and Religious Events	Political Events
1644	Schools dispersed to Le Chesnai. Walon De Beaupuis enters Port-Royal. Lancelot's *Méthode latine.*	Milton's *Tractate on Education.*		
1646	Schools removed to Paris (rue S. Dominique) and organised. Nicole, Guyot, Coustel, Fontaine and D'Andilly enter Port-Royal.			
1648	Arnauld becomes "confessor" to nuns of Port-Royal.			Peace of Westphalia. End of Thirty Years' War. (1648)
1649	Schools dispersed into the three groups.	Dury's *Reformed School.*	Condemnation of the Five Propositions by the Sorbonne. Descartes died.	Wars of the Fronde. (1649–53)
1651		Jean Baptiste De La Salle born.		
1652	Jacqueline Pascal enters Port-Royal.			
1653			Innocent X declares the Five Propositions heretical.	
1655	Blaise Pascal enters Port-Royal. Racine becomes a pupil at the Little Schools. Lancelot's *Méthode grecque.*			

Year	Port-Royal and educational events	General intellectual / scientific events	Literary and religious works	Political events
1656	(March 24) Miracle of the Holy Thorn. (March 30) Dispersion of Schools.		Pascal's *Provincial Letters*. (1656–7)	
1657	Lancelot's *Jardin des Racines grecques*. (Christmas) Death of Mazarin's nephew in a Jesuit College.			
1658		Comenius' *Orbis Pictus* and *Great Didactic* (Latin version).		
1659	(March 10) Final Dispersion of Schools.		Molière's *Les Précieuses ridicules*.	
1660	Lancelot's *Grammaire Générale*. Dispersion of novices and postulants.			
1661	The Port-Royal *Logic*.	Rollin born.		Death of Mazarin; beginning of personal rule of Louis XIV.
1662	Port-Royal girls' schools restored.	Royal Society of London founded.		
1664			Racine's *Le Thébaïde*.	
1666			Molière's *Misanthrope*.	
1667			Racine's *Andromaque*.	
1669			Peace of the Church.	
1670	Nicole's *Traité de l'Éducation d'un Prince*.	Comenius died.	Pascal's *Pensées*.	
1671			Bossuet's *Exposition de la Doctrine Catholique*. Nicole's *Essais de Morale*.	
1672	Lancelot resigns tutorship of the Princes De Conti.			
1677			Racine's *Phèdre*.	

Date	Port-Royal Events	Other Educational Events	Literary, Scientific and Religious Events	Political Events
1678	A girls' school founded by Nicole at Troyes.			
1679	Port-Royal girls' schools dispersed by royal order.			
1681		Thomassin's (Oratorian) *Méthode d'étudier et d'enseigner.*		
1684		Foundation of Brethren of the Christian Schools.		
1685				Revocation of Edict of Nantes (1685)
1686		Mme de Maintenon founds Saint-Cyr.		
1687	Coustel's *Règles de l'Éducation des Enfans.*	Fénelon's *De l'Éducation des Filles.*		
1689			Racine's *Esther.* (1689)	
1691			Racine's *Athalie.* (1691)	
1693		Locke's *Thoughts concerning Education.*		
1694	Death of Dr Arnauld in exile at Brussels.			
1695	Death of Nicole and of Lancelot.	De La Salle's *La Conduite des Écoles.*		
1699	Death of Coustel.		Fénelon's *Télémaque.* (1699)	
1704	Death of Walon De Beaupuis.			
1709	Destruction of Abbey of Port-Royal des Champs. Establishment of First Tabourin School.			
1715				Death of Louis XIV. (1715)

INDEX

Abelard, 194
Academy, founded by Richelieu, 119
Adamson (*Pioneers of Modern Education*), 160
Affection, basis of the teaching relationship, 82, 237; in the Girls' Schools, 184
Age of Port-Royal schoolmasters, 80, 81
Age of pupils in the Little Schools, 29; in the Girls' Schools, 190
Agnès, Mère (Jeanne Catherine Arnauld), 9, 170
À Kempis, Thomas, 203
Alcuin, 194
Algorism, 28 note
Anatomy as a school subject, 149
Angélique, Mère (Jacqueline Marie Arnauld), reforms Port-Royal, 7, 8; her friendship for Saint-Cyran, 9; her dread of death, 54
Anne Eugénie De L'Incarnation ('maîtresse des pensionnaires'), 168, 185
Anschauung, anticipated by Port-Royal, 94, 232
Aristotle read at the University, 195; attacked by Ramus, 200; by De Saci, 211
Arithmetic in the Little Schools, 149; in the Girls' Schools, 173, 176
Arnauld, Antoine (père), his quarrel with the Jesuits, 47
—— Dr Antoine, 16, 42; his treatise *De la Fréquente Communion*, 17, 47; his influence on Port-Royal education, 16, 63; as a teacher, 115, 165; his literary style, 120; favours Cartesianism, 210, 211
Art, Port-Royal's attitude towards, 69-71
Arts course at the University, 195
Ascham (*Scholemaster*), quoted or referred to, 1, 2, 58 note, 92 note
Augustine, Saint, his influence on Port-Royal educational theory, 10, 53, 209
Augustinus (Jansen), 14, 16, 39, 52
Authors, classical, read in the Little Schools, 23, 142; complete list of, 136

Authors, rules for explanation of (Coustel), 137

Bacon, his praise of Jesuit schools, 45; unknown to the Port-Royalists, 216
Bagotists (Jesuit sect), 30
Baptism, Jansenist views on, 53, 55, 56
Basil (Capuchin), converts Mère Angélique, 7
Bean, king of the (Epiphany festival), 159
Benedict, Saint, order of, 6, 7, 49 note
Bernard, Saint, 6, 89
'Berne,' la, 41
Bignon, Jérôme (père), 16
—— —— (pupil at the Little Schools), 161, 166
—— Thierri (pupil at the Little Schools), 161, 166
'Black Sisters,' in charge of a girls' school at Troyes, 169
Boccaccio, 110
Boileau, quoted, 191
Books read in the Girls' Schools, 173, 174
Borel (master at the Little Schools), 33, 41, 165
Bossuet, tutor of the Dauphin, 43; his criticism of style of Port-Royalists, 120
Bouhours (Jesuit), his criticism of style of Port-Royalists, 64, 120
Bourgeois, Dr Jean (friend of Port-Royal), 75
Brethren of the Common Life (or Hieronymians), 11, 203
Brinsley (*Ludus Literarius*), quoted or referred to, 1, 2, 108
'Bulletin administratif' (1872), inspired by Port-Royal, 228
Busby, Dr (Headmaster of Westminster), 96

Cadet (*L'Éducation à Port-Royal*), quoted or referred to, 8 note, 121, 169, 212, 239
Calvin, 53

Cane, use of, in 17th century schools, 96, 237; in the Little Schools, 97–99, 100; in the University, 196

Card Games, 158

Carré (*Les Pédagogues de Port-Royal*), quoted or referred to, 15, 25, 35, 83, 103, 138, 139, 142, 175, 233, 239

Chapel at Port-Royal des Champs, description of, 70

Chapelet Secret, Le (Mère Agnès), 9

Charron (follower of Montaigne), 199

Chesnai, Le. *See* Le Chesnai

Chevreuse, site of Port-Royal des Champs, 6, 9, 238

Christ's Hospital, 126

Church services, attendance at, 84; (the Girls' Schools), 178, 180, 181

Cicero, read in the Little Schools, 23, 136; referred to by Port-Royal educational writers, 215

Ciceronianism, 141, 200

Cistercian order, 6, 8, 70 note; costume of, 49 note

Cîteaux, 6, 8

Classes in the Little Schools, size of, 74

Classics, Port-Royal's attitude towards, 64, 65, 86–88; value of, 147; list of authors read in the Little Schools, 136

Clermont (Jesuit 'collège'), 41, 42, 45

Codret (Jesuit), his Latin grammar, 46

'Colloquies,' 109

Comblat (Franciscan), his praise of the singing and reading at Port-Royal, 69, 117

Comenius, quoted or referred to, 42, 63, 95, 96, 108, 111, 128, 129, 204

Common-place books, 138

Compayré (*Histoire des Doctrines de l'Éducation en France*), quoted or referred to, 4, 44 note, 65, 104, 146, 165, 170, 199, 215 note, 220, 225, 228, 239

Composition, Latin, 133; French, 124, 175

'Compte rendu,' in Language teaching, 137

Confession, public, in the Girls' Schools, 178, 179

Congrégation de Notre Dame, Filles de la, 208

Constitution du Monastère de Port-Royal (Mère Agnès), 170

Contes (master at the Little Schools), 32

Convention, the (1792–3), 3, 227

Conversation, rules for (Coustel), 102

Cordier, Mathurin, 107

Corneille, 67, 119

Correction of Latin proses, rules for (Coustel), 140

Coustel (master at the Little Schools), 22, 31, 92, 165; his *Règles de l'éducation des Enfans*, 35; tutor to nephews of Cardinal De Fürstemberg, 42

Curriculum, variety in, 92, 93, 231

Da Feltre, Vittorino, 110, 141, 158, 195

D'Andilly, Robert Arnauld, introduces Saint-Cyran to Port-Royal, 9; his work at Port-Royal des Champs, 95

Daniel (Jesuit), his criticism of Port-Royal translations, 132

Dante, 110

D'Arcy Thompson (*Daydreams of a Schoolmaster*), quoted or referred to, 92, 125

Date of destruction of the Little Schools, 41, 167, 239–246 (Appendix A)

De Bagnols (friend of Port-Royal), 31, 41, 243, 244

De Bascle (master at the Little Schools), 18, 32, 165

De Beaupuis, Walon (master at the Little Schools), 20, 30, 42, 165

De Beauvais, Vincent (*De Institutione Principum*), 43

De Bernières (friend of Port-Royal), 18, 31, 165, 242

De Bérulle, Cardinal (Oratorian), 61, 205

De Bohebert (pupil at the Little Schools), 89

De Buzenval, Bishop of Beauvais (friend of Port-Royal), 40

De Champagne, Philippe (friend of Port-Royal), 70

De Chazé, Mlle (pupil at the Girls' Schools), 172

De Chevreuse, Duc (pupil of Lancelot), 42

De Condren (Oratorian), 112

De Conti, Princes (pupils of Lancelot), 42, 43, 76, 219

De Fürstemberg, Cardinal, 42

De Guémenée, Princesse, 163

De Guivry, Marquis (friend of Port-Royal), 40

De La Ferté-Milon (pupil at the Little Schools), 163

De Lamoignon, Louise Sainte-Praxède (nun at Port Royal), 8 note

De La Potterie (friend of Port-Royal), 40

De La Salle, S. Jean Baptiste, 4, 219

De Longueville, Duchesse (friend of Port-Royal), 48, 169

De Luynes, Duc (friend of Port-Royal), 33, 48, 164, 168; translator of Descartes' *Meditations*, 211

De Maintenon, Madame, 4, 192

De Maistre, Joseph, quoted, 45

De Monglat, Mlle (pupil at the Girls' Schools), 174, 190 note
De Montauban, Duc (pupil at the Little Schools), 163
De Noailles, Cardinal, 49
De Pomponne, Simon Arnauld, Marquis, 132, 162, 169
De Quincey, his reference to the Port-Royal Greek grammar, 144
De Retz, Cardinal, 48
De Rohan, Duc (pupil at the Little Schools), 163
De Saci, 25, 26, 165; his style, 120; his attitude towards Descartes, 211
Descartes, his praise of the Jesuit schools, 45; his influence on Port-Royal education, 57, 66, 113, 207, 209–215; his services to the vernacular, 110
Des Champs (pupil at the Little Schools), 105, 166
De Séricourt (solitary at Port-Royal), 11, 19, 31 note, 95
Despauterius. *See* Van Pauteren
Despauterius Novus, 46 note, 128
—— *Renovatus*, 127
De Tillemont (pupil at the Little Schools), 20, 23, 29, 39, 51, 166; as a historian, 148, 158, 161
De Vallemont (pupil at the Little Schools), 25
De Villeneuve (pupil at the Little Schools), 18, 61, 103, 163, 166
De Xainctonge, Anne (Ursuline), 192, 208
Dialectic in the University, 195
Discipline in the Little Schools, 97–99; in the Girls' Schools, 188, 189
Disputations, 195, 196
Doctrinaires, 208
Dominique d'Enfer, rue S., school in the, 20, 23, 25, 28, 30
Dress of the Port-Royal nuns, 49 note; of the pupils in the Little Schools, 159
Dübner, his criticism of the *Jardin des Racines grecques*, 146
Du Fossé, Gentien Thomas (friend of Port-Royal), 18
—— Pierre Thomas (pupil at the Little Schools), 18, 19, 29, 33, 39, 161, 166
Duguet (Oratorian), 43
Dumarsais, 222
Du Mont (friend of Port-Royal), 39
Dury (*The Reformed School*), 109

'Écoles grandes' and 'écoles petites,' 28
Egger, his criticism of Lancelot's *Méthodes*, 131

Emulation allowed in the Little Schools, 103–106
Entretiens d'Ariste et de Eugène (Bouhours), 64
Environment, educational importance of, 76, 77, 235, 236
Epigrammatum Delectus, 137
Erasmus, quoted or referred to, 43, 58 note, 74, 203, 215
Essais de Morale (Nicole), 54, 221
Etymology at Port-Royal, 145, 146
Eudes De Sully, Bishop of Paris (founder of Port-Royal), 6
Experience in teaching, value of, 80
Expurgation, 86, 87, 235

Falsehoods, horror of, in the Little Schools, 98; in the Girls' Schools, 189
Fees in the Little Schools, 160
Fénélon, tutor of Dauphin, 43
Fleury, Abbé, quoted or referred to, 43, 101, 113, 140, 219
Fontaine (solitary at Port-Royal), 12, 26
France, Church of. *See* Gallican Church
Free composition in Latin, 139; in French, 124; (Girls' Schools), 175
French contribution to education, 1, 3
French language and literature as a school subject, 119, 122; in the Girls' Schools, 174
Fréquente Communion, De la (Dr Arnauld), 16, 17, 19, 21, 39, 47, 53
Frœbel, anticipated by Port-Royal, 92, 232
Fronde, Port-Royal's attitude towards the, 48, 160

Gallican Church, the, 6, 8
Games in the Little Schools, indoor, 153, 158; outdoor, 153, 155, 156; in the Girls' Schools, 177, 179
Garden of the Soul, 175
'Gentleman,' education of the, 101
Geography, 147, 148
Geometry, 149
Gibbon, his use of De Tillemont's *Church History*, 20
'Giocosa, La' (Vittorino Da Feltre's school), 195
Girls, education of, in France (17th century), 192, 208
Girls' Schools of Port-Royal, history of the, 6, 7, 8, 14, 37, 42, 168; revived after the destruction of Port-Royal, 49; description and criticism of the education given in them, 84, 167–193
Goury (master in the Tabourin Schools), 50
'Goûter,' 153, 180, 182

Grace, doctrine of, 53-55, 57, 60
'Gramères' (Ramus), 201
Grammaire générale, 16, 21, 114; criticism of, 212; recommended by La Chalotais, 225
Granges, Les. *See* Les Granges
Great Didactic (Comenius), 112, 129
Greek, 32, 142-147
Guyot (master at the Little Schools), 22, 42, 165

Habit of the Port-Royal nuns, 49
Hallays (*Le Pèlerinage de Port-Royal*), quoted or referred to, 49, 50, 51
Hamon (solitary at Port-Royal), 27, 63, 186 note; his affection for Racine, 32
Herbart, 1
Hieronymians. *See* Brethren of the Common Life
History, 147, 148, 158
Hodgson, Miss (*Studies in French Education*), quoted, 95, 187
Holidays in the Little Schools, 158
Humanists, their contempt for vernacular languages, 110

Jansen (Bishop of Ypres), 10
Jansenism, 10, 47, 52-57, 83, 141, 209
Jansenist schools (other than the Little Schools), 49-51
Janua Linguarum (Comenius), 111, 112; criticised by the Port-Royalists, 128, 129
Jardin des Racines grecques (Lancelot), 21, 32, 143-147
Jesting, rules for (Coustel), 102
Jesuits, their educational work, 3, 29, 39, 41, 43, 65, 202, (Greek) 142, (physical exercises) 157, (their pupils) 162; their persecution of Port-Royal, 4, 30, 40, 41, 44-48, 168; their quarrel with Saint-Cyran (*Petrus Aurelius*), 11; with Dr Arnauld (*De la Fréquente Communion*), 17, 19, 39, 47; their theological position as opposed to Jansenism, 53; their expulsion from France (1762), 50, 223, 224
Jesus, Society of. *See* Jesuits
Joly (Precentor of Notre Dame), 30 note
Jouvency (Jesuit), quoted or referred to, 46, 58, 220
'Jules, petit.' *See* De Villeneuve

Kant, 1, 187
Keatinge (*Suggestion in Education*), 234
Kindness, education by, in the Little Schools, 82, 83, 97-99, 237; in the Girls' Schools, 186, 187

Labbé (Jesuit), quoted, 143

La Bruyère, 44
La Chalotais, 224, 225
La Ferté-Milon, 15
La Flèche (Jesuit 'collège'), 45
La Fontaine, erroneously said to have been a pupil at the Little Schools, 26 note
Lambert (friend of Port-Royal), 20
Lamy (Oratorian), 140, 207
Lancelot (master at the Little Schools), 11, 14, 16, 21, 26, 32, 42, 149, 165; his criticism of Comenius' *Janua*, 112, 129; his *Nouvelles Méthodes*, 130-132, 143, 144, 150; his *Jardin des Racines grecques*, 21, 32, 143-147; his attitude towards Descartes, 211
Lantoine (*Histoire de l'Enseignement secondaire en France*), 214
Latin, conversational, 107-110; teaching of, 45, 86, 124-142, (in the Girls' Schools) 174, 175; grammars, 46, 125-132; translation, 132-135; authors, 136-139; prose composition, 139, 140; verses, 105, 140, 141
Laurie (*Educational Opinion from the Renaissance*), 96
Learning by heart, 137-139
Le Bon (master at the Little Schools), 31, 165
Le Chesnai, school group at, 19, 31, 39, 40, 41, 163, 164, 165
Le Fèvre (master at the Little Schools), 24, 33, 89, 154, 165
Le Maître (solitary at Port-Royal), 11, 19, 27, 32, 63, 95, 103, 165
Le Mothe Le Vayer, 43
Les Granges, school group at, 31, 32, 33, 39, 42, 164, 165
Les Trous, school group at, 31, 33, 40, 41, 164, 165
'Libido sciendi' and 'libido excellendi,' 64
Lieutenant, police, visits Port-Royal, 30, 39, 41, 240-243
Lily (Headmaster of S. Paul's School), 108
Literary activity during reign of Louis XIV, 119
Literature, Port-Royal's attitude towards, 32, 64-69, 71, 119-124, 141, 142
'Little Schools,' why so called, 28-30
Locke (*Thoughts on Education*), quoted or referred to, 1, 36, 77, 93, 95, 101, 220
Logic, study of, at the University, 195; in the 'écoles grandes,' 28, 29
Logic, The Port-Royal, authorship of, 16, 23, 212; quoted, 85, 201, 213; criticism of, 213, 214; its popularity, 221, 230

Louis XIV, patron of literature, 119, 121; pupil of Péréfixe, 43

Louvain, 10, 15, 126

Luther, his views on teaching, 57

Lying, punishment of, in the Little Schools, 98; in the Girls' Schools, 188, 189

Magny, school group at, 33, 164

Malebranche, 112 note, 206

Malingering, how dealt with in the Girls' Schools, 187

Mancini, Alphonse (nephew of Mazarin), 41

Manners, teaching of, in the Little Schools, 101–103; in the Girls' Schools, 187, 188

Manual Training, 95

Marie Claire (pupil and nun at Port-Royal), 182

Marriage, attitude towards, in the Girls' Schools, 171, 172

Mass, attendance at (Little Schools), 84, 154; (Girls' Schools), 178, 181

Masters at the Little Schools, 20–28, 81, 165, 232, 233; qualifications required of, 79–81, 236

Mathematics, 149; (Ramus), 201; (Oratorians), 206

Mathilde De Garlande (foundress of Port-Royal), 6

Matthieu De Marly De Montmorenci, 6

Mazarin, 39, 41, 43, 48, 119

Meals at the Little Schools, 152, 153; at the Girls' Schools, 177, 179

Meditations (Descartes), 209, 211

Method, Discourse on (Descartes), 210

Méthode espagnole, 150
—— grecque, 143, 144
—— italienne, 150
—— latine, 130, 131

Méthodes Nouvelles (Lancelot), 130–132, 143, 144, 150

Milton (Tractate on Education), 1, 2

Miracle of the Holy Thorn, 40

Misbehaviour in church, how punished, in the Little Schools, 98, 154; in the Girls' Schools, 178, 188

Mistresses in the Girls' Schools, qualifications of, 184, 185, 190; their attitude towards their pupils, 184–187

Modern Languages, 150

Molière, quoted or referred to, 119, 171, 192

Monmouth, Duke of (pupil at the Little Schools), 163

Monroe (History of Education), quoted or referred to, 26 note, 93, 239

Montaigne, quoted or referred to, 77, 101, 108, 110, 121, 157; censures

flogging, 96, 196, 197; his influence on education, 198, 199

Moral instruction in the Little Schools, 83–89, 214, 234–236; in the Girls' Schools, 170, 181–183

MS documents relating to Port-Royal, afterwards printed, 31 note, 241

Mulcaster (Positions), 1, 2

Music in the Little Schools, 69; in the Girls' Schools, 173, 176, 181

Napoleonic system of education, 3, 226, 227

Natural Science, 149, 150

Nécrologes, contemporary documents, 31 note, 241

Needlework in the Girls' Schools, 96, 173, 176

Nicole (master at the Little Schools), 22–24, 32, 42, 49, 165; his style, 120, 121, 123; his views on Descartes, 211

Nouvelles Méthodes. See Méthodes, Nouvelles

Novels, Port-Royal's attitude towards, 68, 69

Number of pupils in the Little Schools, 44, 163, 165, 166; in the Girls' Schools, 190, 191

Nuns, object of the Girls' Schools to make, 170–173

Object Lessons, 94

Oratorians, 11, 61, 112, 140, 205–207, 228

Oratory of Jesus. See Oratorians

Painting, Port-Royal's attitude towards, 70, 71

Pallu (solitary at Port-Royal), 186 note

Parlements, their educational work in 1762, 224–226

Paroissiens, 175

Pascal, Blaise, 24, 26 note, 37–39, 44, 63; his Provinciales, 38, 39, 46, 47; his Pensées, 38, 104; his method of teaching reading, 38, 50, 115; his literary style, 121; his opinion of Montaigne, 199
—— Jacqueline, 37, 38, 67, 115, 170, 187; her Règlement pour les enfans de Port-Royal, 36, 38, 170, 171, 176–190

Patience in teaching, 89, 90

Penances imposed in the Girls' Schools, 182

Pens and nibs, 118

Pensées (Pascal), 38, 104

Péréfixe (Archbishop of Paris), 43

Périer, Marguerite, 40

Pestalozzi, anticipated by Port-Royal, 37, 90, 94, 107, 126, 216, 232; read by Herbert Spencer, 215 note

Petrarch, 110 note

Petrus Aurelius (? Saint-Cyran), 10

Petty (letter to Hartlib), quoted, 149

Philology in the *Grammaire générale*, 213; in the *Jardin des Racines grecques*, 146

Phonetic method of reading, 115, 116

Physical exercises, 155–158

Place-taking in class, 105

Plainsong taught in the Girls' Schools, 173, 176, 181

Plaisted, Miss (*Early Education of Children*), quoted, 116

Play. *See* Games

Poetic composition discouraged, 67

Poland, Queen of (friend of Port-Royal), 30

Politeness inculcated in the Little Schools, 101–103; in the Girls' Schools, 187, 188

'Port-Royal,' derivation of name, 6

Port-Royal des Champs, 6–9, 14, 15, 18, 31, 37, 39, 49, 51, 70, 76, 155, 238

—— de Paris, 9, 16, 20, 40, 74

Potherie, Adrien (master at the Tabourin Schools), 50

Pourchot (Rector of the University), 219

Prayer, as an educational instrument, 99–101, 190; regarded as more important than school-work, 181, 182

Precentor of Notre Dame, 28, 30 note, 218

Predestination, doctrine of, 53–57

Prince, De l'Éducation d'un (Nicole), 23, 36, 42, 43, 221

Princes, education of, 38, 42–44

Prizes, 105

Propositions, the Five, 52

Prose Composition in French, 124, 175; in Latin, 139

Provinciales (Pascal), 38, 39, 46, 47

Psychology as applied to education, 90–95, 231, 232

Public and grammar schools in England, 2, 116, 126, 230

—— Schools Commission (1861), 1, 125

Punishments in the Little Schools, 96–99, 156; in the Girls' Schools, 188, 189

Pupils in the Little Schools, 44, 160–163; number of, 163–166; in the Girls' Schools, 190, 191; in the Jesuit schools, 45, 162

Quick, R. H., quoted, 220

Quintilian, 215

Rabelais, 77, 94, 107, 110, 121, 142, 157; ridicules scholasticism, 196; his influence on education, 197, 198

Racine, 15, 16, 27, 29, 32, 103, 139, 143, 161; his breach with Port-Royal, 67, 68; his praise of the Girls' Schools, 172, 191

Ramus, 110, 127, 200–202

Rapin (Jesuit), 174

Ratio Studiorum of the Jesuits, quoted or referred to, 105, 107, 203; of the Oratorians, 207

Ratke, 1, 110, 111

Reading, teaching of, in the Little Schools, 38, 50, 113–116; in the Girls' Schools, 173, 174; reading aloud, 116, 117

Realien, use of in teaching, 94, 95; (Comenius), 204

Recreations in the Little Schools, 153, 154, 156, 158

Règlement des Écoles de Port-Royal (Walon De Beaupuis), 21, 31, 35, 36, 151

—— *pour les enfans de Port-Royal* (Jacqueline Pascal), 36, 38, 170, 171, 176–190

Règles de la traduction française (Le Maître), 19, 36

—— *de l'éducation des Enfans* (Coustel), 22, 35, 42, 93

Renaissance, the, 65, 141, 157, 194–197

Retard (friend of Port-Royal), 33

Retranslation into Latin, 139

Revivals of learning in France, 194

Revolution, the French, 3, 44, 226, 227

Richelieu, 8, 15, 16, 43, 47, 119

Ritterakademien, 158

Rivalry between pupils in the Little Schools, 103–106

Rochemonteix (*Un Collège de Jésuites*), quoted, 45, 46

Rod, use of. *See* Cane

Rolland, 225, 226

Rollin, 4, 203, 217, 218, 227

Rousseau, 36, 93, 95, 131, 221, 222; his knowledge of Port-Royal books, 4, 103, 221

Royer-Collard, 227

Saint-Ange (pupil at the Little Schools), 18, 61, 163

Saint-Antoine, Frères de (or Tabourin Brothers), 51

Saint-Cyr, 192

Saint-Cyran (founder of the Little Schools), 9–18, 22, 26, 47, 73, 83; his theological and educational views, 52, 53, 57–65, 80, 88, 89, 90, 97, 98, 100; his attitude towards Descartes, 210

St Cyres, Viscount (*Camb. Mod. Hist.*, art. *The Gallican Church*), quoted, 209

Saint-Elme (pupil at the Little Schools), 25

Sainte-Marthe, Sœurs de, 49, 169

Scholasticism, 195, 196, 200, 201, 203, 208, 225

School-books of Port-Royal, 249; their influence, 144, 146, 230

Science, Natural, 149, 150

Secular knowledge, Port-Royal's attitude towards, 62–64, 67, 181

Selle (master at the Little Schools), 18

Seneca, quoted or referred to, 82, 215

Servants, choice of, 76, 77

Sevran, school group at, 33, 76, 164

'Silences' in the Girls' Schools, 182, 183

Silvy, 51

Singing at Port-Royal, 69; as a school-subject, 173, 176, 181

Singlin (confessor at Port-Royal), 10, 13, 37

Sisters of the Christian Doctrine. *See* Doctrinaires

Sleep, hours of, in the Little Schools, 159

Society, Port-Royal's attitude towards contemporary, 73, 235, 236

'Soft paedagogics,' 93

Solitaries of Port-Royal, the, 11, 14

Spencer, Herbert, 2, 36, 215

Sturm, 1, 43, 108, 109, 203

Style, literary, of the Port-Royalists, 119–124

Suireau, Marie Des Anges, 22

Sundays and festivals, time-table for, in the Little Schools, 154, 155; in the Girls' Schools, 181

Supervision of pupils, in the Little Schools, 72, 153, 235, 236; in the Girls' Schools, 186

Syllabic method of reading, 115, 116

Table-manners, rules for (Coustel), 102

Tabourin and his schools, 49–51, 75

Tabourot (follower of Montaigne), 199

Talleyrand, 3, 227

Teaching, Jansenist views on, 57–59, 78–80, 185; in the Girls' Schools, 184–186

Terence, 86, 87

Theatre, Port-Royal's attitude towards, 68

Thomassin (Oratorian), 207

Time-tables for the Little Schools, 151–155; for the Girls' Schools, 176–181

Training, professional, of teachers, 79, 80, 237

Traité des Études (Rollin), 217, 218

Translation, 133–137; extempore, 135; rules for, 134; value of, 122, 123; classical translations ('versions'), 132

'Transparents,' 118

Travel, Port-Royal's attitude towards, 77, 78

Treatises, educational, of Port-Royal, 34–37, 248

Trotzendorf, 108

Trous, Les. *See* Les Trous

Troyes, Nicole's school at, 49, 169

'Tutoiement,' forbidden in the Little Schools, 103; in the Girls' Schools, 188

Tutorial system of the Little Schools, 73–75, 232

—— work of the solitaries after the destruction of the Little Schools, 21, 42

Universal education, Port-Royal's attitude towards, 42, 43, 63

University, the, 28, 29, 47, 107, 194, 195, 200, 202, 203, 219; reformed by Henri IV, 3, 157, 201, 203; reformed by Rollin, 4, 217

Ursulines, 192, 208

Van Pauteren (or Despauterius), 126–128, 130, 131

Varet (*Éducation Chrestienne des Enfans*), 56 note

Vaumurier, 33, 164; conferences at, 34, 210, 211

Vernacular, use of, in teaching, 91, 107, 110–120, 130, 132; (Jesuits), 46, 219; (Ramus), 201; (Comenius), 204; (Rollin), 218; (the University), 219; (elementary schools), 218, 219

Verses, Latin, 105, 140, 141

'Versions,' 132

Vesalius of Padua, 149

Vestments, church, at Port-Royal, 70

Villemain, 228

Vincent De Paul, S., 61

Virgil, 64, 104, 136, 137

Vitart (uncle of Racine), 16

—— (pupil at the Little Schools), 163

Vittorino Da Feltre. *See* Da Feltre, Vittorino

Vives, 108, 195, 215

Walon De Beaupuis. *See* De Beaupuis, Walon

Writing, teaching of, in the Little Schools, 118; in the Girls' Schools, 173, 175

For EU product safety concerns, contact us at Calle de José Abascal, 56–1°,
28003 Madrid, Spain or eugpsr@cambridge.org.

www.ingramcontent.com/pod-product-compliance
Ingram Content Group UK Ltd.
Pitfield, Milton Keynes, MK11 3LW, UK
UKHW010036140625
459647UK00012BA/1414